GUIDE TO CONTRACT PRICING

Cost and Price Analysis for Contractors, Subcontractors, and Government Agencies

4th edition

GUIDE TO CONTRACT PRICING

Cost and Price Analysis for Contractors, Subcontractors, and Government Agencies

4th edition

John Edward Murphy, CPA, CPCM

MANAGEMENTCONCEPTS

Vienna, Virginia

ᏝᏝᏝ
MANAGEMENTCONCEPTS

8230 Leesburg Pike, Suite 800
Vienna, Virginia 22182
Phone: (703) 790-9595
Fax: (703) 790-1371
Web: www.managementconcepts.com

Printed in the United States of America

Library of Congress Cataloging-in-Publication Data

Murphy, J. Edward.
    Guide to contract pricing: cost and price analysis for contractors, subcontractors, and government agencies / John Edward Murphy.—4th ed.
        p. cm.
    Includes index.
    ISBN 1-56726-153-1
    1. Government purchasing—United States—Handbooks, manuals, etc. 2. Public contracts—United States—Handbooks, manuals, etc. I. Title.

JK1673.M87 2005
352.5'3'0973—dc22   2004053896

About the Author

John Edward (Ed) Murphy has more than 40 years of experience in financial management and procurement in the private sector for CPA firms, and in the public sector for the U.S. General Accounting Office (GAO), the Defense Contract Audit Agency (DCAA), the Naval Audit Service, and the Office of Personnel Management (OPM). While with OPM, he managed a governmentwide program providing financial management and procurement training for worldwide federal, state, and local employees. He has received a Presidential commendation and many meritorious service awards and special citations. The Association of Government Accountants (AGA) recognized Ed's achievements by honoring him with its Outstanding Achievement Award and its Distinguished Leadership Award. He has an excellent reputation as a speaker and educator, and as an accomplished writer of manuals, articles, and position papers. Ed obtained his Bachelor of Science in Business Administration from Duquesne University in Pittsburgh. He is a Certified Public Accountant (CPA), Certified Fraud Examiner (CFE), Certified Government Financial Manager (CGFM), and Certified Professional Contracts Manager (CPCM).

Ed is the founder and principal of the Financial Management Institute, a management consulting firm specializing in procurement, finance, public policy, and litigation support. Client service includes acquisition support service, expert witness and forensic accounting service, and trouble-shooting client problems with federal agencies.

Table of Contents

Preface

Guide to Contract Pricing is intended to serve as a reference to answer the day-to-day issues that arise in establishing, evaluating, and negotiating a fair and reasonable contract price. This master reference—now in its fourth edition—puts everything you need to know about government pricing rules and regulations in one easy-to-use volume. The reader will learn how to:

- Apply appropriate formulas to evaluate or negotiate prices
- Identify sources of market intelligence
- Distinguish between market-based prices and cost-based prices
- Know when to apply price analysis, cost analysis, and cost realism analysis
- Apply different techniques of price analysis
- Know what to obtain from contractors and suppliers to determine a fair and reasonable price
- Structure solicitation requirements so that you obtain sufficient cost or pricing information to perform sound cost analysis or cost realism of different cost elements
- Apply the principles and standards of Federal Acquisition Regulation (FAR) Part 31 to determine the allowability, reasonableness, and allocability of proposed or incurred costs
- Perform sound cost analysis or cost realism of different cost elements (e.g., direct labor cost, direct material cost, other direct cost, indirect cost)
- Evaluate proposed facilities capital cost of money
- Apply the "structured profit approach" required by the FAR to evaluate proposed profit or fee
- Calculate an equitable price adjustment for contract changes.

This latest edition of *Guide to Contract Pricing* also contains a new chapter on one of the most challenging pricing issues: equitable adjustments for contract changes.

This fourth edition represents a long-term effort to combine and simplify the body of knowledge contained in two earlier public domain publications: the *Armed Services Pricing Manual* (circa 1986 and 1987) and the *Cost and Price Analysis* manuals used by the General Services Administration in the late 1980s. Like its forebears, *Guide to Contract Pricing* can serve as a ready-reference desk guide as well as a training manual in the classroom and on the job.

John Edward Murphy
May 2004

Acknowledgments

I am very grateful to Beverley J. Goodale, Adjunct Assistant Professor at the University of Maryland, University College, and her students. Thanks for using my text in your curriculum—what a delightful vote of confidence. And certainly thanks for your valuable feedback for the fourth edition.

Also thanks to Barbara Beach of Management Concepts, who encouraged me to embark on the first edition. Thanks, Barbara, for your encouragement over the years and your vote of confidence.

CHAPTER 1
Basic Pricing Policy and Concepts

The government policy is to contract for its products and services at fair and reasonable prices. No matter how the problem is approached, the decision comes down to a matter of good personal judgment on whether or not a particular asking price is fair and reasonable. We have to consider a broad range of factors that exist when the purchase is made.

The problem faced by government contracting people in deciding whether or not a price is reasonable is in many ways like that of an individual making purchases for his or her own private purposes at the local department store or supermarket. We all know that we usually have to pay more for high quality articles than we do for ordinary articles. We realize we are likely to pay more if we make emergency purchases, such as getting the furnace repaired after normal business hours or stopping at the local convenience market so we will not be delayed by a long line at the supermarket. We know that we may have to pay more for name brand items, such as an IBM personal computer rather than a no-name clone, and that an electric "water pic" will cost more than a conventional toothbrush.

PRICING RESTRAINTS IN GOVERNMENT CONTRACTING

Government contracting people encounter some restraints not faced by private individuals when trying to reach a decision on a reasonable price to pay.

Use of Public Funds

The government employee is spending public funds rather than his own money. If we, in our private lives, choose to spend $50,000 for an automobile, we are the ones who bear the expense and no one else is affected. However, the government employee is held responsible for use of good judgment so that excessive prices are not paid.

Promote Full and Open Competition

Federal Acquisition Regulation (FAR) 11.002 (a) provides that agencies

(1) Specify needs using market research in a manner designed to—
    (i) Promote full and open competition with due regard to the nature of the supplies or services to be acquired; and

(ii) Only include restrictive provisions or conditions to the extent necessary to satisfy the minimum needs of the agency or as authorized by law.

(2) To the maximum extent practicable, ensure acquisition officials—

(i) State requirements with respect to an acquisition of supplies or services in terms of—

(A) Functions to be performed;

(B) Performance required; or

(C) Essential physical characteristics;

(ii) Define requirements in terms that enable and encourage offerors of commercial items and nondevelopmental items an opportunity to fill such requirements;

(iii) Provide offerors of commercial and nondevelopmental items an opportunity to compete in acquisition to fill such requirements;

(iv) Require prime contractors and subcontractors at all tiers under the agency contracts to incorporate commercial items or nondevelopmental items as components of items supplied to the agency; and

(v) Modify requirements in appropriate cases to ensure that the requirements can be met by commercial items or, to the extent that commercial items suitable to meet the agency's needs are not available, nondevelopmental items.

Full and open competition, when referring to a contract action, means that all responsible sources are allowed an opportunity to compete (FAR 2.101(a)). Note also that the FAR citation above encourages the use of commercial items and nondevelopmental items to encourage maximum competition. Government contracting officers do not have the luxury of buying from one or even a very few sources, based on good business relations in the past. They cannot restrict their sources to suppliers who are already known for quality products and on-time delivery. The government does not have product or supplier loyalty. They must extend the opportunity to compete to all responsible sources. This approach is in marked contrast to that of private individuals and businesses who may well return to the known vendors repeatedly, rather than take a chance on some vendor with whom they have no experience.

PRICING ADVANTAGES IN GOVERNMENT CONTRACTING

Government buyers have some significant advantages in getting fair and reasonable prices. Some of these advantages are mentioned below.

The Government Is the Only Buyer

For certain commodities such as spacecraft and weapons systems, Uncle Sam is the only buyer. In these cases, the government has a strong negotiating position on pricing because the seller cannot turn to other consumers who are willing to pay a higher price.

High Volume Purchases

Private suppliers like to deal with high-volume buyers and are inclined to give better prices to such buyers. Government agencies typically deal in fairly large quantities, as much or more than individual buyers in the private sector. The government's small purchase activity (i.e., individual orders less than $500,000 each) alone is a major revenue source, particularly to small businesses near federal installations. This major revenue source for private businesses helps the government in securing reasonable prices for the products and services that it buys. The benefits are even greater when heavy competition exists to get government business.

The Government Pays Its Debts

Large volume buyers who are also good credit risks tend to get better prices because the seller runs less risk of taking a financial loss. It is taken for granted that the government pays its legal obligations. The Anti-Deficiency Act requires that government agencies have money to pay for contract work before signing the contract. It is not necessarily certain that the private sector buyer actually has all the funds required to pay for a buy "up front." That commercial buyer may itself have to pass on the goods or services to another buyer and obtain payment before it has the money to meets all its own bills. The problem of cash flow is a very real concern to all businesses, large or small, and it takes cash in hand to pay bills. A government agency, on the other hand, has the money needed to pay its bills from the outset; otherwise it cannot contract to buy products or services. If the government decides not to buy after the contract is placed, the contractor is protected against financial loss without having to resort to expensive legal actions. Contractors do not need to "up their prices a shade" because their government customers may not pay.

Prompt Payment of Bills

The Prompt Payments Act is another factor that helps the government, already known for paying its legal debts, to get more reasonable prices. In almost all cases, the government contractor is very certain to be paid somewhere around 30 days after submission of a proper invoice. A fairly common practice among firms in the private sector is to alleviate their cash flow problems by paying suppliers late. This practice provides a way to have the use of money interest-free for a longer time. Such firms may even deliberately lose discounts. It may be better to delay paying the full amount, even though interest is added, than be short of cash to pay more pressing obligations such as payroll. In the worst cases, private firms may wait as long as possible to pay their bills and then take the offered discount long since expired. Such firms are depending on the fact that, as a practical matter, the most the supplier can do is refuse to sell to them again, and lose business in the process.

Most Favored Customer Treatment

The government is often in a good position to obtain "most favored customer" treatment from vendors because of its high-dollar value buying practices. It is common practice in the commercial sector for suppliers to grant special price concessions to customers who are favored because they buy in very large quantities, or pay very rapidly or provide other benefits to the supplier. The government is very often in the position of being able to buy large quantities with the promise of rapid payment and can successfully use that leverage to obtain price concessions not available to ordinary buyers. FAR 13.303-2 (b) requires that after determining Blanket Purchase Agreements (BPA) would be advantageous, contracting officers shall:

> Consider suppliers whose past performance has shown them to be dependable, who offer quality supplies or services at *consistently lower prices*, and who have provided numerous purchases at or below the simplified acquisition threshold. (*Emphasis added.*)

It is important to understand that no supplier is forced to give the government "most favored customer" treatment; no one forces the supplier to deal with the government in the first place. The requirement merely says that the supplier must give that pricing advantage to the government if it desires to enter into a BPA. The supplier knows that a BPA (a type of charge account) will very likely result in some government purchases.

Cost and Pricing Data

Under some conditions (covered in more detail in Chapter 5) the government may receive cost and pricing data from offerors prior to selecting one of them for an actual contract. These cost and pricing data give the government detailed information about how the offeror developed the asking price in its proposal. Government examination of that information is a major help in judging the reasonableness of the offeror's price proposal. The Truth in Negotiations Act (PL 87-653) provides the legal basis for obtaining this information under prescribed conditions. Private companies and individuals do not have this advantage as a legal right in private contracting.

WHAT IS A FAIR AND REASONABLE PRICE?

A fair and reasonable price is different things to different people. The buyer tends to think on the low side, and the seller tends to think on the high side. The seller wants to make as much money as possible and the buyer wants to save as much as possible.

Although the FAR talks about payment of fair and reasonable prices, it does not define the term. The reason the term goes undefined is that whether or not a price is reasonable depends on great many factors, and it simply is not possible to define the term in a few words. However, you will see as we progress through this text that (1) the government prefers market-based pricing over cost-based pricing to judge fair and reasonable price, and (2) cost-based pricing is appropriate only when the forces of the marketplace cannot judge fair and reasonable price. The determination depends heavily on good personal judgment and experience, no matter how the problem is approached. One purpose of this text is to help you understand how to approach the problem.

It is a good idea to look at five means normally identified to establish a fair and reasonable price. Four of the means are market-based, and one is cost-based.

Market-Based Prices

Competitive Offers—Prices arrived at through this means are:

- In response to solicitations encouraging competing offers;
- Prepared with no effort by the buyer to suppress a known source;
- Submitted by multiple responsible offerors who can satisfy the buyer's requirements with priced offers responsive to the solicitation's expressed requirements; and
- Submitted by offerors who are competing independently for a contract to be awarded to the responsible offeror submitting the lowest evaluated price.

Sellers proposing prices that are too high risk seeing the business go to a competitor. The forces of the market push each offeror to propose a fair and reasonable price.

Established Catalog Price—Prices established by this means are:

- Published by the seller in a regularly maintained catalog or price list;
- Available for inspection by potential buyers; and
- State current prices, including discounts and other price-related terms, for offered goods and services.

The published catalog or price list is the seller's message that:

- They are willing to offer goods and services at the prices published;
- All competing offerees may either accept the prices as published by placing an order, or decline the prices as published by refraining from placing an order; and
- Market forces make it disadvantageous to use their income producing capacity to sell goods and services at lower prices than those published.

The seller is in effect saying, "other customers are willing to meet our price. We plan to continue servicing them with these prices that they find satisfactory. Therefore, it is not to our advantage to offer a lower paying customer (like you) the benefits of our income producing capacity." The forces of the market push the buyer to accept a fair and reasonable price.

Established Market Price—The seller believes and is able to show to their satisfaction (and if necessary, to the customer's satisfaction) that their proposed price for comparable goods and services is either better than or equal to prevailing prices for comparable goods and services in the marketplace.

The seller is in effect saying, "other customers are willing to meet our price. We are confident that current and potential customers will be satisfied to pay these prices. Therefore, it is not to our advantage to offer a lower paying customer (like you) the benefits of our productive capacity." The forces of the market encourage the buyer to accept a fair and reasonable price.

Established by Law or Regulation—Prices are established by legislative or regulatory authority usually to protect buyers, punish buyers (for example, a fine or penalty), or to achieve some socioeconomic goal.

In these cases, the seller is able to demonstrate that (1) other authorities have established a ceiling or floor on their prices; and (2) all customers are consistently impacted by the established prices.

The seller is saying in effect, "other authorities regulate our prices. We are blameless. Presumably the regulating authorities have judged the price to be fair and reasonable under the circumstances." Regulatory forces in the market encourage (or force) the buyer to accept a fair and reasonable price.

The four means above rely on the marketplace to determine a fair and reasonable price. However, when there are no competing sources or the competing sources are ineffective, the marketplace cannot be relied upon to produce a fair and reasonable price. In those cases, cost-based pricing serves as a surrogate to the market in determining a fair and reasonable price.

Cost-Based Prices

When the buyer cannot rely on the competitive forces of the market economy, it will often make extraordinary efforts to judge a fair and reasonable price. If the order is significant, the buyer may encourage or even demand that the seller prepare a detailed cost and price breakdown showing the composition and basis or estimate of the total cost by: Direct Cost; Indirect Cost; Profit; and Total Price. The cost and pricing data submitted is analyzed, and serves as a basis to negotiate a fair and reasonable price.

The seller's cost and price breakdown is presumably the seller's best estimate of what it feels it *will cost* to produce the goods and services called for in the solicitation, and the requested profit margin. The buyer then challenges the seller's *will cost* position with its own *should cost* position. The buyer may also challenge the seller's proposed profit.

The seller is forced to disclose data that may be challenged by the buyer. Ineconomies, inefficiencies, and ineffectiveness inherent in the seller's proposal are hopefully disclosed and discussed. By analyzing such data as labor hours and labor mix, the buyer may also determine if the seller's proposed effort is responsive to the buyer's solicitation. Differences between buyer and seller positions are worked out through negotiation before contract award.

As we have seen, the definition of a "fair and reasonable price" is complicated. At this point, we turn to the simpler task of defining "price."

$$Cost + Profit = Price$$

As shown by the above equation, price is made up of two component parts: cost and profit. Any definition of price must first define cost and profit.

Definition of Cost

For purposes of this text, cost is defined as the expenses a contractor will incur in performing contract work. It is important to clearly understand this definition from the outset so that the term "cost" is not mixed up with the term "price." It is true that "cost" is often used, even in government publications, when "price" is really meant. You can save yourself a lot of trouble if you accept that there is a difference between "cost" and "price."

Readers who have previous contracting experience are already accustomed to the term "cost" as described above. For example, they know about cost-reimbursement contracts and their general meaning. FAR 16.301-1 defines cost-reimbursement contracts as follows:

> Cost-reimbursement types of contracts provide for payment of allowable incurred costs, to the extent prescribed in the contract. . . .

Unfortunately this definition (and others in the FAR) reuses the word cost when defining a term containing the same word; however, the meaning is clear. The government says that it will reimburse the holder of a cost-reimbursement contract for its costs expended (expenses) to do the work as long as they are allowable, reasonable, and properly allocable to the contract. The government recognizes that contractors incur costs when doing government work. Normal government pricing policy is to ensure that the contractor recovers its reasonable costs.

A contractor's costs comprise a wide variety of expenses that may have to be paid. Some are a direct result of accepting the contract work. The most common of these are the costs of labor and materials. Other costs that may be directly related to contract work include expenses such as travel and consultant costs. Other costs fall into the category of general operating expenses, such as costs for furniture and equipment, utility costs, pay of management personnel, property taxes and insurance, and a wide variety of other costs. Although these costs may not be directly related to specific contract jobs, they nevertheless have to be paid if the contractor is to stay in business.

Consider building occupancy costs. All contractors, except the very few whom operate in government facilities, need buildings to perform their government and commercial work. If the contractor rents the building, it is an expense, which has to be met by the business firm, an out-of-pocket expense. If the contractor owns the building, it did not get it without cost. There was an out-of-pocket expense at the outset to acquire the building. Since the building presumably will be usable for a considerable number of years, generally accepted accounting principles require that the business "charge off" the building expense over a number of years so that each year carries a part of the total cost. Accountants call this charge-off procedure depreciation.

The above discussion is an introduction to cost. Chapters 4, 6, 7, and 8 provide detailed coverage of cost.

Definition of Profit

In the broad sense, business profit is whatever monies are left after all costs have been paid. When talking about a particular contract, profit is the additional amount a contractor receives above out-of-pocket costs; profit makes it worthwhile to do the particular contract work. It is the reward for undertaking the contract task in the first place. As is obvious, if customers (including the government) pay prices that merely repay contractors for the costs to do work, it would be pointless for them to be in business. The owners of the firm would be better off to invest their money so it would earn interest, and go to work for someone else to draw a reward for their work.

All contractors, except the narrow category of not-for-profit institutions, are primarily interested in profit. The expectation of adequate profit is what makes it reasonable to invest money in a business at the outset and to let money stay in the business. The stockholders in a business receive dividends or see their capital investment grow as a direct result of the profit the business makes. If their invested money does not earn at least as much as it would invested in the money market or a savings account, they would be foolish to leave their money in the business.

The government fully understands that profit is a basic motivation for all private businesses. Government pricing policy provides for contractors to receive a fair and reasonable profit. Chapter 10 will cover methods for determination of a proper profit.

Definition of Price

We previously defined price as the sum of cost and profit. Now that we have learned more about the real meaning of cost and profit, we are in a better position to discuss price. We will do this from the standpoints of the government and the seller (contractor).

Price, to the government or any other buyer, is the financial outlay, which is made to pay for a product or service. In terms of our basic formula, a reasonable price is the sum of reasonable costs to do the work and a reasonable profit. It is very important to establish clearly at the outset (if possible) what the price will be for the work to be performed. It is possible to establish the price at the outset in many types of contract actions. In some cases, including much research and development (R&D) work, it is not practical to try to determine the ultimate price at the outset.

As we have mentioned previously, the government policy is to pay a fair and reasonable price for whatever it buys. This text will help you approach the difficult matter of determining a fair and reasonable price for a particular contract job.

The government knows well that a failure to pay reasonable prices will result in contractors selling their outputs in the private sector where they will be treated more fairly. On the other hand, if the government pays excessive prices, it is a waste of taxpayer money. When excessive prices have already been paid, it is not possible for the government to recover overpayments except in very limited circumstances.

Price to the contractor (seller) means the total payment received for work performed. In the normal course of events, the contractor expects to receive enough to repay it for actual costs expended to do the work plus a profit for doing the work. The determination of the price to charge (i.e., to bid or propose) is a very complex subject, which will be discussed in the next sections.

Cost-Plus-Profit Pricing

Almost all companies decide on the price to charge for their products or services by determining the cost to make or provide the product or service and then adding a profit. We will use a small bakery to illustrate this type of pricing called cost-plus-profit pricing.

A bakery produces a wide variety of bread and pastry products. It can determine the cost of the flour, sugar, and other raw materials used to make these products. The labor costs can also be established. The bakery has to consider all its other operating costs such as those for working space, equipment, utilities, taxes, and numerous other expenses. By using methods to be described later in this text, the bakery can establish a total cost for each output product. It can then calculate unit costs. It has to sell its products for at least that much just to break even. Since it wants to make a profit, it will add a profit figure to establish a selling price. If the bakery operates its own sales outlet, its costs must also include its selling expenses. If the bakery sells all its output to a grocery store, the price that the bakery receives is a cost to the grocery, i.e., and an out-of-pocket expense. The grocery goes through a similar cost-plus-profit pricing procedure to decide on the price to charge its customers.

Any firm that manufactures products uses certain specifications and standards for making its products. These specifications may be formal or informal but whatever they are the company must know (if it is to survive) its costs to perform its work. For the bakery, the specification is the recipe for each product. A company that manufactures electric appliances follows detailed drawing specifications and standards for making or buying various parts for the appliances and for assembling them into finished products. It can then calculate what it costs to produce each product and establish a price by adding a profit figure to the cost.

The same general analogy applies whether we are talking about bakery products, electric appliances, complex machine tools, or a new building. It also applies to services. A firm, which provides services, calculates the cost of providing the service and then adds a profit to establish the price to be charged.

The discussion above is satisfactory for the present; however, later parts of this text will bring out details that show price calculation is not as simple as this discussion has indicated. The appliance manufacturer may well go through all the calculations above to establish cost, profit, and price, and then discover that its price is higher than prices charged by competitors for comparable appliances. If so, the manufacturer will not be able to sell many appliances at that calculated price. Something must be done. The manufacturer may have to settle for a smaller profit, find ways to reduce costs, or get out of the appliance business. It may also discover that it is not calculating certain costs correctly, especially if it is producing various other products.

More on the Pricing of Commercial Products

The Manufacturer-Distributor-Retailer Chain: Primary manufacturers of commercial products will, for the most part, use the cost-plus-profit approach described above to arrive at prices for their products. Most of these primary manufacturers provide their products to the market-place through distributors who in turn sell to retailers. The manufacturer's price is a cost to the distributor. To determining its selling price, the distributor considers the cost of the product itself and adds its storage and handling costs plus a profit. This distributor price is a cost to the retailer who in turn adds its handling costs plus a profit. It is obvious that there is considerable pyramiding of costs and profits by the time most items find their way to the ultimate consumer.

(Note: Some very large mass-production companies use a method called rate-of-return pricing. This entails pricing so that a given percent of return on capital investment will be achieved. This particular approach will not be further described in this text.)

Heavy users of commercial items, whether private companies or the government, prefer to find ways to avoid the effects of pyramiding of costs and profits through the manufacturer-distributor-retailer chain. The government and most private companies solicit bids or proposals when their requirements are a high-dollar amount or for large quantities or both. Retailers are not generally in a position to compete with either the manufacturers or the distributors in these circumstances. Consequently, bids come in from manufacturers or distributors and the government and the private companies achieve price savings. The General Services Administration places contracts for thousands of commercial items used by various government agencies on this basis. These sources are published in the Federal Supply Schedules and, with rare exceptions, provide major price savings to government agencies compared to retail purchases.

"What the Traffic Will Bear": Around the turn of the century, railroad operators coined this expression to describe their method of setting prices. Overland shippers had to use the railroads because no other overland mass transportation was available. The railroads took advantage of the situation by charging outrageous shipping rates. It was purely and simply "price-gouging." The government corrected this and similar situations with legislation providing for public regulation of prices charged by monopolistic industries for essential services and with various pieces of anti-trust legislation.

In present usage, the term basically means that suppliers are likely to charge whatever they think they can reasonably get. If this bothers you, stop and consider how you would set your asking price if you decided to sell your house or car. The tendency to set prices at "whatever the market will bear" is one of the most fundamental rules of all pricing and one which the government buyer does well to remember. The government buyer also must remember that although people groan at the high cost of government, they take advantage of any opportunity to benefit personally from that vast storehouse of public funds.

Adapting to Established Prices: This pricing approach is commonly seen for commercial items and services. The supplier who sells products or services essentially the same as those sold by other sellers in the same marketing area is generally forced to conform to established prices. The penalty for charging more is that buyers will soon drift away to other sellers. The auto industry is a good example of adapting to established prices. Each car manufacturer attempts to come out with various models of their own product, which will compete with similar cars built by their competitors. This results in very heavy competition in the auto industry even though there are very few major automobile manufacturers.

Product Differentiation: Sometimes large companies are able to convince some buyers that their particular product or service is worth the extra price. Such efforts generally require heavy advertising and selling expenses, which themselves add to the cost of the products being sold. The Xerox Corporation is an excellent example of this approach. Many of us are inclined to think of Xerox copiers as the ultimate in reliability and technology, even though we may not actually have first-hand knowledge to support that belief. Smaller companies are much more likely to base their prices on established market prices because they cannot afford massive expenditures for advertising and selling.

One reason for government emphasis on minimum requirement specifications and purchase descriptions is that such emphasis tends to reduce requirements to actual needs rather than "nice-to-have" features.

Price Leadership: Some very large firms, such as Microsoft, may take the initiative by setting prices for the products they sell in their own catalogs and price lists. If they lower prices, other companies in the industry have little choice except also to lower prices, since the giant can easily take on the added business. If the leader raises prices, the other companies will often follow suit as a way to increase profits. This practice is not collusion in the anti-trust law sense unless the sellers have preagreed on the pricing arrangement as a price-setting scheme.

Customary or Convenient Prices: Small consumer-type items such as candy bars, soft drinks, chewing gum, and similar items are often individually priced for over-the-counter or vending machine sales at customary or convenient prices (e.g., 25 or 50 cents each). These prices remain pretty much the same for considerable periods of time regardless of fluctuations in the cost of materials and labor to make and distribute the products. This practice is rapidly spreading to other types of merchandise such as minor office supplies and small hardware items (e.g. pens, paper clips, wood screws, and bolts). Much of the price of these items is consumed by packaging. In almost all cases, significant price reductions can be achieved by purchasing the items in reasonable bulk quantities.

Variable (Incremental) Cost Pricing

The earlier discussion of cost-plus-profit pricing may have led you to believe that suppliers always price their outputs based on their total costs for the products or services plus a profit. Suppliers do not always do their pricing that way. For example, a supplier may have slow-moving items in its inventory and may choose to sell them at cost, or even a little less, just to recover the money invested in them so it can be used for other purposes. Or, a supplier may deliberately sell at cost plus a less-than normal profit level.

A similar type of pricing occurs when a firm's business is temporarily down. The firm may not be getting enough work to keep it going at its usual profit levels, or for that matter at any profit level. Meanwhile its general operating expenses continue to exist and they have to be paid if the company is to exist at all. Examples are rent, taxes, utility bills, pay of owners and clerical staff, and similar expenses. There is a practical limit to how low these expenses can be pared if company doors are to stay open.

Under these circumstances, some business is better than no business. If the company can get work that recovers its variable costs to do the work plus makes a contribution to other costs, it is generally better to take that work. The example below will make this point more clear.

ACME Constructors, Inc., estimates the following costs for a job that will take 30 days:

Labor costs (including fringe benefits)	$20,000
Material requirements for the job	14,000
Equipment rental for the job	5,000
Total incremental cost for the job	$39,000

Normally the company would price out this job as below, before adding its profit:

Job cost shown above	$39,000
Fixed overhead pro-rated to the job	
(Its "normal" share of the firm's total operating expenses)	11,000
Total "normal" cost for the job	$50,000

The company could get the job at a price of $43,000; the customer refuses to pay more because he has a $43,100 price from another offeror.

The company might well take the job because it will clear $4,000 over the actual costs caused by undertaking the work ($43,000–$39,000). It will have $4,000 toward its fixed costs (building rent, taxes, utilities, etc.) which go on in any case and have to be paid. If it turns down the job, it loses the $4,000 it would have had toward these expenses which must be paid.

Obviously the firm cannot continue for a long period taking a loss on all its jobs because it will fail to meet its total expenses. For the short-run, it may be acceptable to do so and survive on savings while waiting for a business upturn.

A firm might also take a job at less than full cost recovery if it has lots of other jobs going that are recovering all its general operating costs plus proper profit levels. The firm might undertake such work to establish a reputation for good work with new customers or to keep work crews busy who would otherwise be laid off. It might, in some cases, also do it to "buy-in," a method of getting a contract by submitting a below-cost offer and then making up the money later using overpriced change orders. The FAR states that "buy-ins" are an improper business practice.

Price Analysis

Price analysis is a set of methods for determining whether an asking price is reasonable without examining the details of the cost or profit included in the price. We do price analysis almost daily in our private lives. Every time we make a purchase, we consciously or unconsciously make a price analysis, which satisfies us that what we are paying, is reasonable. Rarely, in our private lives, do we know the actual costs and profit, which stand behind a quoted price. All we know is the "bottom line" price we see and we reach a judgment on whether or not to buy based on that quoted price. We may haggle about the price and may get a reduction to a new and lower price. Then we repeat the mental process of price analysis to decide if the new price is acceptable.

The government does a significant amount of contracting based on getting a price alone, with no information on how much cost and profit is included in the price. Such contracting will result in the award of a fixed-price type contract, in which the government commits itself to pay the asking price when the work is satisfactorily performed. The government buyer must be as certain as he or she can be that the asking price is fair and reasonable before committing the government to pay that price.

Before going further, one point must be emphasized. When some contract types are used, we cannot do price analysis prior to awarding the contract. In some circumstances, the government contracts to reimburse a contractor for its allowable costs of performance plus (in most cases) a fee or profit. In such cases, the actual costs for the work will not be known until the work is completed. This means that the actual price for the work is also unknown until the work is complete. In such cases, we are not in a position to do price analysis prior to awarding the contract. The only recourse is to do cost analysis.

Cost Analysis

Cost analysis is a set of procedures used to determine the reasonableness of proposed costs to do contract work. Of course we cannot do cost analysis unless we know what the costs are. Under certain conditions (to be discussed in Chapter 5) the government is entitled to receive complete details on the estimated cost and profit built into a bottom line asking price. The government is then in a position to examine the reasonableness of the estimated costs and profits and can determine whether the asking price is realistic for the firm in question.

Over time, the term "cost analysis" has come to mean the government's analysis of proposed costs *and* profits. Strictly speaking, the analysis of proposed profit to determine if it is reasonable would be called "profit analysis," and sometimes it is called by that term. For the most part, however, the term "cost analysis" is taken to mean analysis of proposed costs and profits.

Moreover, the fact that cost analysis shows that costs and profits for a given firm to do a job are reasonable does not automatically prove that the *price* is reasonable. For example, a firm located in a high labor cost area might well be able to justify the reasonableness of a $100,000 price to do the contract work in their own situation. If a firm located in a lower labor cost area offers to and can do the same work for $95,000, we would be foolish to go with the higher priced firm just because their price was reasonable *for their firm.* Obviously, we will not contract with a higher priced company simply because they are able to justify their own excessive costs.

We always do price analysis when dealing with prices, even though we may have already done cost analysis. In the cases above, we have two firms with proven reasonable prices of $100,000 and $95,000 for their own situations; however, we might have other valid evidence to show that neither price is reasonable, for example a highly reliable government cost estimate. Both cases might have resulted from a misunderstanding of the work required, perhaps because of a faulty government work description. Or maybe neither company was anxious to get the work, but no one else bothered to make an offer. Cost analysis alone is not a sufficient basis for determining price reasonableness and contract award.

Cost analysis is covered in detail beginning in Chapter 4. Profit analysis is covered in Chapter 10.

Adequate Price Competition

The government relies on adequate price competition to get fair and reasonable prices. The concept is that if offerors are competing against each other to get the work based on lowest price, the pressures of the competition itself will result in a reasonable price. The concept is correct and true *only if* actual adequate price competition exists.

FAR 15.403-1 (c) states

(1) A price is based on adequate price competition if—
   (i) Two or more responsible offerors, competing independently, submit priced offers responsive to the Government's expressed requirement and if—
      (A) Award will be made to the offeror whose proposal represents the best value where price is a substantial factor in source selection; and
      (B) There is no finding that the price of the otherwise successful offeror is unreasonable. Any such finding that the price is unreasonable must be supported by a statement of the facts and approved at a level above the contracting officer;
   (ii) There was a reasonable expectation, based on market research or other assessment, that two or more responsible offerors, competing independently, would submit priced offers responsive to the solicitation's expressed requirement, even though only one offer is received from a responsible offeror and if —
      (A) Based on the offer received, the contracting officer can reasonable conclude that the offer was submitted with the expectation of competition, e.g., circumstances indicate that—
         (1) The offeror believed that at least one other offeror was capable of submitting a meaningful offer; and
         (2) The offeror had no reason to believe that the other potential offerors did not intend to submit an offer; and
      (B) The determination that the proposed price is based on adequate price competition, is reasonable, and is approved at a level above the contracting officer; or
   (iii) Price analysis clearly demonstrates that the proposed price is reasonable in comparison with current or recent prices for the same or similar items, adjusted to

reflect changes in market conditions, economic conditions, quantities, or terms and conditions under contracts that resulted from adequate price competition.

Notice that the FAR provides the following important features of "adequate price competition":

FAR 15.403-1 (c) (i) highlights the traditional presumption of competition if two or more responsible offerors, competing independently, submit priced offers responsive to the Government's expressed requirement.

FAR 15.403-1 (c) (ii) acknowledges adequate price competition even when a single offeror prepares a price offer. Provided the buyer, in preparing a solicitation, anticipated multiple priced offerors from responsive sources. And the offeror, when submitting a priced offer, operated under the assumption that a (known or unknown) competitor(s) may also be simultaneously preparing a competing price offer. In effect, the FAR is saying that an offeror tendering an offer in ignorance of the absence of competition is tendering a competitive offer.

FAR 15.403-1 (c) (iii) acknowledges that reasonableness of a proposed price can be judged by comparison with current or recent prices for the same or similar items purchased in comparable quantities, under comparable terms and conditions under contracts that resulted from adequate price competition.

Note that the description above is based on having actually received priced offers, i.e., the time when we finally have to determine if the price is reasonable. A complete analysis of this very detailed description above would be almost a book in itself. For our purposes, the following points need emphasis:

1. The customarily heard phrase "at least two offerors" does not in itself guarantee that adequate price competition exists. Numerous other conditions have to be met.
2. There must be at least two offerors who can actually satisfy the requirement (responsible) and they must be *responsive* (promise to do what the government says it wants).
3. The offerors must have competed independently. There must be no reason to believe that any collusion existed, or that anyone was under any pressure to make or not to make an offer.
4. The offerors must have known from the outset that the award would be made to the offeror with the lowest price meeting the criteria of responsibility and responsiveness. The lowest price is not always the sole criterion for contract award (for example, many negotiations for R&D) even though cost and profit must always be considered. When contract award is based on factors other than lowest price, the price effect has been diluted and price competition is not governing.
5. Adequate price competition may not exist if one or several firms known to be qualified for the work did not have a reasonable opportunity to compete. Maybe they were not given adequate time to make up their proposals or were deprived of an opportunity to compete because of unduly restrictive qualification requirements which, in effect, confined the award to a selected few.
6. Adequate price competition does not exist if one or a few offerors have a lock on the job. Often the incumbent contractor is fully aware of the precise and the risky pricing areas, whereas the stranger to the contracting action does not have that advantage. One offeror may already have fully amortized the cost of the special machinery needed to do the work.

That offeror may be in a position to bid unreasonably high for his own costs, knowing full well that he can still beat other offerors who will include the cost of expensive machinery. The offeror who controls the sale of some major assembly has a great advantage over all other offerors who must come to him to get that major assembly.

A Single Reasonable Offer

What does the government do if it receives only one offer but the price is reasonable? FAR 15.403-1 (c) (ii) acknowledges adequate price competition when a single offeror prepares a price offer—provided the buyer, in preparing a solicitation, anticipated multiple priced offerors from responsive sources and the offeror, when submitting a priced offer, operated under the assumption that a (known or unknown) competitor(s) may also be simultaneously preparing a competing price offer. In effect, the FAR is saying that an offeror tendering an offer in ignorance of the absence of competition is tendering a competitive offer.

Certificate of Independent Price Determination (FAR 3.103-1)

FAR 3.103-1 requires the insertion of a Certificate of Independent Price Determination in all solicitations when the government anticipates the award of either a firm-fixed-price contract or fixed-price a contract with economic price adjustment. The provision itself is stated at FAR 52.203-2.

In summary, the offeror is required to certify that:

1. It arrived at the offered prices independently and without consultation with other offerors or competitors for the purposes of restricting competition. This portion of the certificate covers price discussions, intent to submit a price, and methods of calculating a bid price.
2. Prices have not and will not knowingly be disclosed to any other possible offeror prior to bid opening time or, in the ease of negotiation, prior to contract award time.
3. No attempt has been made to influence any offeror or competitor to submit or not submit an offer.

In addition, the certificate contains certain other statements designed to show that the person or persons who sign the certificate are responsible for determining the offered prices and that they have not, and will not, violate the terms of the certificate.

The certificate is not required for acquisitions for (1) small purchase procedures, (2) utility services, (3) requests for technical proposals under Step 1 of two-step sealed bidding, and (4) work performed outside the United States, its possessions, and Puerto Rico.

Precautions against Buy-Ins

FAR Subpart 3.5 covers "buy-ins" as one of several improper business practices. The offeror engaging in a "buy-in" submits a below-cost offer just to get the contract and plans on making up the shortfall after award by unnecessary or overpriced change orders or by receiving follow-on contracts at artificially high prices.

FAR 3.501-2 states that the government should minimize the possibilities for a "buy-in" by seeking price commitments for as much of a total program as is practical. Some of the suggested means are:

- Multi-year contracting using prices for the total quantity;
- Priced options for additional quantities that considered with the basic quantity add up to the total requirement; and
- Other safeguards such as referral of unreasonable quotations to higher level authorities for determination.

In practice, it is often difficult to know whether an offeror is engaging in a "buy-in" or exercising its right to provide a good faith below-cost offer (see Variable (Incremental) Cost Pricing). The Comptroller General has repeatedly ruled that a below-cost bid or proposal is not in itself a basis for rejection of an offer. An offeror may submit such a below-cost offer to keep people employed that he would otherwise have to discharge, to fill in work during a temporary lull in overall business, and for other legitimate reasons. The receipt of a known below-cost offer raises several questions:

- Is it a mistake in the offer itself? If so, the FAR contains procedures for calling the offeror's attention to suspected errors (FAR 14.407 and 15.508).

If the offeror reaffirms the stated price, the remaining questions are:

- Is it a good faith intentional below-cost offer by a *responsible* offeror with no improper intent in mind?
- Is it a below-cost offer caused by failure to understand fully the work to be done? If so, the offeror may not be responsible and hence would be ineligible for contract award. Award would very likely result in later contract administration problems.
- Is it an actual "buy-in" submitted as an improper business practice? If so, the offeror is very unlikely to admit that fact openly.

Chapter 2
Contracting Methods and Contract Types: Pricing Implications

This chapter will briefly review the major contracting methods and the broad categories of contract types used by the government. The subjects will be covered primarily from a pricing standpoint. We will not attempt to cover all aspects of these subjects in this text; however, this chapter should suffice to bring those readers without prior experience to essentially the same level as more experienced readers.

Those readers who desire to learn in more detail about contracting methods should refer to additional texts on basic acquisition or types of contracts. FAR Parts 12, 13, 14, and 15, respectively, provide detail on acquisition of commercial items, simplified acquisition procedures, sealed bidding, and contracting by negotiation. FAR Part 16 covers contract types in detail.

CONTRACTING METHODS

FAR 6.401 identifies two acceptable procedures for obtaining competitive prices:

- *Sealed Bidding.* A process by which government needs are made known by a solicitation called an Invitation for Bids (IFB). The government will use sealed bidding when (1) it feels confident that award can be made to the lowest price offeror who is responsive and responsible and (2) the government's requirement is reasonably well defined in the form of drawings and specifications. Award by sealed bidding exploits the presumed existence of adequate price competition.
- *Competitive Proposals.* A process by which government needs are made known by a solicitation called a Request for Quotation (RFQ) or a Request for Proposals (RFP). Offerors respond by submitting priced offers for the work, product, or service described in the solicitation. However, FAR 15.304 (c) (2) provides that offerors' responses may—and in some cases, must—provide other relevant information to enable the government to consider such noncost evaluation factors as past performance, compliance with solicitation requirements, technical excellence, management capability, personnel qualifications, and prior experience. The government evaluates the proposals and generally, but not always, holds individual discussions with each offeror. Offerors have an opportunity to change their proposals. Final contract award is made to the offeror or offerors who provide the "best overall deal(s)" to the government. Award may or may not be primarily based on the lowest price, but cost or price must always be a factor in the final choice. This process, normally referred to as contacting by negotiation, is described in FAR Part 15. The processes of competitive proposals, as they apply to acquisition of commercial items, and simplified acquisition procedures are described in FAR Parts 13 and 14, respectively.

Sealed Bidding (FAR Part 14)

Sealed bidding is used when the government contracting officer decides that adequate price competition exists and that the specification or statement of work is well enough defined to enable offerors to bid on a fixed-price basis.

In sealed bidding, the using activity prepares an acquisition request that describes its needs and cites funds for the acquisition. The contracting activity prepares an IFB to inform prospective bidders of the government's needs. It is made up in accordance with a standard format prescribed in the FAR and contains a description of the supplies or services required, any special inspection and acceptance criteria, certain required bidder certifications, and copies of (or references to) the clauses applicable to the final contract.

The upcoming acquisition is publicized through distribution to prospective bidders, posting in public places such as electronic bulletin boards, and by other means. The IFBs are mailed to firms on the solicitation mailing list, which is a list of firms who have already advised the government of their interest in getting the type of work on the IFB. Publicizing enables firms not on the solicitation mailing list to be aware of the acquisition and request a copy of the IFB. Those firms interested in the work will submit bids. The bids are kept in a secure place until the bid opening time stated in the IFB and are publicly opened at that precise time. (Late bids are not considered unless the bidder can prove, under very stringent criteria, that its bid was delayed through no fault of the bidder, by mail delays, or by mishandling within the government.)

The price that was bid by each offeror becomes publicly known once the bids are opened. The government starts the evaluation of the bids at this point, beginning with the apparent low bidder. To be eligible for award, the bidder must be both responsive and responsible. To be responsive, the bidder must not have taken exception to any material aspect of the specification, work statement, or other terms of the proposed contract. To be responsible, the bidder must be judged capable of performing and meeting the terms stated in the IFB. Both determinations are made by the contracting officer. If the apparent low bidder meets both criteria, that firm gets the contract award as long as the bid price is reasonable. If the criteria are not met, the next low bidder is evaluated. The process continues until the lowest responsive, responsible, and reasonably priced bid is determined. The bidders have agreed, by submission of their bids, to keep their bids open for acceptance during this evaluation period, normally 60 days.

Contract award will not be made by this procedure unless the price of the low responsible bidder is determined to be reasonable. This determination is made by price analysis techniques, since the bid price is the only information available. The bidder is not required to furnish information on cost and profit to support its bid price; the government has depended on adequate price competition to get a fair and reasonable price. There are no individual discussions with any bidder during the process, and no price discussions occur.

Sealed bidding always leads to a firm-fixed-price contract or fixed-price with economic adjustment contract. Once the contract has been awarded, the government is firmly committed to paying the price that was bid and accepted. This practice requires that great care be taken to assure that the price is reasonable. The government cannot later go back and demand a refund or otherwise reduce the contract price on the pretext that it made a mistake in the price reasonableness determination.

Negotiation (FAR Part 15)

In many instances sealed bidding is needlessly time consuming and cumbersome. The government recognized this concern with the passage of The Federal Acquisition Streamlining Act (FASA) of 1994 (Public Law 103-355). FASA established the government's preference for the acquisition of commercial items by setting out policies more closely resembling those of the commercial marketplace and encouraging the acquisition of commercial items and components. FAR Part 12 prescribes the policies and procedures for the acquisition of commercial items.

The government also recognizes that certain acquisitions of relatively low dollar value do not warrant the time-consuming efforts of sealed bidding. FAR Part 13 prescribes the policies and procedures for the acquisition of supplies and services, the aggregate amount of which does not exceed the "simplified acquisition threshold." Past editions of the FAR referred to these items as "small purchases." The designation "small purchases" no longer shows up in the FAR. Indeed the current simplified acquisition threshold is $100,000 for most items, but can be a high as $5 million for certain commercial items. Regardless, to avoid the time-consuming procedures of sealed bidding, the government exploits the existence of multiple sources in the marketplace to obtain competing offers.

In still other instances, the specification or statement of work may not be well-enough defined to enable offerors to bid on a fixed-price basis, the buying activity may find it desirable to hold individual discussions with offerors before making a final source selection, or, in some rare instances, multiple sources may not exist.

Negotiation is the contracting method that may be used when sealed bidding is inappropriate. The process of negotiation starts in a way similar to sealed bidding. The using activity states its requirements in an acquisition request, including specifications for needed products and a statement of work for needed services. The contracting activity converts the acquisition request into a solicitation—usually into an RFP. The forthcoming acquisition is publicized through distribution to prospective bidders, posting in public places, electronic bulletin boards, and other readily accessible places, and by other means. The RFPs are sent to firms on the solicitation mailing list. Firms not on the list have an opportunity to request copies of the RFP because of the publicity given in the public postings. Interested firms make offers in response to the RFP. There is no formal public opening of the offers (as in sealed bidding), but they must be received by the date and time stated in the RFP. Offers are then evaluated in light of the solicitation requirements.

But, in marked contrast to a sealed bid award, a negotiated award:

- Need not be made to other than the lowest priced offeror;
- Is not restricted to a firm-fixed-price contract or fixed-price with economic adjustment contract;
- May result in any of the wide selection of contract types permitted by FAR Part 16, and
- May be preceded by changes to the original offer up to the time of contract award, based on discussions and negotiations.

Also, in contrast to sealed bidding, offers are sometimes subjected to an early screening to qualify for the competitive range. The competitive range consists of those offerors who, based on initial proposal evaluation, are believed to have a reasonable chance of getting the final award. This determination is the result of:

- Evaluating technical proposals by systematic procedures to determine their strengths and weaknesses and their relative order of excellence;
- Evaluating the pricing proposals by price analysis techniques to determine their reasonableness and the offerors' apparent understanding of the contract requirements; and
- If applicable, evaluating management proposals and any other special requirements which may have been stated in the RFP.

Offerors who are determined to be outside of the competitive range based on evaluation of their initial proposals are notified that they will not be considered further.

The competitive range establishes the list of offerors with whom individual discussions will be held; the discussions may be written or oral, or both. The purpose of these discussions is to advise offerors of deficiencies in their proposals, resolve any uncertainties that exist, and give offerors a reasonable opportunity to revise their proposals in light of the discussions. Obviously, the government must prepare for individual discussions with each offeror by completing a detailed and thorough examination of each proposal. This requirement applies to technical and pricing content of the proposals, and to any other information that sheds light on the offerors' ability to perform at a reasonable cost or price.

FAR Part 15 prescribes the policies and procedures governing competitive and noncompetitive negotiated acquisitions.

FAR 15.002 distinguishes between two types of negotiated acquisition: competitive and sole source acquisitions.

Competitive Acquisition

As the name implies, competitive acquisitions rely on market forces to obtain the best value to the government. FAR 15.002 (b) states that procedures for competitive acquisitions should "minimize the complexity of the solicitation, the evaluation, and the source selection decision, while maintaining a process designed to foster an impartial and comprehensive evaluation of offerors' proposals, leading to selection of the proposal representing the best value to the Government."

RFPs for competitive acquisitions exploit the competitive marketplace to obtain the best overall deal to the government. The *issuance of an RFP to multiple suppliers*, in and of itself, *shows that the buying agency is trying to promote adequate price competition.*

FAR Subpart 15.1—Source Selection Processes and Techniques, provides considerable flexibility to the buying activity in evaluating competitive proposals. An agency can obtain best value in negotiated acquisitions by using any one or a combination of source selection approaches. In different types of acquisitions, the relative importance of cost or price may vary. For example, in acquisitions where the requirement is clearly definable and the risk of unsuccessful contract performance is minimal, cost or price may play a dominant role in source selection. The less definitive the requirement, the more development work required, or the greater the performance risk, the more that technical or past performance considerations may play a dominant role in source selection.

A tradeoff process may be appropriate when it is in the best interest of the government to consider awarding to other than the lowest priced offeror or other than the highest technically rated offeror. However, when using a tradeoff process:

> All evaluation factors and significant subfactors that will affect contract award and their relative importance shall be clearly stated in the solicitation; and

> The solicitation shall state whether all evaluation factors other than cost or price, when combined, are significantly more important than, approximately equal to, or significantly less important than cost or price.

This process permits tradeoffs among cost or price and noncost factors and allows the government to accept other than the lowest priced proposal. The perceived benefits of the higher priced proposal shall merit the additional cost, and the rationale for tradeoffs must be documented in the file

The government conducts discussions with each offeror in the competitive range to be sure that all deficiencies have been pointed out and that areas of possible misunderstanding have been cleared up. Offerors are given full opportunity to revise their proposals. The government then notifies all offerors still in the competitive range to submit their "best and final" offers (BAFOs) by a certain time and date. This time and date must be met for the offeror to be eligible for final award. The government makes a final source selection based on the content of the BAFO.

Sole Source Acquisition

When contracting in a sole source environment, the RFP should be tailored to remove unnecessary information and requirements—e.g., evaluation criteria and voluminous proposal preparation instructions.

Contrary to popular opinion, awards for sole source acquisitions may be based on price analysis. Indeed, FAR 15.403-1 forbids the contracting officer from even requesting cost and pricing data for acquisitions below the simplified acquisition threshold or for the acquisition of commercial items. Nor can the contracting officer request cost and pricing data if the sole source supplier's price is set by law or regulation. And as we learned in Chapter 1, FAR 15.403-1 (c) acknowledges that reasonableness of a proposed price can be judged by comparison with current or recent prices for the same or similar items purchased in comparable quantities, under comparable terms and conditions under contracts that resulted from adequate price competition.

As we will see in Chapter 5, the requirement for the submission of cost and pricing data is to be the exception rather than the rule. Nevertheless, in some unusual circumstances, the RFP for sole source acquisitions may require that offerors submit detailed cost and pricing data in their pricing proposal. Or in some instances, the contracting officer may require limited information other than cost and pricing data to support a determination of price reasonableness or cost realism. This requirement means that the offerors will provide detailed estimates of the expected costs of performance and the expected profit or fee. This detailed cost and profit information enables the application of cost analysis principles. We will cover cost and pricing data in detail in Chapter 5.

This text covers the detailed procedures needed to perform an adequate cost, profit, and price analysis. Failure to do this job thoroughly and properly may well result in the payment of excessive prices, or in awarding a contract to an offeror who cannot do the work. Be aware, however, that issues related to proposal evaluation other than cost, such as offerors' technical competency and understanding of the solicitation requirements, are also essential to proper discussions and to source selection. You may wish to refer to other texts on source selection and technical evaluation of proposals.

The preceding discussion has presented a general sequence of events for negotiated procurements; however, negotiation is a flexible process and may be modified, within reason, to meet special requirements.

GOVERNMENT CONTRACT TYPES (FAR PART 16)

FAR Part 16 lists five categories of contract types used by the government.

- Fixed-Price Contracts   FAR Subpart 16.2
- Cost-Reimbursement Contracts   16.3
- Incentive Contracts   16.4
- Indefinite-Delivery Contracts   16.5
- Time-and-Materials, Labor-Hour,
  and Letter Contracts   16.6

This text will review the major characteristics of the first two contract types from a pricing standpoint. The other types listed are special modifications of either fixed-price or cost-reimbursement contracts.

Impact of Cost or Price Evaluation on Contract Type (FAR 15.305 (a) (1))

Normally, competition establishes price reasonableness. Therefore, when contracting on a firm-fixed-price or fixed-price with economic price adjustment basis, comparison of the proposed prices will usually satisfy the requirement to perform a price analysis, and a cost analysis need not be performed. In limited situations, a cost analysis may be appropriate to establish reasonableness of the otherwise successful offeror's price. When contracting on a cost-reimbursement basis, evaluations shall include a cost realism analysis to determine what the government should realistically expect to pay for the proposed effort, the offeror's understanding of the work, and the offeror's ability to perform the contract.

Fixed-Price Contracts (FAR Subpart 16.2)

This contract category includes firm-fixed-price contracts and fixed-price with economic adjustment contracts. These fixed-type contracts can result from either sealed bidding or negotiation.

The basic criterion for use of a firm-fixed-price type contract is that the costs of performance can be predicted with great accuracy. We must understand from the outset that no one can predict exactly what it will cost in the future to do anything. Material and labor costs may change, or unexpected problems may arise to increase costs. FAR 16.202-2 states that a firm-fixed-price type contract is suitable for use when we are buying commercial or commercial-type products and other products and services on the basis of *reasonably definite* functional or detailed specifications. This statement can be better understood if we define the key words and phrases as follows:

- *Commercial products*: The manufacturers and suppliers of these items already have a lot of experience in making and selling these products on the open market. When any customer, including the government, requests a price for future delivery (a bid or proposal), it is possible to use past experience to project a very close estimate of the costs of supplying the order.
- *Commercial-type products*: Commercial-type products are items on which some changes have been made to a purely commercial item to adapt it to government-peculiar uses. For example, standard vehicles may be painted with a particular color paint and a few decals added for use by the National Park Service or the Marine Corps. The added costs to make these changes can be closely estimated for future delivery.
- *Acquiring products or services on the basis of reasonably definite functional or detailed specifications*: Functional specifications describe what a product is to do. Detailed specifications state exactly how to make the product. Work statements define the work to be done to render services. In all such cases, there is some level of uncertainty about what it will actually cost to provide the work. A competent offeror takes that uncertainty into consideration when preparing its proposed price. The government can afford to take the risk when the built-in cost to cover the uncertain aspects is comparatively low.

Firm-fixed-price contracts place the total cost risk on the contractor. The offeror who bids or proposes a firm fixed price to do work is guaranteeing to deliver the work to meet requirements for that amount of money. When the government accepts the offer, it is obligated to pay that amount of money and the contractor is similarly obligated to deliver or perform the work for that fixed price. If unexpected costs arise, the contractor's profit decreases. In some cases, the contractor's profits may disappear or the contractor may even sustain a loss to meet the contract requirements. On the other hand, the contractor may be able to get the required work done for less than originally estimated costs. If so, the contractor keeps the extra profit earned. It is unlawful to give the contractor extra money simply because the costs have unexpectedly exceeded the contractor's original estimate. We cannot increase the contract price unless we get something special in return; more money to deliver what was already promised does not meet the test. On the other side, the contractor is very unlikely to give the government a refund if the actual profit is higher than expected because of decreased cost.

From the above discussion, you can see that we must do our cost and price analysis as accurately as possible before committing the government to paying a firm-fixed price. Once the contract is signed, the government can almost never recover if it belatedly discovers that the price was too high. (The possible exception will be covered in more detail in Chapter 5. If the government relied on noncurrent, incomplete, or inaccurate cost and pricing data at the time of price agreement, the government may effect a recovery of the amount by which the contractor unjustifiably enriched itself. Public Law 87-656, the Truth in Negotiations Act (TINA), enables the government to negotiate a recovery of the overpricing. This exception applies only to negotiated fixed-price contracts when detailed cost data was provided by the offeror and certified.)

Cost-Reimbursement Contracts (FAR Subpart 16.3)

Cost-reimbursement contracts are always awarded as the result of negotiations, never as the result of sealed bidding. Cost-reimbursement contracts provide for payment of the contractor's allowable incurred costs to the extent prescribed in the contract. There are several types of basic cost-reimbursement contracts. The *cost-plus fixed-fee* contract reimburses the contractor for allowable incurred costs and pays a fixed fee (profit) for doing the work. The *cost* (no fee) contract reimburses the contractor for allowable costs but has no fee. The *cost-sharing* contract reimburses the contractor for an agreed-upon share of its allowable costs. (FAR Subpart 16.4, Incentive Contracts, covers several types of incentive cost reimbursement contracts in which the fee is adjusted based on the contractor's actual costs or on how well the work is performed.)

Cost-reimbursement contracts are used when the costs of performing the contract work cannot be predicted with high accuracy at the time of signing the contract. For example, it is rarely possible at the time of contracting for goal-directed R&D work (developing an advanced state-of-the-art space vehicle or a cure for lung cancer) to estimate costs with enough accuracy for fixed-price contracting to be practical. Certain types of services, including maintenance, may fall into the same category. If the government insisted on a fixed-price contract in such situations, offerors would have no choice except to pad costs and prices heavily just to protect themselves.

A cost-reimbursement contract establishes an estimate of total costs for purposes of obligating funds and stating a ceiling that the contractor must not exceed except at its own risk. The contractor is obligated to provide a best effort to get the required work done within the estimated cost. If the contractor gets the work done for less than the estimated cost, the government has funds left for other purposes. If the contractor fails to finish the work within the estimated cost, the government's choices are (1) modify the contract to increase the estimated cost, or (2) settle out the contract and take whatever work has been completed.

The government is carrying all, or essentially all, the cost risk in a cost-reimbursement contract. If the contract calls for a fixed-fee, the government must pay that fee. The fee is the contractor's reward (profit) for taking on the work or engagement. Note that in a cost-plus-fixed-fee contract, the contractor cannot increase its profits no matter how efficiently the work is performed. (It is true that the contractor's profit as a percent of costs increases if the actual cost is less than the estimated cost; however, that fact is of little practical importance to a company interested in earning more profits.) The *cost-plus-incentive-fee* contract (an incentive contract described in FAR 16.405-1) does, within limits, allow for increase or decrease of the fee based on the contractor's actual costs compared to a target cost.

People inexperienced in the proper use of cost-reimbursement contracts often view them with general distrust or even as a license to steal. Generally these people are most experienced in situations where firm-fixed-price contracts are the usual type because their agency purchases well-defined products and services. Properly used and managed cost-reimbursement contracts are a perfectly acceptable contract form. We can draw an analogy in a government installation where in-house personnel perform work of very uncertain and changing content. For example, a government facility would probably budget a set amount each year for exterior building maintenance, including lawn care and clearing snow. That budgeted amount is an estimate. In a given year it may be necessary to remove far more snow than expected, and building maintenance costs may soar because of several storms (both result in an unexpected volume of work). The fact that the budgeted amount (estimated cost) is exceeded does not in itself say that the in-house workforce is wasteful or improperly motivated. It merely means that the cost forecast was wrong.

It is sometimes helpful to readers who do not have experience in using cost-reimbursement contracts to regard them as a way to pay a contractor "by the day" to do government work, and also to pay for the material that the contractor uses. The government must closely administer the work to ensure that it is for proper purposes and is done in an effective and efficient manner. The government will reimburse the contractor for its allowable costs in doing the work required; the contractor is paid only for that work. If work is unnecessary, it should not be done and there should be no reimbursement. In this sense, it is similar to doing work in-house. Here too, the government pays only for the work actually done.

SIMPLIFIED ACQUISITION PROCEDURES (FAR PART 13)

These procedures apply to purchases below the small purchase limitation, presently $100,000 for all agencies. These procedures do not apply to ordering from Federal Supply Schedules or to delivery orders placed against existing contracts. The small purchase and simplified purchase procedures emphasize simplicity and minimal administrative costs. Oral solicitations are normally used, although very simple written quotations may be used under certain circumstances.

Price analysis, covered in detail in Chapter 3, is always used in small purchases and other simplified purchase procedures because we do not attempt to, or need to, get cost and profit data.

PRICE ANALYSIS FOR PURCHASES BELOW $100,000

FAR 13.106 covers the procedures used for determining price reasonableness for purchases under the simplified acquisition threshold (currently $100,000).

For acquisitions below the simplified acquisition threshold, the contracting officer has broad discretion in determining the price reasonableness. But the contracting officer's determination can only be based on some form of price analysis. FAR 13.106-3 provides that whenever possible, price reasonableness be based on competitive quotations or offers.

If only one response is received, the contracting officer must include a statement of price reasonableness. The contracting officer may base the statement on: market research; comparison of the proposed price with prices found reasonable on previous purchases; current price lists, catalogs, or advertisements; a comparison with similar items in a related industry; personal knowledge of the item being purchased; comparison to an independent Government estimate; or any other reasonable basis.

In those few instances when supplies can be obtained only from a supplier that quotes a minimum order price or quantity that either unreasonably exceeds stated quantity requirements or results in an unreasonable price for the quantity required, the contracting officer should inform the requiring activity of all facts regarding the quotation or offer and ask it to confirm or alter its requirement.

CHAPTER 3
Price Analysis

Price analysis is defined in FAR 15.404-1 (b) (1) as the "process of examining and evaluating a proposed price without evaluating its separate cost elements and proposed profit."

As discussed at the beginning of the Chapter 1, we all do price analysis in our daily lives for our own private purposes. Rarely, do we have anything other than a general idea of the cost and profit built into anything we buy. When we buy a house, the largest single purchase most of us ever make, it never occurs to us even to attempt to learn the cost of the materials and labor that went into the house. Even if it did, how many of us would also remember that the builder has more costs than simply the labor and material in the house? The builder has an investment in tools and equipment that it seeks to recover over time by charging off some of those costs to each house built. The builder borrowed money or used capital already available to finance the cost of the land and the construction of the house. You can bet that the labor force and the suppliers did not wait for sale of the house to be paid. Interest on that money, if borrowed, and lost interest if taken from the builder's savings, is a part of the cost too. We make no attempt to learn these built-in costs, and could not get them if we tried. Nor do we have any idea of the profit the builder makes.

So what do we do in our daily lives, whether we are buying a house, car, or refrigerator, or getting the rugs cleaned? We do what the government acquisition regulations call price analysis: we attempt to learn what competitive prices are. If it is a major purchase, we shop around to see what various people are charging. The bigger the purchase, the more shopping and comparing we do. We do not go to a lot of trouble for our very small purchases. Very few people will travel ten miles to save 10¢ on a head of lettuce. But they might well travel ten miles to reduce the weekly grocery bill from $100 to $80. Notice that we do this "price analysis" based primarily on price comparison. The government uses price comparison too. The government has an advantage because it can sometimes use other fairly reliable methods not conveniently available to private individuals. Actually, we could use any of the various methods the government uses but it would cost us more than we would be likely to save for the type of purchases most individuals make.

PURPOSES OF PRICE ANALYSIS

Forecasting the Likely Price of an Acquisition

When a government agency needs to acquire various products and services, it must forecast the price of those products and services in its budget and convince the reviewing authorities that the forecast is reasonable. The agency uses price analysis methods for the forecast, whether it thinks of it in those terms or not. Once the funds are appropriated, the agency is in a position to actually buy the products and services. For example, if a small computer is needed for stock management in the maintenance department store room, the required funds (within an available appropriation) must be cited before the acquisition request even reaches the contracting office. This requirement means that someone has to develop the expected price for the computer. The estimate is likely to be done by comparing with generally known costs for similar computers, perhaps using catalog prices.

Evaluating Bids, Proposals, and Quotations

The bids, price proposals, and quotes received by the government in response to solicitations and requests for quotations must all be evaluated for price reasonableness. The extent of the evaluation necessary depends on the amount of competition that existed and the size of the acquisition action. A small purchase will typically receive a limited amount of price analysis. A $20 million buy for 200 special-purpose vehicles is likely to get very close unit and total price scrutiny, especially if the competition is limited.

Selecting the Bidder or Offeror for Award

Price analysis must be done when selecting a contractor for award of a firm-fixed-price or fixed-price with economic adjustment contract; we must do what we can to assure that the price is reasonable because when the government commits itself by contract signature to pay a price, there is no opportunity to amend the price unless the contract work is changed.

(Note that we have deliberately confined this discussion to fixed-price type contracts. Price analysis, *as such,* is not done for cost-reimbursement contract awards because no price is stated in the contract; it states an estimated cost plus a fee. Our administration of cost-reimbursement contracts provides a second chance to help assure that the ultimate price, known only after completion of the work, is reasonable. We attempt at the outset to get some idea of what the final price will be, but that attempt is not price analysis in the sense described in this chapter. See Chapter 2, "Cost-Reimbursement Contracts," for further discussion.)

Preparing for Price Discussion in Negotiation

When we use negotiation to reach a fixed-price type contract, we normally hold discussions on pricing and technical aspects with each offeror in the competitive range. (The government may award based on proposals as submitted without holding any discussions *if* the solicitation specifically states that possibility; however, this approach is not common, even when the government right is expressed in the solicitation. Obviously, the benefits of negotiation are lost if you don't negotiate. Furthermore, the time commitment of negotiations is often token. Consider, for example, the time commitment of a telephone call requesting a best and final offer.)

Regardless of the size of the acquisition, detailed cost and pricing data are not sought if a determination is made that the award will be based on adequate competition. In such a case, we use price analysis alone to assess the reasonableness of each proposed price. This preliminary price analysis is necessary to be properly prepared for price discussions with the offerors. In other cases, detailed cost and pricing data are obtained. We use cost analysis, covered in a later part of this text, supplemented by price analysis in preparing for cost and price discussions with each offeror.

METHODS FOR PERFORMING PRICE ANALYSIS

FAR 15.404-1 (b) describes in very brief terms several possible methods for doing price analysis. It points out that one or more of these may be used in a specific case. The methods are:

- Comparison of proposed prices received in response to the solicitation;
- Comparison of prior proposed prices and contract prices with current proposed prices for the same or similar items;
- Application of rough yardsticks (e.g., dollars per pound) to highlight significant inconsistencies that warrant additional pricing inquiry;
- Comparison with competitive published price lists, published market prices of commodities, similar indexes, and discount or rebate commitments;
- Comparison with independent government estimates.
- Comparison with prices obtained through market research for the same or similar items.
- Analysis of pricing information provided by the offeror.

The first two techniques above are the preferred techniques. However, if the contracting officer determines that information on competitive proposed prices or previous contract prices is not available or is insufficient to determine that the price is fair and reasonable, the contracting officer may use any of the remaining techniques as appropriate to the circumstances of the acquisition.

Price Analysis

The next sections will describe the price analysis methods in more detail.

Comparison of Proposed Prices Received in Response to the Solicitation
This method consists of comparing offered prices to each other to decide which are reasonable. In the simplest case, all you need do is arrange bids in order and select the best offer. For example:

C	$1,213,140	B	$1,295,030
A	$1,230,970	F	$1,369,870
D	$1,258,990	E	$1,444,460

C is the low bidder at $1,213,140. The range of bid prices in the lowest four bids is fairly close ($1,213,140 to $1,295,030), approximately $80,000. This represents a variance of about 8% from the lowest to the highest. The range is even tighter if we consider the lowest three bids only. In most cases, a tight range of prices shows that adequate price competition exists.

As a general rule, we would expect offered prices to be fairly close together, but not the same, if adequate price competition has occurred. Examination of the range (spread) of prices will give us added confidence that the lowest offered price is reasonable. If all the evidence points to intense price competition for the award, we may not need to do any other price analysis. Our job is finished because adequate price competition has occurred.

However, be careful when using comparison with other prices offered as the *only* price analysis method. An extremely low price, compared to others, may indicate that the offeror did not fully understand the requirement or that a mistake was made. The government is required to point out apparent or obvious mistakes to offerors if it has reasonable basis to suspect they are present. (FAR 14.407 covers the handling of suspected errors in bids resulting from sealed bidding; FAR 15.508 covers errors in offers for negotiation.) This requirement does not obligate the government to conduct a painstaking examination of every offer to double-check every detail. Offerors are basically subject to the consequences of their own errors. However, it is improper to deliberately take advantage of a known or suspected mistake simply to entice the offeror into a contract which is actually underpriced. Also, protracted disputes, even if the government ultimately wins, are not an effective use of government time.

If adequate price competition exists, competitive evaluation may be all that is needed to determine price reasonableness; however, sometimes the circumstances require additional work. For example, we are less confident that adequate price competition exists if the prices at the low side of the range are not closely grouped. When a doubt exists, you need to use other price analysis methods to decide if price is reasonable.

Comparison of competitive bids with each other is the best of all the price analysis techniques when conditions are right for its use. It bases the reasonableness decision on current market price relative to the specific government requirement. However, the circumstances must fit. If the specification is restrictive, you will often fail to get enough bids for the technique to work well. There must be at least two independent offers, preferably more. You need many producers even though not all may choose to bid. Finally, it is important that none of the bidders have a marked advantage over the others.

Comparison to Prior Prices Paid

This method is one of the most frequently used for government price analysis. It is useful when the agency has had a history of contracting for the *same* products or services. For discussion purposes, consider the pricing history and current lowest bid price for a particular product, as shown in Exhibit 3-1.

Exhibit 3-1

Pricing History and Current Lowest Bid for a Product

Quantity	Unit Price Paid	When paid
214	$751.46	3 years ago
297	763.59	2 years ago
290	795.14	1 year ago

The present low unit bid price is $815.04 for a quantity of 305.

We have to decide whether the low unit bid price of $815.04 is reasonable in light of the pricing history. Several factors must be considered.

Reasonableness of Base Price: We are comparing the present unit price bid with some price paid in the past. Most of the time, we are comparing with what we paid the last time, in this case $795.14. Presumably it was considered reasonable a year ago, or we would not have paid it. The base price used for comparison must have been reasonable if this price analysis method is to work properly.

But stop and think about this for a moment: maybe we made the last buy under urgent conditions. If so, we may well have paid a higher-than-normal price because of urgency. Ideally, we would have made a note in the record to show that the price was paid under urgent circumstances. In such a case, we are better off to use the price paid two years ago as a base price when trying to decide on the reasonableness of the current offered price.

Time Since the Last Buy: We have become used to the general upward trend of prices. It does not surprise us that the unit price for a product is somewhat higher than it was a year ago because of the gradual upward movement of many costs in our economy. We might well look at the history and decide that $815.04 is reasonable.

Suppose in the example shown in Exhibit 3-1 that the pricing history had been for prior quarters rather than years. It would mean that, three months ago, we paid a unit price of $795.14, and now we are being asked to pay $815.04. This price would seem unwarranted, as the quantities are about the same. We might well decide that something is wrong and that the asking price is unreasonable.

Another caution is in order. Although general price trends are upward over the years, not every product follows this trend. For example, we can now buy commonplace hand-held calculators for a fraction of the price paid 10 years ago. The prices paid 10 years ago may have been reasonable at that time; the circumstances have now changed. It is not enough to be aware of general price trends. The buyer needs to be aware of the price trends that apply to the particular items being bought.

Relative Quantities: Most of us are aware that we are likely to get a better unit price when we buy larger quantities, and that we will pay more per unit if the quantity decreases. There are several reasons for this price difference. The supplier is more likely to give us a lower unit price on larger quantities because more products are sold, and although the unit profit is less, the overall profit is more. The paperwork cost for the supplier is about the same regardless of the quantity. Shipping and handling costs may not be all that much more for a large quantity than a small quantity.

Our example was deliberately made up to show about the same quantities for the current buy as for the two prior buys. We look at the $815.04 for 305 items and might well decide that although the quantity is up (indicating lower unit price), price trends for the industry are also up and the $815.04 looks reasonable. We are even more convinced because this is the lowest bid price we received.

Suppose the low current bid price is $840.98 rather than $815.04. This is a whole new picture. We might decide to cancel the IFB because of unreasonable bid prices and go to negotiation so we can hold price discussions with the offerors.

Type of Product—Shelf Item vs. Special Production: We all understand that special production items are likely to command a higher price than items held on a supplier's shelf for general sales. For instance, we know we will pay much more for a tailor-made suit than for a ready-made suit on the rack.

Whenever a producer sets up to manufacture an item, special set-up costs are incurred. For example, it may require an outlay of $20,000 to obtain the special tooling and checking equipment needed to make a production run of a particular gear used as a repair part. The manufacturer may decide that it can sell 20,000 of the gears in the next 8 to10 months. If so, it will make a production run of 20,000 gears to put on the shelf waiting for orders. The cost of each gear will include its share of the set-up cost, one dollar. The total cost will include set-up cost plus all other costs to make the gear (e.g., labor and materials) and the total cost for the gear may come to $10. The manufacturer will sell the gear at some price above $10 in order to achieve a profit.

Suppose the producer figures it will be able to sell only 500 gears. Now the set-up cost is $40 per gear ($20,000 for 500 gears). On the same basis as the above, the actual cost to produce each gear is around $49 (set-up cost $40 plus $9 for labor and materials). Now, because of set-up costs and more limited sales, the price per gear is far higher than before. The cost and price continue to increase as the expected sales volume decreases. Eventually the gear price could get so high that the user is better off to buy a new piece of equipment rather than to repair the one it already owns.

Special design items peculiar to government use with no commercial counterparts may well produce significant pricing problems for the government, especially in the area of parts replacement. The parts peculiar to the equipment require a special set-up for production each time they are ordered. The manufacturer is not going to make up a lot of these parts to store on the shelf, hoping the government will order more. Good business sense says to make whatever quantity is ordered. If the government orders in small quantities, the unit prices are often out of line with what common sense would indicate the parts are worth. The cure for this problem falls into the areas of equipment acquisition policy and supply management, not price analysis.

Acquisition Methods: Competitive acquisition methods are far more likely to result in reasonable prices than repetitive use of sole sources. The sole source, particularly when it knows it is a sole source for a necessary item, has no real motivation to keep prices down, except the possibility that the customer may find cheaper substitutes or refuse to buy at all. Sometimes we have little choice except to buy from the sole source, but this circumstance does not mean that we have to keep on "shooting ourselves in the foot." Government policy requires that we justify sole source contracting and that we do all we can to get out of the sole source predicament.

Repetitive buying from single sources may have pricing effects similar to sole source procurement, but less severe. The single source may become complacent in its view that the government will always come to it. This is most likely to occur in the misuse of the simplified acquisition procedures (FAR Part 13). The buyer who avoids or does not know the rules may habitually use the same sources for items, even though competitive purchasing is possible. FAR 13.104 requires the contracting officer to solicit at least three sources. Moreover, FAR 13.104 (b) states that the contracting officer should request quotations or offers from two sources not included in the previous solicitation.

Comparison to Prior Quotes

This method is similar to comparing a present offer to prior prices paid for the same item. However, it compares the present asking price to the prior quotes, not just a price paid. The considerations are essentially the same as those for comparing to prices previously paid.

Comparison to Prices Paid for Similar Items

This situation is similar to that previously discussed except that now we have the added complication of comparing something *similar* rather than the same. This requires us to make adjustments to the price we have previously paid. We add an estimated amount for features that are added and subtract for features that are no longer being bought.

For example, consider a proposed unit price of $297 for an overhead projector that is different in two major ways from previous purchases. It has a device for manually moving a new bulb into position when a bulb burns out, and it has a plastic case and lamp housing. We paid a unit price of $250 a year ago for a projector built with all-metal components but without the bulb changing device. The steps one might take in doing the comparison are:

1. If we were buying the same type projector, it would probably be up to around $270 by now.
2. We don't really know much about how the bulb changing device works, but it's probably a fairly simple metal device made so an outside lever will swing a new bulb into the required position and make a new electrical contact to power the bulb. That device might add another $25 to the price, raising the new estimate to $295.
3. This projector is mostly plastic. We have a feeling that plastic is cheaper than metal, and we adjust the estimate down by about $10, making the final estimate in the order of $285.
4. We compare this estimate of $285 to the actual asking price of $297. This buyer might decide the asking price is close enough to the estimate (actually 3.5 percent higher) to be reasonable.

Note that the comparison described above is all based on the buyer's judgment and is far from a precise mathematical calculation. If the buyer is buying ten projectors for a training center, and the $297 price is the best of three quotes, this information would be all most of us need to believe the price is reasonable. If it is a General Services Administration (GSA) buyer considering a contract which will be published in a Federal Supply Schedule that might result in purchases of 10,000 projectors by various agencies ($2,970,000), some further checking might be in order. (Note: This example is used to illustrate the approach. Let's not worry about why the buyer at the training center was going "off-schedule." There are acceptable reasons.)

You are probably thinking by now that comparing with prices paid for similar items in the past is a very imprecise method. It is, if you are comparing with prices paid several months or a year ago. However, this method may be precise if you are comparing to the price you paid very recently for a similar item. The level of precision depends on how accurately you can estimate the price change related to the differences in design.

Use of Estimating Relationships

The FAR refers to this method as "use of rough yardsticks." Estimating relationships are measures such as dollars per pound for finished products and dollars per square foot for finished construction. For example, a construction activity could maintain data on the total price and square footage for finished office construction in an area. The agency can accumulate the data for each type of construction such as "single-story brick with standard roof." The activity can use the data to generate an average cost for finished construction of the selected type, perhaps $75 per square foot. Then it can use this relationship to forecast reasonable costs for new construction. It can also use it to help verify that bid prices are reasonable.

You need to continually update estimating relationships so they will retain their usefulness. The example in the previous paragraph cited a finished construction price of $75 per square foot. This relationship must be updated to reflect prices as they gradually change. These changes will occur over time because of changes in cost of materials, labor, and other inputs.

Agencies experienced in buying complex items may develop rough yardsticks for use in estimating prices, determining price reasonableness, or detecting significant variations from estimates which justify further checking. Such yardsticks are often used for construction. For example, an agency may develop estimating factors, based on typical construction in the area and past experience, as shown in Exhibit 3-2.

Exhibit 3-2
Estimating Factors

Type of Construction	Cost per Square Foot
Office	$43.85
Warehouse	$23.85

The agency plans construction of an office building to occupy 100,000 square feet. The estimated cost of the construction would be $4,385,000 ($43.85 x 100,000). This cost estimate, adjusted for any special considerations and reasonable profit, can be used for obligating funds for the construction acquisition and for checking price reasonableness of the bids received.

The cost estimate shown above is developed based on the construction agency's experience in the recent past for typical construction in the area. The total cost is the sum of the costs for various parts of the construction effort (foundations, substructure, superstructure, exterior closure, roofing, interior construction, etc.). The total cost can be adjusted for changes peculiar to the specific construction project, like a change from an asphalt to a metal roof. The cost figures are averages for the area. No one considers the total cost to be exact, but it is close enough for "yardstick" measuring purposes.

Similar yardsticks are developed for other applications. For example, a vehicle procuring activity may develop a dollars per pound estimate for vehicles of various classifications such as sedans, buses, utility trucks, and cargo trucks. All such yardsticks are rough indicators and help disclose significant inconsistencies in offered prices.

Comparison of Offers to Published Prices

We are all familiar with catalogs put out by major retail companies and some discount houses. Even though purchases from traditional catalogs have fallen, catalogs still give us a general idea of the retail prices being charged for various items like clothing, hardware, computers, and appliances. These catalogs are recognized as fairly reliable guides on current prices being paid by consumers in general because catalogs are kept up to date by periodic revisions, and because many people buy from catalogs. We know that the company is unlikely to give any discounts from those prices. Hence, the prices are what people are actually paying for items that are bought in substantial numbers; otherwise the item would not be in the catalog.

The government is not normally interested in buying items at retail prices. It prefers to buy at commercial prices such as those made available to retailers or wholesalers. Manufacturers and distributors issue catalogs and price lists for large buyers like the government. Under the proper conditions, these catalogs reflect prices actually being paid and can be a reliable basis for determining price reasonableness.

We can do price analysis on a case-by-case basis to determine if the price is reasonable based on (1) an established catalog or market price; (2) the price paid for commercial items; and (3) the price for items sold in substantial quantities to the general public. If the price meets all these criteria, it is presumed to be reasonable because it is based on competition in the marketplace. However, the analysis involves more than may be immediately apparent. Let's examine each of the criteria.

An Established Catalog or Market Price: This is a price that is identified in a printed catalog, price list, schedule, or other form. The catalog must be regularly maintained; if it is out-of-date it is not useful to the question at hand. It must be readily available to a wide number of commercial customers. Finally, it must contain prices at which a large number of the listed items are actually being sold. It is no secret that suppliers regularly give discount prices to large or special customers. If it turns out that the bulk of the sales by a firm are being made at prices cheaper than the catalog prices, those catalog prices are not useful for determining price reasonableness. The reasonable price is whatever price most customers are actually paying. If most customers are not paying the listed price, they are in effect saying "we can do better elsewhere and we should be given a discount."

The Price Paid for Commercial Items: This entire price analysis approach is based on what commercial buyers are willing to pay for the items they buy. Commercial buyers are buying commercial items, not items that are peculiar to the government. If we are talking about government-peculiar items, the prices paid for commercial items are useful only as a starting point for price comparisons for similar items (see the discussion above).

The Price for Items Sold in Substantial Quantities: The items in the commercial catalog or price list must actually be sold in large enough quantities to show that customers are actually paying those prices. If an item is listed in a catalog at a given price, and it turns out that few people ever buy it, we have no way to know whether the catalog price is reasonable.

As a practical matter, how is the government buyer going to know if the price shown in the catalog put out by GBM Products Company (a fictitious company) meets all the criteria? First, we better find out something about GBM. Is it an established company with reasonable sales volume for its size? Are the prices comparable to those shown in the price lists of other companies in the same business? If GBM is an established company or a "going concern," it is unlikely to have many items in its inventory which do not sell. It is also not likely to use up space in its catalog for things that do not sell (the printing and widespread mailing of catalogs is an expensive matter). Is the catalog up to date? Going concerns keep their catalogs up to date, especially in times of rising prices, and their catalogs show prominently the date of issue.

Is the company discounting a lot of its catalog prices? This may be a tough question to get answered, especially by the company. If the price offered was obtained by competitive methods, and is the lowest price, these two factors are probably enough to establish reasonableness for smaller purchases. If we are buying major amounts, we do well to check the offered prices against the price lists published by several companies in the same business.

Comparing published prices depends on the economic principle embodied in perfect price competition: the market will reflect reasonable prices. The concept is that we can determine whether an offered price is reasonable by comparing it to the price set by the market. Although price competition is never perfect, there are many situations in the imperfect marketplace that are good enough for this method to work. When there is adequate price competition in the market, the comparison of an offered price to published catalog prices or established market prices will result in successful price analysis.

Published catalog prices are defined as prices in regularly maintained catalogs available to the general public. They must be prices that significant numbers of buyers who represent the general public are actually paying. The published prices do not meet the test if they are being substantially discounted. Established market prices are prices established between large numbers of buyers and sellers who are free to bargain. Some farm product sales meet this criterion. *The Wall Street Journal* publishes prices for certain raw materials and commodities traded in the commodities exchanges. Catalog and market prices are reliable indicators of reasonable prices when they meet the criteria discussed above. They result from market interactions of many buyers and sellers.

Comparison of offered prices to published catalog prices or established market prices is a primary technique, and it is an excellent technique when the conditions are right. However, do not be misled. It is not enough merely to establish that the catalog prices are being paid by large numbers of customers. You need to know the circumstances under which those sales are being made. Do they correspond to the circumstances in your solicitation? Your local lumber yard may make many sales at its over-the-counter price to walk-in customers with home projects. Assume that your government purchase action covers twenty line items of building materials estimated at $100,000. You are not in the same circumstance as those walk-in customers. You should get prices far better than those stated in the published catalog. Retail customer prices may well be reasonable for the situations where they are normally used, but they are not likely to be reasonable for a typical high-volume government acquisition.

Large business firms often have multitiered pricing arrangements, with different price lists for different customer groups. They often undercut their own prices for various reasons. Examples include special pricing for favored customers, price reductions to increase market share in particular areas, and inventory reductions. You need to be aware of these possibilities whenever you are comparing offered prices to those in commercial catalogs.

As we have previously covered, sometimes you may not have enough bids to be confident of the results of comparing bids with each other. You can supplement that method by comparing the lowest prices with those in catalogs or the market. You may sometimes compare offered prices with those in published catalogs or established markets as your primary method. You might well do this when you receive only one bid or quote. For example, assume that you receive only one quote, $970, for an item needed by the pathology laboratory. You compare this quote with the price stated in a medical supply catalog from another firm. You know that many commercial customers use this catalog and pay the prices listed in it. If the catalog price is $975.78, you would probably decide that the price quote you received is reasonable.

This method is useful when you compare an offered price with the catalog or market price for the same item. It is not as useful when there are differences among the items whose prices are compared.

Comparison with Independent Government Estimates

Some form of a Purchase Request (PR) is prepared to initiate most procurement actions. The PR shows the anticipated dollar value of the procurement action, to ascertain the availability of budgetary authority. Depending on the dollar value, complexity, and sensitivity of the forthcoming purchase, these estimates can range from simple budgetary estimates to complex estimates based on inspection of the product itself and review of such items as drawings, specifications, and prior data.

For example, FAR 36.203 (a) requires that an independent government estimate of construction costs be prepared and furnished to the contracting officer at the earliest practicable time for each proposed contract or modification expected to exceed $100,000. The contracting officer may request an estimate for amounts less than $100,000.

Construction price estimates prepared by organizations like the GSA Public Building Services, the Army Corps of Engineers, and the Bureau of Reclamation, are fairly reliable. These organizations specialize in construction activities, and have trained and experienced estimators and various data sources that enable them to do a creditable job in construction and A-E price estimating.

Government cost estimates may not be very reliable in other cases. One of the problems is that the people attempting the estimate, no matter how conscientious, may lack the complete and up-to-date data that must be available for reasonably accurate estimating. On the other hand, the purchase request estimate may be quite reliable.

The Armed Services Pricing Manual's discussion of this issue is still pertinent:

> The PR (Purchase Request) estimate may be a valid standard for comparison if it is based on a realistic engineering analysis or if the originator has used a reasonable past purchase price and identified the quantity. A realistic engineering estimate of what an item should cost could be one developed after study of the drawings, after physical inspection or teardown of a sample or by analysis of similar work and projection of price based on the findings of the analysis. Again, however, the buyer should compare earlier estimates developed in the same fashion with the resulting purchase prices before he decides on the reliability of the estimate.

Aside from construction and other areas where highly competent estimating staffs are available, comparison with government estimates alone is usually not a good idea. If comparison with a government estimate is the only method of price analysis, we need to establish that the estimate was arrived at in a systematic way, generally as described in the quotation above.

None of the above says that government people lack the intelligence to do good price estimating. The facts are much more likely to be that they lack the complete and current information essential to do reliable price estimating. Sometimes the estimator, needing something to put on the purchase request, may make an outright guess, which is obviously not a good basis for price comparison.

You need to be cautious when using this method. You must know the basis for the estimate and have a good idea about its reliability. You need to know how the estimate was made, what information and tools were used to formulate it, and where the information came from. Perhaps equally important, you need to know whether the estimator has the experience and training needed to make good estimates. Some estimators may be reasonably good at forecasting likely labor and material costs, but may have little knowledge and experience on matters such as tooling costs, overhead, and reasonable profit.

Comparison with Market Data

Market data consists of a broad collection of information about the market for the product or service being bought and is derived from trade journals, newspapers, economic indexes, and a variety of other sources that provide market information. Comparison with market data, like other secondary methods, is not a precise technique for price analysis. However, use of market data will help one become a better informed buyer.

Price index numbers represent changes in price occurring over periods of time. Various federal agencies develop price indexes for their areas of interest to show general price trends for products and services over time. The Federal Reserve Board, for example, publishes the Index of Retail Sales which shows the changes in quantities and prices of items sold across the country. Most of us have heard of the Consumer Price Index which shows the trends in prices for consumer products and services. The Bureau of Labor Statistics (BLS) of the Department of Labor publishes indexes for a wide variety of commercial products. The Producer Price Index (PPI), a very useful index for price analysis purposes, is published each month for a wide variety of commercial products. One of these PPI indexes covers ethical prescription drugs. The table in Exhibit 3-3 shows the indexes for representative months in 20X2.

Exhibit 3-3
PRI Indexes for Ethical Prescription Drugs

January	286.0	September	305.2
March	293.6	October	300.8
May	300.4	December	308.2
July	299.3		

The index shows there were some minor fluctuations during 20X2. Overall, there was a gradual price increase in this family of products.

Here's how to use the index: In January 20X3, we received a bid price of $73.94 per 1000 tablets for a specific prescription drug. The January 20X3 index is projected to be 311.0. We last bought this drug in September 20X2 and paid a competitive bid price of $72.50 per 1000 tablets.

The price index has increased by 5.8 points since September 20X2, representing a 1.9 percent increase in the index. We would expect the price to have increased around 1.9 percent if the index is a reliable indicator. For $72.50 per 1,000 tablets in September 19X7, a predicted January 20X3 price would be $73.88 ($72.50 x 101.9%). The actual bid price of $73.94 is fairly close to the calculated price, providing another assurance that the January bid price is reasonable. We would probably accept it as reasonable, especially if this bid price is the lowest of several received and the bids were tightly grouped.

In another example, assume that the BLS has published the indexes for hardware products as shown in Exhibit 3-4:

Exhibit 3-4
Indexes for Hardware Products

	Period		
Index	One Year Ago	3 Months Ago	Current Index
	105	111	112

The index in Exhibit 3-4 tells us that there has been a gradual upward trend in hardware prices over the past year. By a simple calculation, we can determine that hardware prices have increased by 6.67 percent over what they were a year ago. This gives us another tool to check current prices. If we bought a small lathe last year for $1,056, we would not be surprised if this year the same lathe is priced around $1,126 ($1056 x 106.67% = $1,126). Another, more direct way to calculate this figure is to multiply the old price by the current index divided by the old index. For example:

$$\$1056 \times \frac{112}{105} = \$1126$$

Economic indexes are useful to confirm the reasonableness of bid prices when other information shows that prices are reasonable. However, be very cautious in using economic indexes alone to reject a price as unreasonable. You need more indications of unreasonableness to be sure of your decision. Economic indexes show the economic trends for families of products. They are averages, calculated using on prices for the specific items that make up the index. The items chosen are intended to be representative of the commodity area. However, considering the hardware index above, not every item within the total list has gone up by 6.67 percent. Most went up but some may have gone down. Factors such as temporary shortages of raw materials and significant shifts in demand due to advertising promotions affect products individually. The 6.67 percent is an overall average, which does not guarantee that every item within the index went up by 6.67 percent.

Indexes are not worth the bother in small purchase procedures. They have some usefulness in buying activities that repetitively buy large quantities of the same items. Such activities can develop their own indexes based on the price trends they observe in their commodities. Indexes help, but they are not a mathematical shortcut that allows us to discard other methods of price analysis.

Pricing Information Provided By the Offeror

Vendors can sometimes provide information to demonstrate that their proffered price is a market-based price. For example, an offeror may prepare an analysis demonstrating that there is a market in the private sector of the economy willing to meet their offered market-based price.

Auxiliary Techniques for Price Analysis

Two auxiliary techniques can sometimes be useful to assist price analysis. Neither price analysis method should be used alone.

Value Analysis

FAR 15.404-1(b)(4) says that value analysis can give insight into the relative worth of a product, and the government may use it in conjunction with other price analysis techniques. This method is used to learn why prices are different for products of the same basic type and whether they are worth the difference. Value analysis consists of evaluating the item being bought in two ways. First, you list the required functions and compare them to the functions of competing products. You would expect an item that does less to have a lower price. Next, you identify and compare the aesthetic requirements. Aesthetics and usefulness that indicate a higher value will support a higher price. However, if a higher price is supported by nothing except the aesthetics, the price difference is hard to justify.

Visual Analysis

Visual analysis consists of looking at an item and using our experience to estimate its value. It is most useful with common commercial items or government items closely resembling commercial items and may be used with the drawings of an item or with a sample of the item. Most people have seen overhead projectors commonly used to show transparencies in classrooms. Our common sense tells us that this is basically a metal box with a light source, a fairly simple lens system, a switch, and a reflector. Most of us would guess that it is far simpler and easier to make than a sophisticated 35mm camera. We might be shocked if we received a price quote for the overhead projector at three times the price for the 35mm camera. For similar reasons, the public is shocked when they read in the newspapers about items such as $600 hammers.

This method is particularly useful when making small purchases for repair parts and accessories, especially when they are available from only one known source. For example, suppose we receive a purchase request for a cable whose only source is Minnesota Cable, Inc. We contact the firm and get a price quote of $95.56. If all we know about this item is that it is a cable, that description covers a broad range of possibilities. It could be anything from a steel cable used in construction to a very complex electrical connector used with computer equipment. Now assume we have a picture of the item and can see that it is a long electrical cable with very complicated looking receptacles at each end. We might be justified in accepting $95.56 as reasonable, lacking any further information. Or suppose it turns out to be a simple steel cable with a metal hook at each end. We would be justified in questioning the price. The picture helps us in the judgment.

THE BEST WAY TO DO PRICE ANALYSIS

Again, let's revisit FAR 15.404-1 (b), which identifies the following two preferred techniques:

- Comparison of proposed prices received in response to the solicitation; and
- Comparison of prior proposed prices and contract prices with current proposed prices for the same or similar items.

But as we stated earlier, FAR 15.404-1 (b) also recognizes that we may have to use a combination of methods. If we have good reason to believe that adequate price competition has occurred, as in, for example, having many bids all fairly close together, then we probably have a reasonable price. It is always wise to compare the bids with what we have previously paid for the same or similar items. Using published catalog prices, government estimates (if reliable), and other comparison methods discussed in this chapter will also help. Experience in the commodity area is very valuable. Good price analysis is a matter of good personal judgment. The problems faced by government buyers are identical to those faced by buyers in private companies, except that the government buyer may be exposed to heavier oversight and criticism because the government uses public funds.

CHAPTER 4
Cost Principles and Cost Classifications

FAR Part 31 contains the cost principles and procedures for:

> (a) the pricing of contracts, subcontracts, and modifications to contracts and subcontracts whenever cost analysis is performed (see 15.404-1(c)); and (b) the determination, negotiation, or allowance of costs when required by a contract clause. (FAR 31.000)

You use the cost principles and procedures to price contracts, subcontracts, and contract modifications whenever you must use cost analysis. You will use cost analysis any time you cannot depend on price analysis alone to establish a reasonable price. This could happen when you are negotiating a fixed-price contract with a single source or any time you do not have enough reliable price information to determine what a proper price for the effort should be.

If you are negotiating a cost-reimbursement contract, for example, the cost estimate is far less certain than it is with a fixed-price contract. You use a cost-reimbursement contract because the resources needed to perform the work are very unpredictable; the government cannot reliably predict the final price because it does not know fully what must be done. The contractor is no better off. One cannot establish the *price* for a cost-reimbursement contract until the contract work is finished. Once the work is finished, pricing can be done. The price consists of the costs and the fee (profit) paid to the contractor during contract performance. Cost, not price, discussions are held before a cost-reimbursement contract is awarded. The cost principles and practices are used in these discussions to negotiate contracts. Among other things, the cost principles help you to evaluate the offeror's estimated costs. This evaluation, in turn, helps to set the fee terms for the final contract. The cost principles also make it possible to reach an understanding in advance on the costs that the government will be willing to pay to get the work done.

You will use the cost principles and procedures to determine, negotiate, and allow costs when a contract clause requires these actions. Again, cost-reimbursement contracts are the most common instance. FAR 52.216-7, Allowable Cost and Payment, provides for periodic payments of allowable costs during performance of a cost-reimbursement contract. You will use the contract cost principles and procedures to review the contractor's periodic claims for cost reimbursement.

COST ACCOUNTING

Cost accounting is a procedure which enables firms to keep track of the costs that apply to each individual contract or major task they undertake. It is not the same as financial accounting. Financial accounting is the accumulation of information that enables the firm to know how much *total* cost and profit they made in a particular period of time. Financial accounting, standing alone, does not tell the firm what each individual job cost or the profit or loss taken on that particular job.

Some form of cost accounting is used by all firms who are reasonably well established. It provides them a means to know which product lines are profitable or incur losses and, hence, where to concentrate their efforts. Cost accounting is used by firms to:

1. Estimate the cost of work before actually undertaking it. It is a logical first step in preparing an offer.
2. Track the cost incurred for doing a specific work task. This tracking, among other things, provides a means to keep costs under control and tells the company how well it did in its estimate. If the estimate is far off from actual costs, the company needs to revise its cost accounting system or its method of estimating or both.
3. Decide whether or not to continue in certain product lines or services. If the firm's costs are so high for some tasks that they cannot effectively compete, they may do well to concentrate their energies elsewhere.

Under some conditions, the government is vitally interested in the adequacy of a firm's cost accounting methods. If, for example, the government places a cost-reimbursement contract with a firm, it is important for the government to be sure that the costs billed to it are a direct outgrowth of the costs incurred for that government contract. The government does not want costs for other contractor work to get mixed in with the costs billed to the government. The government also needs to be sure that the firm uses the same methods for estimating costs as for accumulating the costs for each job. Otherwise it will be difficult, or maybe impossible, to establish an audit trail.

Any time the government enters into a contract (such as a cost-reimbursement contract, a fixed-price-incentive contract, or a fixed-price-redetermination contract) in which the final price paid will depend on actual cost incurred, we must be sure that the contractor has an adequate cost accounting system. The failure to have such a system is a basis for disqualifying a contractor from receiving any cost-reimbursement contract.

If the government places a firm-fixed-price contract by sealed bidding, the price is fixed from the outset because the bid price was reasonable. In that case, we need not concern ourselves with the adequacy of the contractor's cost accounting system. It is the contractor's internal concern. However, if the government places a firm-fixed-price contract by negotiation, and the award is not based on adequate price competition, we are concerned that the contractor have an adequate cost accounting system to help assure us that the proposed costs are reasonable.

When negotiation is used, with final award not based on adequate price competition, we also expect offerors to use the same cost estimating methods (cost accounting systems) for government work that they use for their private work. Otherwise the government runs a risk of paying unfair costs.

COST CLASSIFICATIONS

There are three major classifications of costs that we need to understand fully before proceeding with the remainder of this book. These are: (1) reasonable, allowable, and allocable costs; (2) variable, fixed, and semi-variable costs; and (3) direct and indirect costs.

Reasonable, Allowable, and Allocable Costs

Reasonable Costs

The government has a policy to repay a contractor for its actual costs to do work under a contract, so long as the costs are reasonable. However, the term "reasonable" means different things to different people. There may be considerable differences of opinion between what government and contractor people perceive as reasonable. FAR 31.201-3 defines a reasonable cost as follows:

> A cost is reasonable if, in its nature and amount, it does not exceed that which would be incurred by a prudent person in the conduct of a competitive business.

This is an excellent definition of the term; we will break this definition into its parts and discuss each part.

The *nature of the cost,* combined with other factors in the definition, may make it unreasonable. For example, the use of first class air travel is normally considered to be unreasonable. The requirement for air travel may be perfectly valid and the government does not object to it in a particular case if the need to travel long distances applies. However, the nature of the cost of first class air travel is unreasonable, and under normal circumstances, there is no need to incur the extra cost. In another case, the contractor might propose a cost for very high quality materials when materials meeting lesser standards would be acceptable.

The *amount of the cost* may be unreasonable, even though the nature of the cost is acceptable. A material may be proposed that, in itself, is satisfactory for the purpose. However, we may find that the cost to be incurred for the material is unnecessarily high. This could happen because the proposer did not check around to find adequate material at a lower cost. It may be that the contractor is planning to buy the materials from one of its own divisions. If so, we are not willing to go along with the cost unless it is no higher than that obtainable by competitive procedures outside the company.

The *cost should not exceed what a prudent person would pay in a competitive business*. A prudent person does not spend money unnecessarily. However, the definition adds "in a competitive business." A firm selling items that people must have, with little or no competition, has no strong incentive to save on costs. Their costs are merely passed to the customers as a part of the overall price. However, the prospect that customers might go to a competitor if the price is too high adds a different light to the matter. Now the contractor is highly motivated to keep costs down so the price will be competitive.

The determination of cost reasonableness in specific cases requires skilled judgment. FAR 31.201-3 (b) requires the contracting officer to consider the following factors:

- Is it the type of cost generally recognized as *ordinary and necessary* in the contractor's business or in performing the particular contract? Answering this question may require us to have some experience in the type of costs that are ordinarily incurred by the type business in question. As one example, contractor payments toward an employee pension fund are not, in themselves, beneficial to our contract work. However, that type of expense has become an ordinary expense to many firms and is necessary once it is initiated. We would not argue about the nature. We might question the amount if we regarded it as too high. It isn't enough simply to regard it as too high with no rational basis. We need to compare the amount with that paid by similar companies.

- Is the cost a result of *sound business practice, arms-length bargaining, application of federal and state laws, or contract terms and specifications?* Sound business practice results in paying only the cost that is really necessary to obtain satisfactory materials or services. Arms-length bargaining means arriving at costs by straightforward business procedures without favoritism. Certain costs are mandatory because of state and federal law. Compliance with the public law makes them reasonable (as in, for example, the requirement to pay Social Security (FICA) taxes on employee pay and to pay minimum or prevailing wage rates). If the contract specifications force the incurrence of certain costs, they are reasonable under the contract.

- Is it what a prudent person would do when properly considering *responsibilities to the business owners, the employees, the government, and the public at large?* The owners have a right to see their business operated economically and efficiently. Employees should receive fair wages and reasonable working conditions. The government is entitled to get its products and services at a reasonable price. The public at large pays the taxes and is entitled to fair prices. The public is also entitled to reasonable social and economic benefits from business in general. Some of these benefits are required by law, such as freedom from the effects of toxic waste, polluted water and air, and public nuisance. A firm has to spend money to make these safeguards possible, and such costs are reasonable.

- Is the cost a *significant deviation from established practice?* A question arises about cost reasonableness if the cost was not incurred until the firm started to do government business. If, for example, a new or greatly expanded pension plan suddenly arises at the same time that government business is rising, it may be an unreasonable cost. The judgment depends partly on what portion of the total extra cost is borne by the government.

Determination of cost reasonableness is mostly a matter of common sense. When a firm is in a highly competitive business, their costs are likely to be reasonable because they are motivated to keep them reasonable. If the business is not highly competitive, or if the government is contracting for specially designed products and services, we may need to be more vigilant.

Allowable Costs

Specific cost principles for contracts with commercial organizations are found in FAR Part 31.205. Currently, there are 52 generally applicable cost principles (Exhibit 4-11 at the end of this chapter summarizes the current cost principles in FAR Part 31.205). The number and wording of these principles are continually changing as circumstances change. Cost principles are affected by changes in:

- Business practices (e.g., the large number of business takeovers in the 1980s);
- Public law (e.g., specific legal prohibitions on lobbying costs);
- Legal precedent as established by the court system and the boards of contract appeals.

Each cost principle defines a particular type of cost and establishes it as an allowable cost, unallowable cost, or allowable cost with restrictions. Most ordinary business expenses are allowable under FAR Part 31. A cost is allowable if:

- It is expressly identified as allowable in the cost principles, and meets the relevant tests for the terms of the contract: reasonableness, allocability, and proper application of accounting principles, practices, and standards; *or*
- It is not addressed in the cost principles, but meets the requirements of the three relevant tests cited above.

If a cost is deemed unallowable by the above principles and standards, then it is not recognizable on government contracts as a proposed cost or as a reimbursable expense. If a cost is allowable but with some restrictions, then it is recognizable on government contracts either as a proposed cost or reimbursable expense up to the stated limit. Consult with the cognizant auditor if there is any question.

The allowability of a particular cost under cost principles must be determined using FAR Part 31 (see Exhibit 4-11 at the end of this chapter). Each principle is based on laws and policies. Additionally, the specific wording and interpretation of a principle is affected by case law. In fact, cost principles have been rewritten or added as a result of case law. For example, the cost principle disallowing "goodwill" (FAR 31.205-49) was created to address an Armed Services Board of Contract Appeals opinion on a related issue alluding to the possible recognition of "goodwill" as an allowable cost. Goodwill in this case refers to a corporate takeover in which the acquiring company pays more for the company it is purchasing than its balance sheet value. The difference between the purchase price and the company's value on paper is called goodwill and is recognized as an intangible asset. Procurement authorities felt that it was inappropriate for the government to subsidize corporate takeovers and developed the cost principle expressed in FAR 31.205-49.

The decision for determining the allowability of a particular cost ultimately rests with the contracting officer. In making cost principle judgments, you need to work closely with the cognizant administrative contracting officer and auditor.

The following guidelines may be helpful in addressing questions concerning cost principles and their application:

1. In considering the allowability of a particular cost, more than one cost principle may apply. Consider all possible alternative cost principles in your deliberations.
2. Consult with the cognizant auditor for immediate guidance and assistance.
3. If questions still exist on proper interpretation or classification of a cost issue, contact your legal counsel.

For some cost categories, allowability is not so clearly defined. A cost may be unallowable under certain circumstances, but allowable or allowable with restrictions under other circumstances. As mentioned above, Exhibit 4-11 at the end of this chapter summarizes the cost principles in FAR Subpart 31.205.

Advance Agreements
The cost principles are stated in general terms. They apply to a broad range of contractors, each with their own cost accounting systems and business practices. Under the circumstances, it is possible that the contractor and the government will not interpret a cost principle the same way for a specific situation. If differences of opinion arise after contract award, the results are often very disruptive.

FAR 31.109 suggests that contracting officers and contractors reach advance written agreements on how special or unusual costs will be handled when they do arise. The advantages of using these advance agreements are obvious. Advance agreements are not mandatory, nor can they be used to make a cost allowable if it is specifically unallowable under the cost principles.

You can negotiate advance agreements prior to contract award or after award. You should make a strong effort to identify these costs and reach agreement on them well in advance of their actual occurrence. The agreements must be in writing and signed by the contracting officer and the contractor. They are incorporated into the contract so that both parties are contractually bound. When you generate an advance agreement with a firm, you must be sure that it is consistent with advance agreements between the firm and other federal agencies.

FAR 31.109(h) lists examples of expenses that might be covered in advance agreements. They include employee compensation (such as incentive and hardship pay), use charges for fully depreciated equipment, specific selling and distribution costs, and training and education costs.

Allocable Costs

FAR 31.201-4 states the principles for determining allocability of costs.

> A cost is allocable if it is assignable or chargeable to one or more cost objectives on the basis of relative benefits received or other equitable relationship.

For those of us without cost accounting backgrounds, this definition and the rest of FAR 31.201-4 could use some translation into plain English. For our purposes, think of "cost objectives" as a proposed contract, a change to an existing contract, or a task order. As a broad definition, costs are allocable if they are the types of costs that it makes sense for the government to pay for a particular contract effort. As long as they are reasonable and allowable, costs are allocable (FAR 31.201-4) if:

1. *They are incurred specifically for the contract effort.* If a contractor states that the estimated cost for people to do the work (labor cost) is $219,456.00 and the government agrees with that estimate, none of us would quibble with that amount being something our contract should pay for. We could cite other examples such as material and travel costs caused by the contract effort.
2. *They benefit both the contract and other contract work, and can be reasonably divided among the various contracts.* Certain supervisory costs are examples of this type of expense. Consider a company division chief who manages effort devoted to a wide variety of contracts. That supervisor's efforts benefit our contract and all other contracts. In many cases, it would be impractical to try to figure the actual supervisory cost devoted to each contract (if we could do so, the cost would be allocable under #1 above). The pay of the supervisor is a cost to the company and the company has to recover such cost as a part of the billings to its customers. Since in many cases it is not convenient to determine the exact cost for supervision for each contract, we say that it is allocable because it benefits all the work. The actual cost to be charged to our contract will have to be based on some fair method of dividing the supervisor cost among all contracts.

3. *They are necessary to the overall operation of the business.* This criterion applies even though we cannot determine a direct relationship to our proposed contract effort. For example, property taxes are imposed by state and local taxing authorities and meet the definition of reasonableness. We do not get any direct or indirect benefit from the offeror's requirement to pay taxes, nevertheless the cost is allocable because it is necessary to the overall operation of the business. In this case, like #2 above, our contract will carry a reasonable portion of the property tax. Numerous other normal business expenses fall into this category, including costs for rents, top level management, accounting, and personnel administration.

We have separated reasonable, allowable, and allocable costs in the above material for purposes of definition and explanation. In actual usage, the terms are tied closely together, and it is very often difficult, and needless, to try to separate them. Part of a cost may be unallowable because it is unreasonable or because it is not allocable to our work. Some costs are unallowable because the government has determined that it is unreasonable to pay them.

Variable, Fixed, and Semi-Variable Costs

Each type of cost incurred may also be classified in terms of how the *total* of that cost changes with the volume of business a company has or, stated in another way, how much work the company produces.

Variable Costs

Variable costs are expenses that go up or down depending on the total volume of work. Labor and material costs incurred as a direct result of doing work are the most common examples of variable costs.

Labor Costs: Assume that the labor cost for one unit of a product is $20. Exhibit 4-1 shows the costs for various output levels:

Exhibit 4-1
Labor Costs per Units Produced

	Units Produced				
	1	10	20	30	50
Total Labor Cost	$20	$200	$400	$600	$1000

The total labor cost goes up as the output increases. Exhibit 4-2 shows how the total cost of labor grows with the number of units produced.

Exhibit 4–2
Labor Costs by Volume

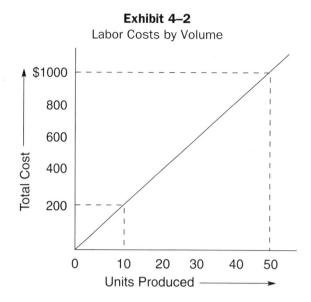

The above graph shows a straight line relationship between the total cost for labor and the volume of production. Note that the graph and the table are displaying *total* costs. We can use the graph to find the total cost for any quantity produced, up to 50. For example, the dotted lines show that the total labor costs for producing 10 units and 50 units are $200 and $1000, respectively.

The Learning Curve: By now you may be thinking that labor does not really cost the same for the 50th unit as it does for the first; you are right. When a company produces a considerable number of the same items, workers find quicker ways to do things, and the company will introduce labor-saving devices, which reduce costs. Consequently, the unit cost will decrease. This "learning curve" effect applies any time a large quantity of identical, or very similar, products or services are produced. The graph below (Exhibit 4-3) illustrates this effect.

Exhibit 4–3
Labor Costs (with Learning Curve)

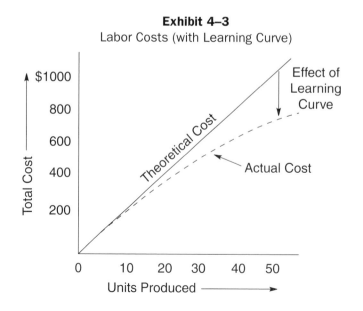

The dashed line in the graph shows the actual total cost of labor based on volume of production. It shows that the total labor cost for 50 units is around $760, or approximately $15.20 per unit compared to $20 per unit. The difference between the theoretical cost line (solid) and the actual cost line is the saving resulting from the learning curve effect. Notice that this effect becomes more pronounced as the production increases.

"Improvement curve" would be a better term than "learning curve" because the decrease in unit cost as more units are produced is due to a variety of factors, not just learning. However, the term "learning curve" has been with us for a long time and will likely stay. Learning curve theory and its applications are very useful and important to government cost analysts who are involved in high volume production. Many high-volume production companies develop learning curve statistics to assist them in predicting production costs. We will provide more detailed coverage of learning curve theory and application in Chapter 6. The next paragraphs will cover the subject enough to give you the general idea behind use of the learning curve.

The concept is that the number of labor hours per unit decreases by a set percentage each time the production quantity doubles. For example, a firm on the 95 percent learning curve has a first unit requiring 1,000 hours of manufacturing labor, as shown in Exhibit 4-4.

Exhibit 4-4

Labor Hours Required on a 95 Percent Learning Curve

Unit 1			1000.00 hours
Unit 2	95% of 1000.0	=	950.0 hours
Unit 4	95% of 950.0	=	902.5 hours
Unit 8	95% of 902.5	=	857.4 hours
Unit 16	95% of 857.4	=	814.5 hours

You may be thinking that we will reach a point when no time is needed. This does not happen because the production quantity continues to double and the time savings per unit continues to decrease. By continuing the above calculations, you can see that the time required for the 512th unit is 630.3 hours and for the 1,024th unit is 598.7 hours.

Unit 32	95% of 814.5	=	773.8 hours
Unit 64	95% of 773.8	=	735.1 hours
Unit 128	95% of 735.1	=	698.3 hours
Unit 256	95% of 698.3	=	663.4 hours
Unit 512	95% of 663.4	=	630.3 hours
Unit 1024	95% of 630.3	=	598.7 hours

Like all efforts to project the future, the learning curve approach has its limitations. Nevertheless it is useful as another method for helping us project total labor hours, and from that the total labor cost. It is usable only when we are concerned with high volume production of identical, or very similar, items.

Material Costs: Material costs are another variable cost. The total cost of material rises as production volume increases and falls as the volume decreases. Exhibit 4-5 illustrates total cost behavior when the cost of material is $10 per unit:

Exhibit 4-5
Effect of Volume on Total Cost

	Units Produced				
	1	*10*	*20*	*30*	*50*
Total Material Cost	$10	$100	$200	$300	$500

The following graph (Exhibit 4-6) is very similar to that for labor costs (see Exhibit 4-2) and can be used the same way to project the total material cost of any production quantity from 1 to 50 units. In practice, the learning curve will fall off from the straight line, like labor costs in the learning curve figure shown earlier. As experience is gained, ways are found to reduce the materials cost per unit. However, the savings in materials cost per unit will generally level out much earlier.

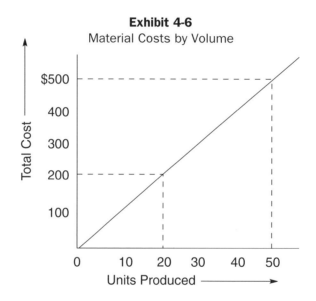

Exhibit 4-6
Material Costs by Volume

Fixed Costs

Fixed costs remain pretty much the same regardless of the amount of production. Building rent is an example. The rent will remain the same whether the company is producing no work or 50 units or 100. Of course, a time may come when we outgrow the building we have rented because of increased volume. At that point we will rent another building. The rental cost will rise to a new fixed level and stay there unless we outgrow our space again. Other costs that tend to remain fixed are top level management costs, property insurance, and property taxes.

Semi-Variable Costs

Semi-variable costs are costs that are partly fixed and partly variable, depending on the amount of production being done. Utility costs are a good example. We will pay a certain fixed cost just to have electricity available, and we will pay that even if we don't turn on a light bulb. On top of that base charge, we will pay for electricity based on the amount of usage, or, in broad terms, the production volume. Exhibit 4-7 illustrates how this works for utility costs in general:

Exhibit 4-7
Utilities Cost per Units Produced

	Units Produced			
	1	10	30	50
Fixed Utilities Cost	$50	$50	$50	$50
Variable Utilities Cost	2	20	60	100
Total Utilities Cost	$52	$70	$110	$150

The total of all costs that a company has will be a mixture of variable costs, fixed costs, and semi-variable costs. However, the semi-variable costs are actually a mixture of variable and fixed costs. Exhibit 4-8 summarizes all the cost examples we have used to illustrate variable, fixed, and semi-variable costs. However, this table does not show the semi-variable costs themselves. These semi-variable costs (utilities) are separated into fixed and variable components.

Exhibit 4-8
Fixed, Variable, and Semi-variable Costs per Units Produced

	Units Produced			
	1	10	20	50
Labor Costs (Variable)	$20	$200	$400	$1,000
Material Costs (Variable)	10	100	200	500
Utility Costs (Fixed)	50	50	50	50
Utility Costs (Variable)	2	20	40	100
Total Costs	$82	$370	$690	$1,650

Exhibit 4-9 illustrates the information in the table above.

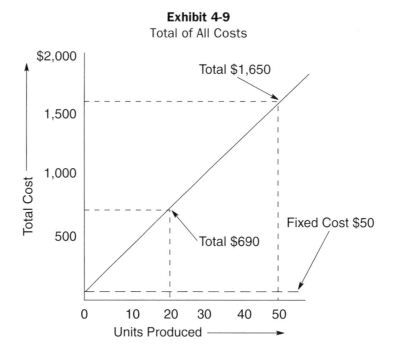

Exhibit 4-9
Total of All Costs

The costs shown in Exhibit 4-9 are, of course, not all the costs the company will have. However, we can learn some useful facts from this information. We note that the total costs increase as the volume of work increases, and that does not surprise us. We also note that we have a cost of $50, even though no work is produced. That is the fixed part of the utility costs. Now calculate the unit cost of the product for various production levels, using the figures in Exhibit 4-8; Exhibit 4-10 shows the results of this calculation.

Exhibit 4-10
Total Unit Cost by Volume

	Units Produced			
	1	*10*	*20*	*50*
Unit Cost	$82	$37	$34.50	$33

The tabulation proves what we have always heard: When the volume of production increases, the unit cost decreases because the fixed costs are spread over a larger number of units.

Many people already know about how costs vary, though they may not have thought about it in the terms we have used. We know from our personal experience that we pay a fixed cost just to have electricity in our home, and we will pay it even though we use no electricity. We know too that use of electricity (a variable cost) will add to the basic charge. We know that other costs, such as house rent or payments, remain the same (a fixed cost) unless we decide to move to another house. We also know that if we consume twice as much food as normal because guests arrived, the grocery bill (a variable cost) is likely to be around twice as high.

We use this general knowledge of cost behavior, as it is called, to evaluate cost proposals. We know, for example, that if a company's work force increases, the cost of fringe benefits will also rise, usually in proportion to the increase in labor costs. We also know that, within reasonable limits, the cost of top level supervision will remain pretty much the same regardless of work force size or volume of business.

The concepts of variable, semi-variable, and fixed costs are not exact. They are rough indicators of how costs change when a company changes the amount of work it produces. We should not get the idea that a company will necessarily come to cost and price discussions with a full set of charts and graphs like those we have used to illustrate the cost principles involved. Companies may not bother with such charts and graphs, but they use the principles involved to project various costs. If they have done their job right, they will give us cost breakouts and cost histories with their pricing proposals. Our understanding of the general ideas of variable, fixed, and semi-variable cost will help greatly in determining how valid their cost figures are.

Direct and Indirect Costs

All costs may be classified as either direct or indirect. Costs are not direct part of the time and indirect at other times. The total cost of a company for some period of time, such as a year, is the sum of all the direct and indirect costs they have paid for that year. The company has to get these costs back just to break even on their total cost of doing business. They do so by including these costs in the billings which the customers pay.

FAR 31.202 defines *direct cost* as any cost that can be identified specifically with a particular final cost objective. In non-accounting terms, this means that direct costs are expenses that are *conveniently chargeable* to (or specifically identifiable with) a given job or contract. The labor cost of scientists actually doing the day-to-day work on an R&D contract is conveniently chargeable to that effort. It is fairly easy to keep up with how much time they spend on the job, and we can convert that time to a dollar cost for their labor. If the company buys special materials for use by the scientists on the R&D contract, those materials are classified as direct materials. It is fairly easy to keep up with the amount of the material actually used for that R&D contract and charge its cost to that effort.

FAR 31.203 defines an *indirect cost* as any cost not directly identified with a single, final cost objective, but identified with two or more final cost objectives or an intermediate cost objective. This definition, like that for direct cost above, can stand some translation into nonaccounting terms. Indirect costs are expenses that are *not conveniently chargeable* to (not directly identified with) one particular contract. They are costs that apply across the board to large parts or all of the company's work. For example, consider a supervisor who is responsible for overseeing a large number of contracts. The cost of the supervisor is identified with all the work that the supervisor does, not just one contract. It is not practical to try to determine the fraction of total supervisor cost that goes with each contract supervised. The cost of the supervisor is, therefore, an indirect cost. The company will have numerous expenses that fall into the category of indirect cost. Another example is utility costs. It would be extremely difficult to determine how much of the total utility bill was caused by each customer's work.

As we have said, the company has to recover its indirect, as well as direct, costs just to break even on its total cost; however, the nature of indirect costs makes it difficult, if not impossible, to figure out how much of each indirect cost was caused by a particular customer's work. So the company establishes methods to divide these expenses among their various customers. Each customer pays part of the indirect costs as a portion of their total billed price. If the company divides the costs properly, it will collect enough from its customers to pay the total indirect costs as well as its total direct costs. Chapter 8 will give you more information on allocating indirect cost.

Direct Costs

Direct labor, direct materials, and some other costs specifically associated with particular contracts are classified as direct costs.

Direct Labor: Direct labor cost is the expense incurred for people who can be specifically identified with the contract work, or, as we have termed it, can be "conveniently charged" to the work. Examples are scientists, engineers, carpenters, welders, electronic technicians, and similar persons.

Sometimes people do work that relates to contract efforts, but charging their cost directly is not practical. A supervisor may be responsible for the work on numerous jobs being performed by the company and also for numerous administrative tasks. It may be impractical to keep up with the amount of time the supervisor actually spends dealing with the problems and questions that arise on a given contract effort. A messenger delivers the mail each day to various company offices. How would we keep up with the time, and the cost, for messenger service that is specifically related to each contract the company is doing? Labor costs of this type are charged to indirect labor cost, as part of indirect costs.

Direct Material: Direct materials are products that become a part of the finished work or are consumed in doing the work. Examples for construction work are steel beams, concrete blocks, and roofing materials. Examples for an R&D contract to develop a new aircraft could be sheet metal, gauges to be used in the cockpit, tires, engines, and radio equipment. Again, the test is whether the materials are specifically identifiable with (conveniently chargeable to) the contract.

It may not be practical to keep up with every item of material used on a particular contract. Scientists engaged in an R&D contract effort will generally use writing pads, pencils, and similar products to help get the work done. It may not be worthwhile to maintain records for the purpose of charging each contract with the exact amount of such costs. If it is not practical to carry such costs as direct, they are carried as indirect costs.

Other Direct Costs: Although direct labor and direct material are the most commonly encountered direct costs, sometimes others appear. Direct costs are legitimate if they are incurred specifically for the contract effort and are conveniently chargeable to it. Some common examples are consultant fees, costs for special equipment, and travel costs.

Recovery of Direct Costs: Since direct costs are conveniently chargeable to each contract, the company can expect to recover 100 percent of those costs from the customers who receive the products or services.

Indirect Costs

Indirect costs are any costs that are not direct. This statement may appear to be ridiculous but it is a good definition. As we have already discussed in general terms, indirect costs are the company's general operating expenses that cannot be directly identified with individual contract efforts. Examples include pay of executives, heat, light, rent or building ownership, taxes, insurance, personnel administration costs, accounting, sales expenses, etc. A company must recover these general operating expenses (indirect costs) plus the direct costs it incurs to break even on its total costs.

Indirect costs may be divided into two categories: overhead costs and general and administrative (G&A) costs.

Overhead Cost: This is sometimes called "burden" or "loading." It is commonly the only indirect cost category used by small companies that are not engaged in providing widely different services or lines of products. In such cases, the overhead consists of all the company's general operating expenses. The company recovers these expenses by including a portion of them in the charges made to each customer. The principle is that by charging each customer for a part of the overhead cost, the company will receive enough money from all its customers to meet its total overhead costs.

Larger companies with two or more operating divisions will typically have overhead expenses too. These companies set up overhead cost pools for each of their operating divisions. Below is an example of cost pooling:

The Adams Company has a company headquarters and three operating divisions. The company headquarters and the maintenance division are located in the same company-owned building in an industrial park. The security guard division is located in rented office space in a building a short distance from the company headquarters. The printing division is located in a company-owned building several miles away. Mrs. Adams started by buying the printing business that she supervised full time. Then she bought a going electronics maintenance business from its original owner and retained the manager to be in charge of the maintenance division. Later she bought the security guard operation. This time she brought in a new person to be the division chief.

Mrs. Adams has separate overhead accounts for each of the operating divisions because they are in very different lines of work and have different general operating expenses.

- The maintenance division occupies most of the building owned by the Adams Company, with 10 electronics technicians. Its overhead expenses include the pay of the division chief, a secretary, the cost of the electronic measuring and test equipment it uses, work benches and desks, and a pro-rata share of utilities costs (the company headquarters shares the building). Customers of this division pay for the direct labor and materials used in the work they receive plus an allocated share of the overhead cost of the maintenance division.
- The security guard division has fairly low overhead costs. It employs around 400 guards, and its overhead costs include the pay of the division chief, a secretary, the rental cost of a small amount of office space, telephone costs, two patrol cars, and some communications equipment. Customers of this division pay the direct labor costs for the guard service they get and an allocated share of the overhead costs of the security guard division.
- The printing division employs a typesetter, nine journeyman printers, and a laborer. It has very heavy overhead expenses, including the pay of the division chief and a secretary, the cost of the building, the cost of very expensive printing equipment, and the associated maintenance costs. The customers of this division pay costs for the direct labor and material they get, plus an allocated share of the overhead cost of the printing division.

General and Administrative (G&A) Cost: To continue the Adams Company example, we have not yet accounted for all the expenses this company has. The company headquarters has expenses such as pay of the president and other company officers, a small administrative staff, sales people, advertising, office equipment, utilities, property taxes, insurance costs, building costs, and numerous other expenses.

The cost for individual customers of the Adams Company will include an apportioned share of the total G&A expenses. All customers of the company share in this G&A cost. This means, then, that the costs for a customer of the security guard division include the direct labor cost of the guards themselves *plus* an allocated share of the security guard division overhead *plus* an allocated share of the G&A cost.

The Difference Between Overhead and G&A Costs: As has been stated, small companies operating with one major product line or service normally have overhead costs only, and all general operating expenses fall into this category.

For other companies there are no hard and fast rules to prescribe exactly which expenses shall be in overhead and which shall be in general and administrative costs. Some variation exists from company to company, depending on their particular circumstances. However, most companies follow some general concepts.

Overhead expenses for each division normally consist of only those expenses the division chief is in a position to control. Generally companies that need both overhead and G&A accounts operate on the "profit center" basis, requiring the division chiefs to operate their divisions so that they recover their direct and overhead costs plus make a profit for the company. For example, the division chief is in a position to control fringe benefit expenses, whether these expenses are a part of the hourly rate or a part of overhead, because the division chief controls the number of employees and their efficiency, and hence, that expense. Other controllable costs include secretarial help, equipment and maintenance costs, and, if separately metered, cost of utilities. In total, the division chief is responsible for controlling direct costs and the assigned overhead costs.

G&A costs normally include those general operating expenses that are not controllable at the division levels. Division chiefs have no control over pay of company officers, size and pay of the corporate staff, insurance costs, rental costs, and similar expenses. Another way to look at G&A cost is to consider it as the "top level" cost that a company has, over and above the costs that exist at the operating levels.

The Government View of Direct and Indirect Costs

The government recognizes that companies have direct and indirect costs, and its policy is to pay for the reasonable costs of acquiring products and services, plus a reasonable profit. The government takes this view as long as the resulting price is itself fair and reasonable. We must always remember that costs for a particular product or service may be reasonable for a specific company *in its situation*, and the company may propose a reasonable profit. This factor, in itself, does not guarantee that the price finally arrived at is reasonable. The company could be in an extremely high labor cost area, forcing it to charge higher-than-normal prices.

When the government accepts direct costs as being reasonable, it is implicitly agreeing to pay 100 percent of those particular costs if a contract is awarded. The direct costs must be allocable to the contract in the first place. In the Adams case above, if the government is considering a contract for maintenance services, it will not pick up any of the direct costs of the printing division. Those costs are not allocable to the proposed contract.

The government also recognizes that all companies have indirect costs, and it is willing to pay its share of those indirect costs, providing they meet certain criteria. First, they must be costs that are reasonable, allowable, and allocable to the contract. Second, the government must be sure that it is paying only a fair share of those costs, i.e., the allocation method produces equitable (fair) results.

COST PRINCIPLES

The cost principles have been fine-tuned over many years to their present state by practice, usage, and interpretations of the Boards of Contract Appeals and the federal courts. Changes in their fine points and additions will undoubtedly continue even though the FAR has combined in one place the best features of these principles presented in multiple earlier regulations. The FAR made major changes by eliminating the application to grants (not a FAR concern) and by removal of special subparts for architect-engineer, construction, and industrial facilities contracts.

FAR 31.103 states that the principles shall be used in pricing negotiated supply, service, experimental, developmental, and research contracts, and contract modifications whenever cost analysis is performed. The principles must be incorporated by reference in contracts with commercial organizations for such purposes as determining reimbursable costs in cost-reimbursement contracts, determining costs for termination purposes, and the pricing of changes (see Exhibit 4-11 and FAR Subpart 31.2 for the complete list).

FAR 31.102, Fixed-Price Contracts, states that the cost principles shall be used in the pricing of negotiated fixed-price contracts and their modifications whenever cost analysis is performed. It adds the following:

> However, the application of cost principles to fixed-price contracts and subcontracts shall not be construed as a requirement to negotiate agreements on individual elements of cost in arriving at agreement on the total price. The final price accepted by the parties reflects agreement only on the total price. Further, notwithstanding the mandatory use of cost principles, the objective will continue to be to negotiate prices that are fair and reasonable, cost and other factors considered.

The quotation above could use some translation. The idea is that we do use the cost principles when negotiating fixed-price contracts. However, we will not necessarily reach agreement with every offeror on every element of their costs. Some offerors may adamantly refuse to eliminate unallowables, e.g., interest charges, from their indirect accounts even though they have otherwise been cooperative. We can nevertheless reach a final agreement on the price even though it does contain some unallowables. The entire process is, after all, a matter of reaching an agreement on forecasted (estimated) costs and a profit to go with them. There is no way to know, until the work is finished, what the actual costs and profit will be. The government would be foolish indeed to stand on ceremony and go to a higher priced offeror whose costs are "sanitized" when it can get the same work from a lower-priced offeror whose costs are "unsanitary" (i.e., include some unallowables).

Exhibit 4-11
Cost Principles

This table summarizes the current cost principles in FAR Subpart 31.205.

(A = Allowable, UA = Unallowable, AWR = Allowable With Restriction)

Selected Costs	FAR Ref:	A	UA	AWR
Alcoholic Beverages Costs	31.205-51		UA	
Asset Valuations Resulting from Business Combinations	31.205-52			AWR
Bad Debts	31.205-3		UA	
Bonding Costs	31.205-4	A		
Compensation for Personal Services	31.205-6	A	UA	AWR
Contingencies	31.205-7	A	UA	
Contributions or Donations	31.205-8		UA	
Cost of Money	31.205-10	A		
Depreciation	31.205-11	A		AWR
Economic Planning Costs	31.205-12	A	UA	
Employee Morale, Health, Welfare, Food Service, and Dormitory Costs and Credits	31.205-13	A		AWR
Entertainment Costs	31.205-14		UA	
Fines, Penalties and Mischarging Costs	31.205-15		UA	AWR
Gains and Losses on Disposition or Impairment of Depreciable Property or Other Capital	31.205-16	A		
Goodwill	31.205-49		UA	
Idle Facilities and Idle Capacity Costs	31.205-17	A	UA	AWR
Independent Research and Development / Bid and Proposal Costs	31.205-18			AWR
Insurance and Indemnification	31.205-19	A	UA	AWR
Interest and Other Financial Costs	31.205-20		UA	
Labor Relations	31.205-21	A		
Legal and Other Proceedings Costs	31.205-47	A	UA	
Lobbying and Other Political Activity Costs	31.205-22	A	UA	
Losses on Other Contracts	31.205-23		UA	
Maintenance and Repair Costs	31.205-24	A		
Manufacturing and Production Engineering Costs	31.205-25	A		
Material Costs	31.205-26	A		
Organization Costs	31.205-27		UA	
Other Business Expenses	31.205-28	A		
Patent Costs	31.205-30	A	UA	

Selected Costs	FAR Ref:	A	UA	AWR
Plant Protection Costs	31.205-29	A		
Plant Reconversion Costs	31.205-31		UA	AWR
Precontract Costs	31.205-32	A		
Professional and Consultant				
Service Costs	31.205-33	A	UA	
Public Relations and Advertising Costs	31.205-1	A	UA	AWR
Recruitment Costs	31.205-34	A		
Relocation Costs	31.205-35			AWR
Rental Costs	31.205-36	A		AWR
Research and Development Costs	31.205-48	A	UA	AWR
Royalties and Other				
Costs for Use of Patents	31.205-37	A		
Selling Costs	31.205-38	A	UA	
Service and Warranty Costs	31.205-39	A		
Special Tooling and Special Test				
Equipment Costs	31.205-40	A		
Taxes	31.205-41	A	UA	
Termination Costs	31.205-42	A		
Trade, Business, Technical and				
Professional Activity Costs	31.205-43	A		
Training and Education Costs	31.205-44	A		AWR
Transportation Costs	31.205-45	A		
Travel Costs	31.205-46			AWR

The above interpretation applies to negotiating *fixed-price contracts* only. The cost principles are strictly interpreted and used in connection with pricing changes to contracts, reimbursement of expended costs under cost-reimbursement contracts, and the other situations listed in FAR 31.103. For example, interest expense is unallowable (FAR 31.205-20). We cannot, in the cost-reimbursement situation, reimburse a contractor for claimed expenses if any part of the payment contributes toward interest. We have to ensure that all unallowables have been "stripped out" of the indirect accounts (in the case of interest expense), and then base the reimbursement on whatever is still intact.

COST ACCOUNTING STANDARDS

The Cost Accounting Standards (CAS) contained in 48 CFR (Code of Federal Regulations) Chapter 99 are also included as Appendix B in the looseleaf edition of the FAR. The CAS are complex and apply to relatively few contract actions. Moreover, change imposed by FASA on obtaining cost and pricing data make CAS applicable to even fewer contract actions. Under the current system, companies or contracts meeting one of the following three conditions are not subject to CAS:

1. The subject company is a small business as defined in FAR Subpart 19.1;
2. The subject contract is awarded without the submission of any cost or pricing data;
3. The subject company is not currently performing a contract that is subject to CAS, and the award under consideration is less than $500,000; or
4. Contracts or subcontracts of less than $7.5 million, provided that, at the time of award, the business unit of the contractor or subcontractor is not performing any CAS-covered contracts valued at $7.5 million or greater.

Even a large business that has just received a $500,000 cost-plus-fixed-fee contract might only be subject to Standards 401 (Consistency in Estimating, Accumulating, and Recording Costs), 402 (Consistency in Allocating Costs Incurred for the Same Purpose), 405 (Accounting for Unallowable Costs), and (Cost Accounting Period).

For a large business (small businesses are exempt) to be subject to all the CAS, it must have already either:

- Received a single CAS-covered contract of $50 million or more in the current accounting period; or
- Been awarded more than $50 million in CAS-covered government contracts during the immediate prior accounting period.

These restrictions do not mean that the CAS are unimportant. They are indeed important when they *do* apply. However, we will not cover the CAS in detail in this text; they deserve a separate handbook in their own right. Instead, we provide a listing of the 19 standards and a brief synopsis of their applicability (Exhibits 4-12 and 4-13).

Also, the Cost Accounting Standard Board issued four standards applicable to 99 colleges and universities engaged in large dollar value contracts and grants with the federal government. Since this book is devoted primarily to private sector commercial activities, the CAS standards 501, 502, 505, and 506 are not covered in any detail. Instead, we provide a listing of these four standards and a brief synopsis of their applicability in Exhibit 4-12.

Exhibit 4–12
Cost Accounting Standards (CAS)
48 CFR Part 9904

CONSISTENCY AND MODIFIED COVERAGE STANDARDS

CAS 401—Consistency in Estimating, Accumulating and Reporting Costs. The purpose of this CAS is to ensure that practices a contractor uses in estimating costs for a proposal are consistent with the cost accounting practices it uses to accumulate and report costs. (48 CFR 9904.401)

CAS 402—Consistency in Allocating Costs Incurred for the Same Purpose. This standard requires that each type of cost be allocated only once and on only one basis to any contract or other cost objective. (48 CFR 9904.402)

CAS 405—Accounting for Unallowable Costs. The purpose of this standard is to facilitate the negotiation, audit, administration, and settlement of contracts. It contains guidance on (i) identification of costs specifically described as unallowable at the time such costs first become defined or authoritatively designated as unallowable, and (ii) the cost accounting treatment to be accorded such identified unallowable costs to promote the consistent application of sound cost accounting principles covering all incurred costs. (48 CFR 9904.405)

CAS 406—Cost Accounting Period. This standard provides criteria for selecting the time periods to be used as cost accounting periods for contract cost estimating, accumulating, and reporting. (48 CFR 9904.406)

COST ALLOCATION STANDARDS

CAS 403—Allocation of Home Office Expenses to Segments. This standard establishes criteria for allocating expenses of a home office to the segments of the organization based on beneficial and casual relationship between such expenses and the receiving segment. (48 CFR 9904.403)

CAS 410—Allocation of Business Unit General and Administration Expenses to Final Cost Objectives. This standard provides criteria for the allocation of G&A expenses to final cost objectives and furnishes guidelines for the type of expense that should be included in the G&A expense pool. (48 CFR 9904.410)

CAS 418—Allocation of Direct and Indirect Costs. This standard provides (i) guidelines for consistent determination of direct and indirect costs, (ii) criteria for the accumulation of indirect costs, including service center and overhead costs, in indirect cost pools, and (iii) guidance relating to the selection of allocation measures based on the beneficial or casual relationship between an indirect cost pool and cost objectives. (48 CFR 9904.418)

CAS 420—Accounting for Independent Research and Development Costs and Bid and Proposal Costs. This standard covers the accumulation of such costs and allocation on the basis of beneficial or casual relationships. (48 CFR 9904.420)

ASSET RELATED STANDARDS

CAS 404—Capitalization of Tangible Assets. This standard establishes criteria for determining the acquisition costs of tangible assets that are capitalized. It requires contractors to capitalize the acquisition cost of tangible assets in accordance with a written policy that is reasonable and consistently applied. (48 CFR 9904.404)

CAS 409—Depreciation of Tangible Capital Assets. This standard provides criteria for assigning costs of tangible capital assets to cost accounting periods to enhance objectivity and consistency in their allocation. (48 CFR 9904.409)

CAS 414—Cost of Money as an Element of the Cost of Facility Capital. This standard establishes criteria for measuring and allocating cost of capital committed to facilities as an element of contract cost. (48 CFR 9904.414)

CAS 417—Cost of Money as an Element of the Cost of Capital Assets Under Construction. Covers the cost of money for construction effort as an element of cost of the assets. (48 CFR 9904.417)

LABOR RELATED STANDARDS

CAS 408—Accounting for Costs of Compensated Personal Absence. This standard establishes criteria for measuring and allocating the costs of compensated personal absences to final cost objectives. These costs include compensation paid by contractors to their employees for such benefits as vacation, sick leave, holidays, military leave, etc. (48 CFR 9904.408)

CAS 415—Accounting for the Cost of Deferred Compensation. This standard provides for the measurement of the cost of deferred compensation and the assignment of such cost to cost accounting periods. (48 CFR 9904.415)

CAS 412—Composition and Measurement of Pension Costs. This standard provides criteria for measuring deferred compensation costs and assigning those costs to cost accounting periods. (48 CFR 9904.412)

CAS 413—Adjustment and Allocation of Pension Cost. This standard provides guidance for measuring actuarial gains and losses and assigning such gains and losses to cost accounting periods. (48 CFR 9904.413)

MATERIAL RELATED STANDARDS

CAS 407—Use of Standard Costs for Direct Material and Direct Labor. The purpose of this standard is to provide criteria (i) under which standard costs may be used for estimating, accumulating, and reporting costs of direct material and labor and (ii) relating to the establishment of standards, accumulation of standard costs, and accumulation and disposition of variances from standard costs. (48 CFR 9904.407)

CAS 411—Accounting for Acquisition Costs of Material. This standard provides criteria for the accounting of acquisition costs of materials, provides guidance on using inventory costing methods, and improves the measurement and assignment of costs to cost objectives. (48 CFR 9904.411)

INSURANCE STANDARD

CAS 416—Accounting for Insurance Costs. This standard provides criteria for the measurement and assignment of such costs to accounting periods and its allocation. (48 CFR 9904.416)

STANDARDS FOR EDUCATIONAL INSTITUTIONS

These standards are very similar to their companion standards, CAS 401, 402, 405, and 406; however, they have been modified to reflect the organizational and business environments of educational institutions.

CAS 501—Consistency in Estimating, Accumulating, and Reporting Costs by Educational Institutions. This standard ensures the practices each institution uses to estimate costs for a proposal are consistent with the practices it uses to accumulate and report costs. (48 CFR 9905.501)

CAS 502—Consistency in Allocating Costs Incurred for the Same Purpose by Educational Institutions. This standard requires that each type of cost be allocated only once and on only one basis to any contract or other cost objective. (48 CFR 9905.502)

CAS 505—Accounting of Unallowable Costs—Educational Institutions. This standard establishes guidance for (i) identifying unallowable costs when defined or deemed unallowable by authorities and (ii) the accounting treatment of unallowables. (48 CFR 9905.505)

CAS 506—Cost Accounting Period—Educational Institutions. This standard provides criteria for selecting the cost accounting time period used by the institution for estimating, accumulating, and reporting costs. (48 CFR 9905.506)

Exhibit 4–13
Cost Accounting Standards (CAS)
Applicability and Disclosure Statement Requirements

1. Is the contract:
   – with a small business?
   – with a foreign government?
   – awarded through sealed bidding?
   – $500,000 or less?
   – awarded based on adequate price competition?
   – price set by law or regulation?
   – price based on established catalog or market prices of commercial items sold in substantial quantities to the general public?

If the answer to any of the questions above is **yes**, no cost accounting standards apply. If the answer to all of the questions above is **no**, then continue with the questions below.

2. Is the business unit currently performing any CAS-covered contracts?

If the answer to #2 is **no**, then no cost accounting standards apply. If the answer to #2 is **yes**, then continue with the questions below.

3. Did the contractor receive:
   – a single CAS-covered contract award of $50 million or more in the current accounting period?
   – multiple CAS-covered governmental contract awards during the immediate prior accounting period, totaling $50 million or more with at least one award in excess of $7.5 million?

If the answer to both questions in #3 is **no**, then only cost accounting standards 401 & 402 apply. Insert FAR clauses at 52.230-5 "Disclosure and Consistency of Cost Accounting Practices" and 52.230-4 "Administration of Cost Accounting Standards." If the answer to either question in #3 is **yes**, then all cost accounting standards apply. Insert FAR clauses at 52.230-3 "Cost Accounting Standards" and 52.230-4 "Administration of Cost Accounting Standards."

CHAPTER 5
Obtaining Cost or Pricing Data

This chapter is based primarily on FAR 15.403, Obtaining Cost or Pricing Data. People who do cost and price analysis need to understand the regulatory requirements for obtaining cost or pricing data and the safeguards which are a part of those regulations.

The requirement for obtaining cost or pricing data originated with the passage of Public Law 87-653, the Truth In Negotiations Act (TINA) in 1962. The law is fairly simple. TINA requires the contractor to: 1) submit cost and pricing data showing the facts and judgements used to arrived at the proposed price; and 2) certify that the data are current, accurate, and complete at the time agreement is reached on price.

The completion of these two documents triggers the inclusion of a defective pricing clause in the contract, which in turn allows the government a post-performance audit, or review of contract cost. If the post-performance review discloses that the data were not current, accurate, and complete and the contract was significantly overpriced, the government has a right to reduce the contract price accordingly.

The law as originally passed applied to negotiated contracts and contract modifications exceeding $100,000. Ensuing changes in the FAR raised the threshold amount. The Federal Acquisition and Streamlining Act of 1994 (FASA) established a threshold of $500,000. FASA also provided that the threshold amount is subject to adjustment, every five years from October 1, 1995. The current threshold amount is $550,000.

OBTAINING COST AND PRICING DATA

The most recent changes in the FAR significantly restrict the government's ability to routinely request and obtain cost or pricing data. We can identify two fundamental changes from past practices: (1) hierarchical preferences discouraging requests for cost or pricing data; and (2) exceptions to cost or pricing data requirements.

Hierarchical Preferences

FAR 15.402, Pricing Policy, contains a hierarchical preference for contracting officers to use in obtaining information to determine price reasonableness. Current policy shows a marked preference for reliance on price analysis techniques, rather than cost analysis. Contracting officers are not to obtain more information than is necessary for determining the reasonableness of the price or evaluating cost realism. FAR 15-402 (a) establishes a general order of preference in determining the type of information required:

(1) Price is based on adequate price competition, in which case, usually no additional information is required from the offeror
(2) Information related to prices (e.g., established catalog or market prices or previous contract prices), relying first on information available within the government; second, on information obtained from sources other than the offeror; and, if necessary, on information obtained from the offeror
(3) Information other than cost or pricing data (sometimes referred to as "non-certified" or "uncertified" cost or pricing data)
(4) Cost or pricing data (frequently referred to as "certified" cost or pricing data)

The distinction between "cost or pricing data" and "information other than cost or pricing data," is a relatively new distinction. Possibly cumbersome nomenclature, the distinction is neither whimsical nor frivolous. "Certified" cost or pricing data requires the contractor to: (1) submit cost and pricing data showing the facts and judgements used to arrived at the proposed price; and (2) certify that the data are current, accurate, and complete at the time agreement is reached on price. The completion of these two documents triggers the inclusion of a defective pricing clause in the contract providing for price reduction for defective cost and pricing data.

By contrast, the documentation requirements for "information other than cost or pricing data," are almost always less demanding. And, classifying this type of data as "uncertified" does not trigger the inclusion of a defective pricing clause. Information other than cost or pricing data refers to any type of information that is not required to be certified in accordance with FAR 15.406-2 and that is necessary to determine price reasonableness or cost realism. Such information may include pricing, sales, or cost information, and includes cost or pricing data for which certification is determined inapplicable after submission.

The distinction between "certified" cost and pricing data and "information other than cost or pricing data" is neither whimsical nor frivolous. The submission details for information other than cost and pricing data are less demanding. And, as we will see in a later section, although the FAR prescribes clauses for price reduction for defective cost and pricing data, no such penalty clauses apply to information other than cost and pricing data. Nevertheless, information other than cost or pricing data can be extremely useful to a contracting officer. One of the most prevalent circumstances requiring the submission of "information other than cost or pricing data," is a contracting officer's desire to determine cost realism. Cost realism is a critical evaluation of an offeror's proposed price to determine if the proposal reflects the buyer's requirement, of if the offeror understands the complexity of the proposed work.

Imagine the case of a low-price offer from Kildare Enterprises, one of several competing offerors. Kildare's proposed price is exempt from the submission of cost or pricing data on the basis of "adequate price competition" (one of the exceptions discussed later). The contracting officer realizes that Kildare's low market-based price may be a bargain. On the other hand, it may be an indication that Kildare misunderstood, underestimated, and underpriced the buyer's requirement. Under these circumstances, the contracting officer may ask for information other than cost or pricing data to verify cost realism. The contracting officer, for example, may ask for sufficient information (e.g., labor mix, labor hours, material mix, and material quantities) to determine if the offeror fully understands the requirements of the solicitation.

Notice how the FAR shows "certified" cost or pricing data at the bottom of the hierarchical preferences. The contracting officer should use every means available to ascertain whether a fair and reasonable price can be determined before requesting cost or pricing data. Contracting officers shall not require unnecessarily the submission of cost or pricing data because it leads to increased proposal preparation costs, generally extends acquisition lead time, and consumes additional contractor and government resources.

Exceptions to Cost or Pricing Data Requirements

FAR 15-403-1 and 15-403-2 prohibit contracting officers from obtaining cost or pricing data when the agreed-upon price is:

- Based on adequate price competition (The standards for adequate price competition are covered in Chapter 1.);
- Set by law or regulation;
- At or below the simplified acquisition threshold;
- For the acquisition of a commercial item;
- For the exercise of a contract option at the price established at contract award or initial negotiation; or
- Used solely to fund overruns or interim billing price adjustments.

Contracting officers may obtain cost or pricing data for acquisitions above the simplified acquisition threshold ($100,000) but less than the threshold for obtaining cost or pricing data, $550,000. But the FAR language indicates that such instances should be few. FAR 15.403-4 (a) (2) requires that approval for obtaining cost and pricing data come from the head of the contracting activity. Furthermore, the files must contain a written finding that cost or pricing data was necessary, the facts supporting that finding, and the approval of the finding at a level above the contracting officer.

FAR 15.402 (a) (3) says that the "contracting officer should use every means available to ascertain whether a fair and reasonable price can be determined before requesting cost or pricing data. Contracting officers shall not require unnecessarily the submission of cost or pricing data, because it leads to increased proposal preparation costs, generally extends acquisition lead time, and consumes additional contractor and Government resources."

COST ANALYSIS AND COST REALISM

As we can see from the preceding sections, current policy shows a marked preference for reliance on price analysis, rather than cost analysis, techniques and makes the submission of certified cost and pricing data the exception rather than the rule. But let's not jump to the erroneous conclusion that cost analysis is unimportant. Let's first look at the how FAR defines cost analysis and cost realism. When doing either cost analysis or cost realism analysis, the buyer must have enough information from the contractor to intelligently evaluate some or all of the proposed costs.

Cost Analysis

FAR 15.404-1 (c) defines cost analysis as:

> The review and evaluation of the separate cost elements and profit in an offeror's or contractor's proposal (*including cost or pricing data or information other than cost or pricing data*), and the application of judgment to determine how well the proposed costs represent what the cost of the contract should be, assuming reasonable economy and efficiency. (Emphasis added.)

Notice how cost analysis applies to both *cost and pricing data or information other than cost or pricing data.*

FAR 15.404-1 (c) (2) lists six different cost analysis techniques and procedures to ensure a fair and reasonable price, given the circumstances of the acquisition. These techniques are described below.

1. Verification of cost or pricing data and evaluation of cost elements, including:
   • The necessity for, and reasonableness of, proposed costs, including allowances for contingencies;
   • Projection of the offeror's cost trends on the basis of current and historical cost or pricing data;
   • Reasonableness of estimates generated by appropriately calibrated and validated parametric models or cost-estimating relationships; and
   • The application of audited or negotiated indirect cost rates, labor rates, and cost of money or other factors.
2. Evaluation of the effect of the offeror's current practices on future costs. In conducting this evaluation, the contracting officer shall ensure that the effects of inefficient or uneconomical past practices are not projected into the future. In pricing production of recently developed complex equipment, the contracting officer should perform a trend analysis of basic labor and materials, even in periods of relative price stability.
3. Comparison of costs proposed by the offeror for individual cost elements with: actual costs previously incurred by the same offeror; previous cost estimates from the offeror or from other offerors for the same or similar items; other cost estimates received in response to the government's request; independent government cost estimates by technical personnel; and forecasts of planned expenditures.
4. Verification that the offeror's cost submissions are in accordance with the contract cost principles and procedures in Part 31 and, when applicable, the requirements and procedures in 48 CFR Chapter 99 (Appendix to the FAR loose-leaf edition), Cost Accounting Standards.
5. Review of documentation to determine whether any cost or pricing data necessary to make the contractor's proposal accurate, complete, and current have not been either submitted or identified in writing by the contractor. If there are such data, the contracting officer shall attempt to obtain them and negotiate using them or making satisfactory allowance for the incomplete data.
6. Analysis of the results of any make-or-buy program reviews in evaluating subcontract costs.

Cost Realism

FAR 15.404-1 (d) defines cost realism analysis as

> The process of independently reviewing and evaluating specific elements of each offeror's proposed cost estimate to determine whether the estimated proposed cost elements are realistic for the work to be performed; reflect a clear understanding of the requirements; and are consistent with the unique methods of performance and materials described in the offeror's technical proposal.

Cost realism analyses shall be performed on cost-reimbursement contracts to determine the probable cost of performance for each offeror. The probable cost:

- May differ from the proposed cost and should reflect the government's best estimate of the cost of any contract that is most likely to result from the offeror's proposal;
- Shall be used for purposes of evaluation to determine the best value;
- Is determined by adjusting each offeror's proposed cost, and fee when appropriate, to reflect any additions or reductions in cost elements to realistic levels based on the results of the cost realism analysis.

Cost realism analyses may also be used on competitive fixed-price incentive contracts or, in exceptional cases, on other competitive fixed-price-type contracts when new requirements may not be fully understood by competing offerors, there are quality concerns, or past experience indicates that contractors' proposed costs have resulted in quality or service shortfalls. Results of the analysis may be used in performance risk assessments and responsibility determinations.

OBTAINING COST INFORMATION

When cost analysis is necessary to support a decision on price reasonableness or cost realism, the contracting officer may require an offeror to submit cost information at any time prior to the close of negotiations. The preferred time for such a request is in the original solicitation. Including the cost information requirements in the original solicitation permits the offeror to gather the required information simultaneously during proposal preparation. If you require the data after proposals are received, the contracting process must be delayed while the offeror gathers the required documents and information.

The solicitation must specify:

- Whether cost or pricing data is required and the format in which it is to be submitted;
- Whether information other than cost or pricing data is required, if cost or pricing data is not necessary; and
- The necessary preaward or postaward access to examine the offeror's records.

However, the solicitation's request for cost and pricing data must also include a specification that "... in lieu of submitting cost or pricing data, the offeror may submit a request for exception from the requirement to submit cost or pricing data ..." (FAR 15.403-5 (a) (2)).

Information Other than Cost or Pricing Data (FAR 15.401 and 15.406-2)

Information other than cost or pricing data means any type of information that is not required to be certified in accordance with 15.406-2 and is necessary to determine price reasonableness or cost realism. Such information may include pricing, sales, or cost information, and includes cost or pricing data for which certification is determined inapplicable after submission.

The level of detail required for information other than cost or pricing data may be very limited, requiring information demonstrating that a proposed price is a market-based price or information necessary to perform cost realism analysis (labor mix, labor hours, material mix, and material quantities).

But in some instances, the level of detail required may be essentially the same as that required for "certified" cost or pricing data. For example, FAR 15.404-1 (d) (2) requires that "cost realism analysis shall be performed on cost reimbursement contracts to determine the probable cost of performance for each offeror." Under these circumstances, the offerors may have to provide detailed estimates as required by FAR 15.408, Table 15-2, even though the information is not accompanied by the FAR 15.406-2 certificate.

The submission requirements for information other than cost or pricing data (or non-certified cost or pricing data) are much less demanding than for "certified" cost or pricing data. The information is usually submitted in a format selected by the offeror, unless a specific format has been described in the solicitation (FAR 15.403-5(b)(2). And as we will see in a later section, the FAR prescribes clauses for price reduction for defective cost and pricing data. But, no such penalty clauses apply to information other than cost and pricing data.

Since the amount of data required for information other than cost or pricing data will vary significantly, describing the almost infinite possible scenarios is not practical in this publication. But since analysis of information other than cost or pricing data will incorporate only a portion of the material required for "certified" cost or pricing data, a discussion of the cost or pricing data requirements will provide an understanding of the full process.

Certified Cost or Pricing Data

FAR 2.101 defines "cost or pricing data" as:

> all facts that, as of the date of price agreement or, if applicable, an earlier date agreed upon between the parties that is as close as practicable to the date of agreement on price, prudent buyers and sellers would reasonably expect to affect price negotiations significantly. Cost or pricing data are data requiring certification in accordance with 15.406-2. Cost or pricing data are factual, not judgmental; and are verifiable. While they do not indicate the accuracy of the prospective contractor's judgment about estimated future costs or projections, they do include the data forming the basis for that judgment. Cost or pricing data are more than historical accounting data; they are all the facts that can be reasonably expected to contribute to the soundness of estimates of future costs and to the validity of determinations of costs already incurred. They also include such factors as—
>
> (1) Vendor quotations;
> (2) Nonrecurring costs;

(3) Information on changes in production methods and in production or purchasing volume;

(4) Data supporting projections of business prospects and objectives and related operations costs;

(5) Unit-cost trends such as those associated with labor efficiency;

(6) Make-or-buy decisions;

(7) Estimated resources to attain business goals; and

(8) Information on management decisions that could have a significant bearing on costs.

Unless one of the exceptions applies, the TINA, as amended, requires the contracting officer to obtain cost or pricing data before accomplishing any of the following actions when the price is expected to exceed the applicable cost or pricing data threshold:

- The award of any negotiated contract (except for undefinitized actions such as letter contracts).
- The award of a subcontract at any tier, if the contractor and each higher-tier subcontractor have been required to furnish cost or pricing data.
- The modification of any sealed bid or negotiated contract (whether or not cost or pricing data was initially required) or subcontracts. When calculating the amount of the contract price adjustment, consider both increases and decreases. For example, a $200,000 modification resulting from a reduction of $400,000 and an increase of $200,000 is a pricing adjustment exceeding the current cost or pricing data threshold ($400,000 + $200,000 = $600,000). (Note: This requirement does not apply when unrelated and separately priced changes for which cost or pricing data would not otherwise be required are included for administrative convenience in the same contract modification.)

The contracting officers may: (1) require proposal submission of cost or pricing data in the format prescribed in FAR 15.408, Table 15-2; (2) specify an alternative format; or (3) permit submission in the contractor's own format. FAR 15.408, Table 15-2, provides instructions on preparing a proposal, the backup required, and other information when cost or pricing data are required (see Exhibit 5-1).

Exhibit 5–1

Table 15-2—Instructions For Submitting Cost/Price Proposals When Cost or Pricing Data Are Required

This document provides instructions for preparing a contract pricing proposal when cost or pricing data are required.

Note 1: There is a clear distinction between submitting cost or pricing data and merely making available books, records, and other documents without identification. The requirement for submission of cost or pricing data is met when all accurate cost or pricing data reasonably available to the offeror have been submitted, either actually or by specific identification, to the Contracting Officer or an authorized representative. As later information comes into your possession, it should be submitted promptly to the Contracting Officer in a manner that clearly shows how the information relates to the offeror's price proposal. The requirement for submission of cost or pricing data continues up to the time of agreement on price, or an earlier date agreed upon between the parties if applicable.

Note 2: By submitting your proposal, you grant the Contracting Officer or an authorized representative the right to examine records that formed the basis for the pricing proposal. That examination can take place at any time before award. It may include those books, records, documents, and other types of factual information (regardless of form or whether the information is specifically referenced or included in the proposal as the basis for pricing) that will permit an adequate evaluation of the proposed price.

I. *General Instructions*

A. You must provide the following information on the first page of your pricing proposal:

(1) Solicitation, contract, and/or modification number;

(2) Name and address of offeror;

(3) Name and telephone number of point of contact;

(4) Name of contract administration office (if available);

(5) Type of contract action (that is, new contract, change order, price revision/redetermination, letter contract, unpriced order, or other);

(6) Proposed cost; profit or fee; and total;

(7) Whether you will require the use of Government property in the performance of the contract, and, if so, what property;

(8) Whether your organization is subject to cost accounting standards; whether your organization has submitted a CASB Disclosure Statement, and if it has been determined adequate; whether you have been notified that you are or may be in noncompliance with your Disclosure Statement or CAS, and, if yes, an explanation; whether any aspect of this proposal is inconsistent with your disclosed practices or applicable CAS, and, if so, an explanation; and whether the proposal is consistent with your established estimating and accounting principles and procedures and FAR Part 31, Cost Principles, and, if not, an explanation;

(9) The following statement: This proposal reflects our estimates and/or actual costs as of this date and conforms with the instructions in FAR 15.403-5(b)(1) and Table 15-2. By submitting this proposal, we grant the Contracting Officer and authorized representative(s) the right to examine, at any time before award, those records, which include books, documents, accounting procedures and practices, and other data, regardless of type and form or whether such supporting information is specifically referenced or included in the proposal as the basis for pricing, that will permit an adequate evaluation of the proposed price.

(10) Date of submission; and

(11) Name, title and signature of authorized representative.

B. In submitting your proposal, you must include an index, appropriately referenced, of all the cost or pricing data and information accompanying or identified in the proposal. In addition, you must annotate any future additions and/or revisions, up to the date of agreement on price, or an earlier date agreed upon by the parties, on a supplemental index.

C. As part of the specific information required, you must submit, with your proposal, cost or pricing data (that is, data that are verifiable and factual and otherwise as defined at FAR 15.401). You must clearly identify on your cover sheet that cost or pricing data are included as part of the proposal. In addition, you must submit with your proposal any information reasonably required to explain your estimating process, including —

(1) The judgmental factors applied and the mathematical or other methods used in the estimate, including those used in projecting from known data; and

(2) The nature and amount of any contingencies included in the proposed price.

D. You must show the relationship between contract line item prices and the total contract price. You must attach cost-element breakdowns for each proposed line item, using the appropriate format prescribed in the "Formats for Submission of Line Item Summaries" section of this table. You must furnish supporting breakdowns for each cost element, consistent with your cost accounting system.

E. When more than one contract line item is proposed, you must also provide summary total amounts covering all line items for each element of cost.

F. Whenever you have incurred costs for work performed before submission of a proposal, you must identify those costs in your cost/price proposal.

G. If you have reached an agreement with Government representatives on use of forward pricing rates/factors, identify the agreement, include a copy, and describe its nature.

H. As soon as practicable after final agreement on price or an earlier date agreed to by the parties, but before the award resulting from the proposal, you must, under the conditions stated in FAR 15.406-2, submit a Certificate of Current Cost or Pricing Data.

II. *Cost Elements*

Depending on your system, you must provide breakdowns for the following basic cost elements, as applicable:

A. **Materials and Services**. Provide a consolidated price summary of individual material quantities included in the various tasks, orders, or contract line items being proposed and the basis for pricing (vendor quotes, invoice prices, etc.). Include raw materials, parts, components, assemblies, and services to be produced or performed by others. For all items proposed, identify the item and show the source, quantity, and price. Conduct price analyses of all subcontractor proposals. Conduct cost analyses for all subcontracts when cost or pricing data are submitted by the subcontractor. Include these analyses as part of your own cost or pricing data submissions for subcontracts expected to exceed the appropriate threshold in FAR 15.403-4. Submit the subcontractor cost or pricing data as part of your own cost or pricing data as required in paragraph IIA(2) of this table. These requirements also apply to all subcontractors if required to submit cost or pricing data.

(1) **Adequate Price Competition**. Provide data showing the degree of competition and the basis for establishing the source and reasonableness of price for those acquisitions (such as subcontracts, purchase orders, material order, etc.) exceeding, or expected to exceed, the appropriate threshold set forth at FAR 15.403-4 priced on the basis of adequate price competition. For interorganizational transfers priced at other than the cost of comparable competitive commercial work of the division, subsidiary, or affiliate of the contractor, explain the pricing method (see FAR 31.205-26(e)).

(2) **All Other**. Obtain cost or pricing data from prospective sources for those acquisitions (such as subcontracts, purchase orders, material order, etc.) exceeding the threshold set forth in FAR 15.403-4 and not otherwise exempt, in accordance with FAR 15.403-1(b) (i.e., adequate price competition, commercial items, prices set by law or regulation or waiver). Also provide data showing the basis for establishing source and reasonableness of price. In addition, provide a summary of your cost analysis and a copy of cost or pricing data submitted by the prospective source in support of each subcontract, or purchase order that is the lower of either $10,000,000 or more, or both more than the pertinent cost or pricing data threshold and more than 10 percent of the prime contractor's proposed price. The Contracting Officer may require you to submit cost or pricing data in support of proposals in lower amounts. Subcontractor cost or pricing data must be accurate, complete and current as of the date of final price agreement, or an earlier date agreed upon by the parties, given on the prime contractor's Certificate of Current Cost or Pricing Data. The prime contractor is responsible for updating a prospective subcontractor's data. For standard commercial items fabricated by the offeror that are generally stocked in inventory, provide a separate cost breakdown, if priced based on cost. For interorganizational transfers priced at cost, provide a separate breakdown of cost elements. Analyze the cost or pricing data and submit the results of your analysis of the prospective source's proposal. When submission of a prospective source's cost or pricing data is required as described in this paragraph, it must be included along with your own cost

or pricing data submission, as part of your own cost or pricing data. You must also submit any other cost or pricing data obtained from a subcontractor, either actually or by specific identification, along with the results of any analysis performed on that data.

B. **Direct Labor**. Provide a time-phased (e.g., monthly, quarterly, etc.) breakdown of labor hours, rates, and cost by appropriate category, and furnish bases for estimates.

C. **Indirect Costs**. Indicate how you have computed and applied your indirect costs, including cost breakdowns. Show trends and budgetary data to provide a basis for evaluating the reasonableness of proposed rates. Indicate the rates used and provide an appropriate explanation.

D. **Other Costs**. List all other costs not otherwise included in the categories described above (e.g., special tooling, travel, computer and consultant services, preservation, packaging and packing, spoilage and rework, and Federal excise tax on finished articles) and provide bases for pricing.

E. **Royalties**. If royalties exceed $1,500, you must provide the following information on a separate page for each separate royalty or license fee:

(1) Name and address of licensor.

(2) Date of license agreement.

(3) Patent numbers.

(4) Patent application serial numbers, or other basis on which the royalty is payable.

(5) Brief description (including any part or model numbers of each contract item or component on which the royalty is payable).

(6) Percentage or dollar rate of royalty per unit.

(7) Unit price of contract item.

(8) Number of units.

(9) Total dollar amount of royalties.

(10) If specifically requested by the Contracting Officer, a copy of the current license agreement and identification of applicable claims of specific patents (see FAR 27.204 and 31.205-37).

F. **Facilities Capital Cost of Money**. When you elect to claim facilities capital cost of money as an allowable cost, you must submit Form CASB-CMF and show the calculation of the proposed amount (see FAR 31.205-10).

III. **Formats for Submission of Line Item Summaries**

A. New Contracts (Including Letter Contracts)

Cost elements	Proposed contract estimate— total cost	Proposed contract estimate— unit cost	Reference
(1)	(2)	(3)	(4)

(1) Enter appropriate cost elements.

(2) Enter those necessary and reasonable costs that, in your judgment, will properly be incurred in efficient contract performance. When any of the costs in this column have already been incurred (e.g., under a letter contract), describe them on an attached supporting page. When preproduction or startup costs are significant, or when specifically requested to do so by the Contracting Officer, provide a full identification and explanation of them.

(3) Optional, unless required by the Contracting Officer.

(4) Identify the attachment in which the information supporting the specific cost element may be found.

(Attach separate pages as necessary.)

B. Change Orders, Modifications, and Claims

Cost elements	Estimated cost of all work deleted	Cost of deleted work already performed	Net cost to be deleted	Cost of work added	Net cost of change	Reference
(1)	(2)	(3)	(4)	(5)	(6)	(7)

(1) Enter appropriate cost elements.

(2) Include the current estimates of what the cost would have been to complete the deleted work not yet performed (not the original proposal estimates), and the cost of deleted work already performed.

(3) Include the incurred cost of deleted work already performed, using actuals incurred if possible, or, if actuals are not available, estimates from your accounting records. Attach a detailed inventory of work, materials, parts, components, and hardware already purchased, manufactured, or performed and deleted by the change, indicating the cost and proposed disposition of each line item. Also, if you desire to retain these items or any portion of them, indicate the amount offered for them.

(4) Enter the net cost to be deleted, which is the estimated cost of all deleted work less the cost of deleted work already performed. Column (2) minus Column (3) equals Column (4).

(5) Enter your estimate for cost of work added by the change. When nonrecurring costs are significant, or when specifically requested to do so by the Contracting Officer, provide a full identification and explanation of them. When any of the costs in this column have already been incurred, describe them on an attached supporting schedule.

(6) Enter the net cost of change, which is the cost of work added, less the net cost to be deleted. Column (5) minus Column (4) equals Column (6). When this result is negative, place the amount in parentheses.

(7) Identify the attachment in which the information supporting the specific cost element may be found.

(Attach separate pages as necessary.)

C. Price Revision/Redetermination

Cutoff date (1)	Number of units completed (2)	Number of units to be completed (3)	Contract amount (4)	Redetermination proposal amount (5)	Difference (6)	Cost elements (7)

Incurred cost—pre-production (8)	Incurred cost—completed units (9)	Incurred cost—work in process (10)	Total incurred cost (11)	Estimated cost to complete (12)	Estimated total cost (13)	Reference (14)

(Use as applicable).

(1) Enter the cutoff date required by the contract, if applicable.

(2) Enter the number of units completed during the period for which experienced costs of production are being submitted.

(3) Enter the number of units remaining to be completed under the contract.

(4) Enter the cumulative contract amount.

(5) Enter your redetermination proposal amount.

(6) Enter the difference between the contract amount and the redetermination proposal amount. When this result is negative, place the amount in parentheses. Column (4) minus Column (5) equals Column (6).

(7) Enter appropriate cost elements. When residual inventory exists, the final costs established under fixed-price-incentive and fixed-price-redeterminable arrangements should be net of the fair market value of such inventory. In support of subcontract costs, submit a listing of all subcontracts subject to repricing action, annotated as to their status.

(8) Enter all costs incurred under the contract before starting production and other nonrecurring costs (usually referred to as startup costs) from your books and records as of the cutoff date. These include such costs as preproduction engineering, special plant rearrangement, training program, and any identifiable nonrecurring costs such as initial rework, spoilage, pilot runs, etc. In the event the amounts are not segregated in or otherwise available from your records, enter in this column your best estimates. Explain the basis for each estimate and how the costs are charged on your accounting records (e.g., included in production costs as direct engineering labor, charged to manufacturing overhead). Also show how the costs would be allocated to the units at their various stages of contract completion.

(9) Enter in Column (9) the production costs from your books and records (exclusive of preproduction costs reported in Column (8)) of the units completed as of the cutoff date.

(10) Enter in Column (10) the costs of work in process as determined from your records or inventories at the cutoff date. When the amounts for work in process are not available in your records but reliable estimates for them can be made, enter the estimated amounts in Column (10) and enter in Column (9) the differences between the total incurred costs (exclusive of preproduction costs) as of the cutoff date and these estimates. Explain the basis for the estimates, including identification of any provision for experienced or anticipated allowances,

such as shrinkage, rework, design changes, etc. Furnish experienced unit or lot costs (or labor hours) from inception of contract to the cutoff date, improvement curves, and any other available production cost history pertaining to the item(s) to which your proposal relates.

(11) Enter total incurred costs (Total of Columns (8), (9), and (10)).

(12) Enter those necessary and reasonable costs that in your judgment will properly be incurred in completing the remaining work to be performed under the contract with respect to the item(s) to which your proposal relates.

(13) Enter total estimated cost (Total of Columns (11) and (12)).

(14) Identify the attachment in which the information supporting the specific cost element may be found.

(Attach separate pages as necessary.)

SUBMISSION OF COST OR PRICING DATA

FAR 15.408, Table 15-2, provides instructions on preparing a proposal, the backup required, and other information when cost or pricing data are required (see Exhibits 5-1 and 5-2). An example of a completed proposal cover sheet (the first page of the proposal) as required by FAR 15.408, Table 15-2, and the associated proposal backup are found in the price proposal model (Exhibit 5-2). It is extremely important to review and prepare proposals in accordance with these instructions when the contracting officer specifies that FAR Table 15-2 is to be used. FAR 15.408, Table 15-2, I., General Instructions, requires that specific information appear on the first page of the proposal.

For the time being, turn to the price proposal model (Exhibit 5-2). Scan the price proposal model and note how the model conforms to the FAR Table 15-2 instructions. Later chapters on the analysis of direct costs, overhead, and general and administrative costs will cover the detailed instructions for submitting each type of data.

These submissions, often called price proposals, are estimates of future costs plus the anticipated profits. No reasonable person expects contractors to estimate the future exactly. The estimates are a combination of presently known information and judgments used to project expected costs from the presently known information.

Notice how the proposal not only shows the details of direct labor and material, other direct costs, the related indirect costs, and profit (fee), but also provides enough supplemental information about the cost figures to make it possible for the government to analyze the pricing proposal in detail.

For example, a contractor may know that labor costs to produce a special-design government product a year ago were $250 per unit. The government contract specialist now asks for a pricing proposal for making a similar quantity. The contractor knows that if it gets the contract it will not actually start making the items for another six months, the lead time between contract award and getting set up to do the work. The previous labor cost of $250 per unit is factual information that appears in the cost accounting records. However, the information is one year old.

Exhibit 5–2
Model Proposal

Advanced Tank Technologies (ATT)
Washington, DC
Proposal Submitted in Response to RFP DAAH01-99-R-0001

ATT was incorporated in the State of Maryland in 1985. ATT is a research and development concern specializing in engineering feasibility studies and surface vehicle design. As recently as 1995, ATT developed a small manufacturing capability that enables it to manufacture prototypes of its basic designs. ATT had to borrow funds from a local lending institution to establish this capability. ATT provides services primarily to major DoD contractors on a firm-fixed-price (FFP) basis.

This procurement solicited by Request for Proposal (RFP) number DAAH01-99-R-0001, calls for the production of 50 prototypes of a new heavy-duty shock absorber. ATT designed this part under another Army contract for the Armored Personnel Carrier Program.

The period of performance is 29 February 1999 to 30 September 2001.

Advanced Tank Technologies (ATT)
Washington, DC
Proposal Submitted in Response to RFP DAAH01-99-R-0001

Proposal Cover Sheet (Cost or Pricing Data Required)

1. *Solicitation/Contract/Modification No.*: DAAH01-99-R-0001

2. Advanced Tank Technologies
   500 East Highway
   Washington, DC 20001

3. Point of Contact
   Jane Doe
   Contracts Manager
   (202) 555-1212

4. Contract Administration Office   Audit Office

   DCMC Baltimore   District Branch Office
   200 Townsontown Blvd., West   8181 Professional Place
   Towson, MD 21204-5299   Landover, MD 20785-2218
   (301) 339-4800   (301) 436-2090

5. Type of Contract Action: New Contract

6. Proposed Cost + Profit or Fee = Total: $938,241 + $93,824 = $1,032,065

7. Government Property
   We will not require the use of any government property in the performance of this work.

8. Cost Accounting Standards (CAS) and Estimating & Accounting Compliance
   a. Our organization is NOT subject to the Cost Accounting Standards Board (CASB) Regulations (Public Law 91-379) as amended and FAR Part 30. We have a Small Business Exemption.

b. This contract action is NOT subject to CAS. We have a Small Business Exemption.

c. NO, we have not submitted a CASB Disclosure Statement (CASB DS-1 or 2).

d. We have NOT been notified that we are or may be in noncompliance with our Disclosure Statement or CAS.

e. NO aspect of this proposal is inconsistent with our disclosed practices or applicable CAS.

f. YES, this proposal is consistent with our established estimating and accounting practices and procedures and FAR Part 31, Cost Principles.

9. This proposal reflects our estimates and/or actual costs as of this date and conforms with the instructions in FAR 15.403-5(b)(1) and FAR 15.408, Table 15-2. By submitting this proposal, we grant the Contracting Officer and authorized representative(s) the right to examine, at any time before award, those records, which include books, documents, accounting procedures and practices, and other data, regardless of type and form or whether such supporting information is specifically referenced or included in the proposal as the basis for pricing, that will permit an adequate evaluation of the proposed price.

10. 21 November 1998

11. Donna Hoffman, President

Advanced Tank Technologies (ATT)
Washington, DC
Proposal Submitted in Response to RFP DAAH01-99-R-0001

Element of Cost	Amount	Reference
Engineering Labor	$452,151	Schedule 1
Manufacturing Labor	26,412	Schedule 1
Direct Labor Overhead @ 56.7%	271,345	Schedule 3
Material	113,175	Schedule 2
Material Handling Overhead @ 5.0%	5,659	Schedule 5
Subtotal	868,742	
G&A @ 8.0%	69,499	Schedule 4
Estimated Cost	938,241	
Profit @ 10.0%	93,824*	
Total Price	$1,032,065	

*Contractors can negotiate profit with the contracting officer. Typically, contracting officers use criteria in FAR 15.404-4 for establishing a profit objective. DoD contracting officers may use the weighted guidelines policy described in DFARS 215.404-4.

Advanced Tank Technologies (ATT)
Washington, DC
Engineering Labor and Manufacturing Labor

Category	1999 Engineering Labor Cost			2000 Engineering Labor Cost			2001 Engineering Labor Cost			Total Engineering Labor	
	Rate/Hr	Hours	Total	Rate/Hr	Hours	Total	Rate/Hr	Hours	Total	Hours	Total
Program Manager	$33.93	683	$23,174	$35.63	760	$27,079	$37.41	507	$18,967	1,950	$69,220
Senior Engineer	26.39	1,200	31,668	27.71	900	24,939	29.10	700	20,370	2,800	$76,977
Junior Engineer	22.12	1,800	39,816	23.23	1,500	34,845	24.39	900	21,951	4,200	$96,612
Engineering Aide	14.50	1,800	26,100	15.23	550	8,377	15.99	50	800	2,400	$35,277
Technical Writer	16.00	—	—	16.80	—	—	17.64	900	15,876	900	$15,876
Metallurgist	18.95	1,900	35,815	19.79	1,200	23,748	20.78	700	14,546	3,800	$74,109
Draftsman	18.95	2,200	41,690	19.90	1,500	29,850	20.90	600	12,540	4,300	$84,080
Total Direct Labor— Engineering		9,583	$198,263		6,410	$148,838		4,357	$105,050	20,350	$452,151

Labor/Category	1999 Manufacturing Labor Cost			2000 Manufacturing Labor Cost			2001 Manufacturing Labor Cost			Total Manufacturing Labor	
	Rate/Hr	Hours	Total	Rate/Hr	Hours	Total	Rate/Hr	Hours	Total	Hours	Total
Fabrication	$10.85	400	$4,340	$11.39	600	$6,834	$11.96	600	$7,176	1,600	$18,350
Assembly	9.25	—	—	9.71	200	1,942	10.20	600	6,120	800	$8,062
Total Direct Labor— Manufacturing		400	4,340		800	$8,776		1,200	$13,296	2,400	$26,412
Total Direct Labor			$202,603			$157,614			$118,346		$478,563
Direct Labor Overhead @ 56.7%			$114,876			$89,367			$67,102		$271,345

All hours proposed are based on historical costs, reference Contract DAAHo1-97-C-0001, account 9271.

The supporting data showing the historical hours and the development of the proposed hours are in file "DAAH01-99-R-0001, Hours" and are available immediately upon request.

The direct labor rates are based on actual average rates as of 31 October 1998 and escalated 5 percent each year.

The supporting data and rate calculations are located in file "DAAH01-99-R-0001, Direct Labor Rates" and are available immediately upon request.

Advanced Tank Technologies
Washington, DC
Proposal Submitted in Response to RFP DAAH01-99-R-0001

Shock Absorber
Bill of Material

Support	Qty (Note 4)	Unit Price	Total	Notes
Sheet Metal	1,600 sq. yd	$25.00	$40,000	(1)
Casings	750 pcs.	8.50	6,375	(2)
Plastic	7,500 pcs.	5.75	43,125	(1)
Springs	1,700 pcs.	4.00	6,800	(2)
Bolts	7,500 pcs.	2.25	16,875	(2)
Total Material			**$113,175**	
Material Overhead at 5.0%			$5,659	**(3)**

Explanatory Notes

(1) These prices are supported by multiple vendor quotes. The proposed prices are those provided by the low bidder who was the ACME Corporation in their quotation dated 21 October 1998. The quotations are included in file "DAAH01-99-R-0001, Vendor Quotations" that are available immediately upon request.

(2) These prices are supported by the Halloween edition of the Springs R Us Catalog. This catalog is available for review in the pricing office.

(3) See Schedule 5.

(4) The proposed quantities are from the engineering drawings for the shock absorber. This drawing is located in file "DAAH01-99-R-0001, Engineering Drawing" and is immediately available upon request.

Schedule 3
Advanced Tank Technologies
Washington, DC
Budget for Fiscal Year 1999 Labor Overhead
Actual Overhead Expenses for Fiscal Years 1996 through 1998

	Budget	Actual Expenses		(Note 1)
Overhead Expenses (Note 2)	**1999**	**1998**	**1997**	**1996**
Indirect Payroll	$260,000			
Payroll Taxes	228,000			
Vacation	120,000			
Holiday	110,000			
Sick Leave	50,000			
Pensions	171,000			
Employee Morale	5,000			
Entertainment	50,000			
Office Equipment	7,000			
Depreciation	5,000			
Subscriptions	1,500			
Travel	22,000			
Miscellaneous	2,000			
Stationery	6,000			
Reproduction	17,000			
Maintenance	5,000			
Rent	202,000			
Telephone	11,000			
Insurance	102,000			
Total Pool	$1,374,500			
Less Unallowable Costs				
Entertainment	$ 50,000			
Net Allowable Expenses	$1,324,500			
Allocation Base				
Direct Labor	$2,336,000		(Note 3)	
Rate	56.7%		(Note 4)	

Explanatory Notes

(1) Provide the prior three years' actual overhead expense and allocation base in the same format as the budget for 1999.

(2) The projected overhead expenses are based on the company's operating budget for 1999. The operating budget supporting data is located in file "DAAH01-99-R-0001, Overhead Operating Budget" and is immediately available upon request.

(3) Includes Bid and Proposal Labor of $5,000.

(4) The same rate is estimated for fiscal years 2000 and 2001. We anticipate minimal inflation and a stable business base. The data and analysis supporting this assertion is located in file "DAAH01-99-R-0001, Overhead Forecast" and is immediately available upon request.

Schedule 4
Advanced Tank Technologies
Washington, DC
Budget for Fiscal Year 1999 G&A
Actual G&A Expenses for Fiscal Years 1996 through 1998

Projected G&A Expenses	(Note 2)	Less Unallowables	Net Allowable Expenses	Actual Expenses (Note 1)		
				1998	1997	1996
Payroll Taxes	$ 16,000		$ 16,000			
Officers' Salaries	165,000		165,000			
Indirect Salaries	21,000		21,000			
Interest	14,000	14,000	0			
Vacation	11,000		11,000			
Holiday	9,000		9,000			
Sick Leave	5,000		5,000			
Contributions	8,000	8,000	0			
Pensions	12,000		12,000			
Office Equipment	1,000		1,000			
Depreciation	2,500		2,500			
Travel	10,000		10,000			
Miscellaneous	2,000		2,000			
Legal Fees	7,000		7,000			
Accounting Fees	7,000		7,000			
Computer	17,500		17,500			
Rent	15,000		15,000			
Advertising	8,500	8,500	0			
Telephone	3,000		3,000			
Insurance	7,000		7,000			
Total Pool	$ 341,500	$ 30,500	$ 311,000			
B&P	8,500		8,500	(Note 3)		
Total G&A and B&P	**$350,000**	**$ 30,500**	**$ 319,500**			

Allocation Base

Labor	$ 2,331,000	
Overhead	1,371,665	(Note 4)
Other Direct Costs	29,000	
Materials	250,000	
Material Overhead	12,500	
Total Base	**$ 3,994,165**	
Rate	8.0%	(Note 5)

Explanatory Notes

(1) Provide the prior three years' actual G&A expenses and the allocation base in the same format as the 1999 budget.

(2) The projected G&A expenses are based on the company's operating budget for 1999. The operating budget supporting data is located in file "DAAH01-99-R-0001, G&A Operating Budget" and is available immediately upon request.

(3) Includes $665 B&P Travel ($5,000 + $2,835 + $665).

(4) Total Pool, excluding $2,835 allocated to B&P Labor ($5,000 x.567) [$1,374,500 $2,835].

(5) The same rate is estimated for fiscal years 2000 and 2001. We anticipate minimal inflation and a stable business base. The data and analysis supporting this assertion is included in file "DAAH01-99-R-0001, G&A" and is available immediately upon request.

Schedule 5
Advanced Tank Technologies
Washington, DC
Budget for Fiscal Year 1999 Labor Overhead
Actual Overhead Expenses for Fiscal Years 1996 through 1998

Material Handling Expenses (Note 2)	Budget 1999	Actual Expenses (Note 1)		
		1998	1997	1996
Purchasing Department	$10,000			
Receiving Department	2,500			
Total Expenses	$12,500			
Less Unallowable Costs	$ 0			
Net Allowable Expenses	$12,500			
Allocation Base				
Materials	250,000			
Material Overhead Rate (Note 3)	5.0%			

Explanatory Notes

(1) Provide the prior three years' actual material overhead expenses and allocation base in the same format as the budget for 1999.

(2) The projected material overhead expenses are based on the company's operating budget for 1999. The operating budget supporting data is located in file "DAAH01-99-R-0001, Material Overhead-Operating Budget" and is immediately available upon request.

(3) The same rate is estimated for fiscal years 2000 and 2001. We anticipate minimal inflation and a stable business base. The data and analysis supporting this assertion is located in file "DAAH01-99-R-0001, Material Overhead-Forecast" and is available immediately upon request.

The contractor's labor costs are currently five percent higher than they were when it made the last production run. That information is also factual. So the contractor estimates current labor cost at $262.50 (5% over $250). The contractor's *judgment* is that it will have to raise labor pay four percent within the next six months; consequently, the contractor proposes a labor cost per unit of $273 (4% over $262.50). The $273 is a combination of factual information and judgment. If you accept the contractor's factual information as correct and agree with the contractor's judgment on the four- percent wage increase, you have established that the labor cost line item in the pricing data is reasonable.

During cost discussions, the government might argue that the contractor has experience making the item (well along on the learning curve) and should be able to produce the item at fewer labor hours than it projected. This argument does not change the factual information regarding the original labor cost of $250 per unit and the present pay level at five percent higher than a year ago. The government's assertion that the contractor "should be able" to make the items at a labor cost less than $273 per unit is its *judgment*; they have no way to prove their assertion, so it is not data. The contractor might agree to reduce its labor cost estimate to $272.12 per unit. The contractor agrees only because it thinks the cost estimate is reasonable.

When the offeror (or contractor in case of a price adjustment to an existing contract) has been required to submit certified cost or pricing data, a certificate must be obtained from the offeror (contractor) immediately after price agreement. (See Exhibit 5-3 for the form of the certificate.) The certificate applies to data submitted by the offeror or contractor, not to the accuracy of any judgments that were inputs to the cost estimates. What happens if the contractor's negotiators did not know about certain factual information that would have changed the agreed-upon price? The contractor is not excused if it had the factual information reasonably available, regardless of whether its negotiators knew about it.

Paper or Electronic Data Submission

Many contracting activities are requiring firms to submit cost or pricing data or information other than cost or pricing data electronically. Most of the data have already been assembled by the offeror as part of the proposal preparation. So the electronic submission requirement seldom places a burden on the offeror. Contracting officers frequently require offerors to submit data on a computer diskette or by Electronic Data Interchange (EDI) (computer to computer transmission). Obviously, this type of submission eliminates unnecessary paper submission and storage as well as the inefficient use of staff and computer time.

IDENTIFYING THE CONSEQUENCES OF CERTIFYING DEFECTIVE DATA

According to FAR 15.407-1(b), defective pricing exists when any price, including profit or fee, for any purchase action covered by a Certificate of Current Cost or Pricing Data is increased by any significant amount because the data were not accurate, complete, or current. Following are examples of defects related to the three different cost or pricing data requirements:

- *Inaccurate Data.* The decimal point was accidentally or purposefully moved one place to the right. As a result, the costs used for trend analysis of a key component were ten times the actual cost.

Exhibit 5-3
Certificate of Current Cost or Pricing Data

CERTIFICATE OF CURRENT COST OR PRICING DATA

This is to certify that, to the best of my knowledge and belief, the cost or pricing data (as defined in section 2.101 of the Federal Acquisition Regulation (FAR) and required under FAR subsection 15.403-4) submitted, either actually or by specific identification in writing, to the Contracting Officer or to the Contracting Officer's representative in support of _____* are accurate, complete, and current as of _____**. This certification includes the cost or pricing data supporting any advance agreements and forward pricing rate agreements between the offeror and the Government that are part of the proposal.

Firm _____

Signature _____

Name _____

Title _____

Date of execution*** _____

*Identify the proposal, request for price adjustment, or other submission involved, giving the appropriate identifying number (e.g., RFP No.).

**Insert the day, month, and year when price negotiations were concluded and price agreement was reached or, if applicable, an earlier date agreed upon between the parties that is as close as practicable to the date of agreement on price.

***Insert the day, month, and year of signing, which should be as close as practicable to the date when the price negotiations were concluded and the contract price was agreed to.

- *Incomplete Data.* The past history of vendor prices did not include two recent purchases with lower prices for the item being procured.
- *Data Not Current.* Actual production costs for last month were available but not provided. Instead estimates were based on higher costs from earlier production.

Defective Cost or Pricing Data

FAR 15.407-1 contains the procedures the contractor uses when the government determines that significant overpricing occurred because of defective cost or pricing data. The action taken when there is reason to believe that submitted cost or pricing data is defective (not current, accurate, and complete) depends on whether the discovery is before or after contract award.

Prior to Award (FAR 15.407-1 (a))

If defective data is detected prior to agreement on price, it must be pointed out to the offeror, whether or not correction of the data would increase or decrease the price. The contracting officer then negotiates using resubmitted data or making proper allowance for known errors in the data. This information is placed in the price negotiation memorandum.

After Award (FAR 15.407-1 (b))

If it is determined after contract award that the data was not current, accurate, and complete at the date of final cost agreement, the government is entitled to a downward price adjustment, including profit, for significant overpricing caused by the defective data. The proper contract clauses (covered in the next section) must be in the contract to ensure this government entitlement.

CONTRACT CLAUSES

The FAR prescribes four clauses relating to cost or pricing data. These clauses, described in very general terms, are:

1. *52.215-10—Price Reduction for Defective Cost or Pricing Data.* This clause is used when contracting by negotiation and it is contemplated that cost or pricing data will be required. It notifies the contractor that the government shall reduce contract value if significant overpricing occurs because of defective cost or pricing data certified by the contractor. It also applies to pricing actions negotiated in connection with the contract, such as the pricing of contract modifications.
2. *52.215-11—Price Reduction for Defective Cost or Pricing Data Modifications.* This clause is used when it is contemplated that cost or pricing data will be required for modifications and the clause above (FAR 52.215-10) is not in the basic contract. Use of this clause enables the government to get cost or pricing data even when the basic contract was subject to one of the exceptions from the submission of cost or pricing data obtained. The clause requires the submission of cost or pricing data if the pricing adjustment is expected to exceed the threshold for obtaining cost or pricing data. If a reduction in the price of the contract arises because of defective data, the reduction is limited to pricing errors for the modification itself, not the entire contract.

3. *52.215-12—Subcontractor Cost or Pricing Data.* This clause is used in conjunction with FAR 52.215-10 above, which applies to negotiation. The clause requires the submission of cost or pricing data by subcontractors when the expected price of the subcontract exceeds the threshold for obtaining cost or pricing data. This clause is not to be used if the subcontract award is subject to one of the exceptions from the submission of cost or pricing data. The basic price reduction clause (FAR 52.215-10) states that the price of the basic (prime) contract shall be reduced if it was significantly increased because a subcontractor submitted defective data. Hence, the prime contractor is well advised to ensure that the data submitted by the subcontractor is not defective.

4. *52.215-13—Subcontractor Cost or Pricing Data–Modifications.* This clause is used in conjunction with FAR 52.215-11 above, the clause that provides for submission of cost or pricing data by the prime contractor in case the contract price adjustments are expected to exceed the threshold for obtaining cost or pricing data. If the prime contractor has obtained defective data from a subcontractor, and that defective data caused significant overpricing of the modification, the prime contractor remains responsible

CHAPTER 6
Analysis of Direct Labor Costs

This chapter gets into the detail of how we analyze direct labor costs. It is important that we have a thorough understanding of what direct labor is before we proceed.

The cost for labor is the money expended by a company for a major resource, the people who work for it. This extends from the president of the firm, whose salary is an expense to the company, on through all its company officers and down to everyone who works for the company.

This cost of labor involves more than just the pay of employees. The company incurs added expense simply by having people on the payroll. It has to pay Social Security or FICA taxes (Federal Insurance Contributions Act) and federal and state unemployment taxes. In addition, the company pays numerous other costs for employee benefits, like pension plans, health insurance, and disability insurance. The sum of all these costs is the total cost of labor. Various ways of accounting for these costs are described in later parts of this text.

Labor cost is divided into two major categories: direct and indirect. Even though this chapter is primarily concerned with direct labor, we will also discuss indirect labor. The two subjects go hand in hand and we need to understand the difference from the outset.

Even highly trained and experienced government cost analysts sometimes spend too much time focusing on unallowability of costs and not enough on direct cost analysis. Yet we are likely to get much greater price savings by concentrating on the analysis of direct cost. Careful analysis of direct labor and material costs often results in major savings in the direct cost itself plus savings in the related overhead costs. This chapter concentrates on the analysis of direct labor costs. The next chapter will cover direct material and certain other direct costs.

Direct costs, especially direct labor costs, do not often contain unallowable costs, but they may very well contain costs that are unreasonable or, on occasion, not allocable. This factor frequently causes direct costs to be very difficult to analyze properly because you are not able to challenge many of them as unallowable under the cost principles. The problem is to determine whether they include unreasonable or unallocable costs. In most cases, you will be unable to find a clear-cut basis in the cost principles to help you decide. Analysis often becomes even more complicated because some of the cost is probably reasonable and the rest is not.

Cost analysts have only some of the basic skills needed to examine direct labor costs. Except in unusual situations, they do not have enough knowledge to do the entire job by themselves and need technical support from people intimately familiar with the methods for performing the work covered by the cost proposal. Sometimes cost analysts also need the support of field audit personnel. The analysis is usually on a case-by-case basis. The cost principles provide broad general guidance on basic ideas of reasonableness, allowability, and allocability but very little detailed help on how to determine the reasonableness of proposed direct labor costs.

ANALYZING DIRECT LABOR COSTS

The government places many contracts for physical products; the FAR calls these products "supplies." FAR 2.101 defines supplies as all property excepting land or interest in land. Supplies include public works, buildings, ships, aircraft, aircraft parts and accessories, etc. The modern definition of supplies refers to the entire range of physical products that the government buys, including raw materials, parts, components, assemblies, end items, missiles, and space systems. This text will refer to these as products or equipment, rather than supplies.

Fundamentally, all products and equipment sold contain labor inputs of some kind. Labor converts raw materials into finished items. In some cases, the government buys finished products from distributors or other commercial outlets. In other cases, the government buys products directly from their manufacturers. Physical labor is an input into all of these manufactured products.

The government often does price analysis by itself when buying products. When the government uses price analysis only, it does not need labor cost information.

DIRECT LABOR COST

Direct labor cost is the cost of labor specifically identified with a particular contract that a company is doing. Actually, it is a cost that is specifically identified with a particular final cost objective, as FAR 31.202 puts it. A final cost objective is a major project, task, contract, or other end objective for which a contractor accumulates direct and indirect costs. For simplicity, we will refer to these "final cost objectives" as contracts or jobs or tasks.

It is general practice to refer to the following types of labor costs as direct labor:

1. *Labor directly associated with the work being produced.* Examples are a carpenter cutting boards and nailing them together or a laboratory technician personally running chemical analyses. On the other hand, company maintenance people who repair and maintain the equipment being used by the carpenter or the technician are not directly associated with the work itself.
2. *Labor readily identifiable with a particular objective such as a contract.* Generally people in the direct labor category are assigned to a particular job or assignment, and they stay on that job throughout its duration. A timekeeper, for instance, can keep records of the time workers spend on major jobs. Recorded time can then be converted to a dollar cost using a rate per hour approach. However, a timekeeper would have a difficulty readily identifying the time spent by a messenger carrying mail for each individual contract or job. Such tracking probably could be done, but the effort would be inefficient. Accordingly, messenger time would be treated as an indirect cost rather than a direct cost.

3. *Labor important enough to warrant identifying and measuring so we can keep up with its cost.* The painter who is painting a large completed end-item is doing work that is worth charging to that particular end-item. The person who comes along with a stencil to mark a serial number on each item is not staying at each one long enough to charge stenciling costs to each item.

INDIRECT LABOR COST

Indirect labor is different from direct labor because it is not specifically identifiable to a given job or contract. Consider a supervisory chemist overseeing work performed by fifteen chemists working on five major tasks or contracts. Some of the tasks will not require much direct supervision and some will require a lot. In addition, this supervisor spends some time on purely administrative tasks, such as attending meetings not directly concerned with any particular contract. It would be very difficult to apportion the supervisor's time, and hence cost, to the individual contracts being worked on. It would be improper simply to say that a fifth of the supervisor cost should be charged to each contract because some contracts are bigger than others, and some require more attention than others.

ALLOCATION OF LABOR TO DIRECT OR INDIRECT COST

Some types of labor can be categorized with very little room for argument. The man painting the house is certainly direct labor. The company president, who works on a wide variety of contracts for short periods each (unless one is in a lot of trouble), could hardly be called direct labor.

There are some types of labor that can be either direct labor or indirect labor. Inspection is an example. Some companies assign their inspectors on a job basis, and the inspector stays on that job most or all the time until it is finished. Other companies' inspectors move from job to job; it would be very difficult to keep track of the time they spend on each job. From a management standpoint, both methods have advantages and disadvantages. Some companies do it one way and others, even comparable companies in the same type of business, do it another.

The government is normally quite happy to let companies charge up individual workers any way they please, with a couple of restrictions. The government gets upset if the company charges workers to them one way and to their commercial customers in another way. Also, the government expects the company to reach a decision and keep it that way, as it is quite possible to change total costs by shifting people from direct to indirect labor or vice versa.

The Cost Accounting Standards (CAS) do not tell companies which type of employees should be direct labor and which indirect, except in very broad terms. The standards, if they apply to the company at all, require the company to tell the government how they categorize people as direct or indirect labor and require that the company let the government know if they want to make a change.

HOW COMPANIES ESTIMATE DIRECT LABOR COSTS

You can bet that companies don't estimate labor costs by reaching up into the sky and pulling out a magic figure. The risks are too great. It does not matter whether they are bidding or proposing on private work or government work; if their "guesstimates" are too high, they will lose out on a lot of work, and if they are too low, the companies will lose their shirts. They use systematic procedures.

Any company proposing to do work for anyone, government or private, must first know what it is that they are supposed to do. The government, no different from any other customer, spells out the requirement so the offerors will know the task. Section C of the uniform contract format contains the description, specification, or work statement (or some combination), which states the nature of the work to be done. For products, this description is a performance specification, a design specification, or a combination of the two. For services, it is a work statement which describes the nature of the service to be performed.

Prior to submitting a bid or proposal, competent contractors examine thoroughly the engineering drawings, schedules, specifications, and standards to determine exactly what is to be done. Then, for each type of skill (engineers, scientists, draftsmen, bricklayers, carpenters, plumbers, etc.), they estimate the direct labor hours that they believe will be needed to do the work. Their estimate combines past experience in similar work with an adjustment based on another analysis for the job at hand.

After determining the estimated labor hours, direct labor cost is calculated by multiplying each type of labor hour by an appropriate hourly rate. Companies know the current hourly rate for each labor category because they know what they pay their people, the additional costs that go with salary payments, and the total number of working hours they get from each employee. The company will also consider the probability that by the time they are actually doing the work, some of these rates may be different (e.g., pay increases may occur). The estimator multiplies the number of hours for each skill by the rate per hour for that skill. When all these figures are added together, the company has estimated direct labor cost.

Companies proposing work for anyone, government or private, must first know what it is that they are supposed to do. The government, like any other buyer or customer, spells out the requirement so the offerors will know what the task is. Section C of the uniform contract format (FAR 14.201-1 and 15.406-1) contains the description, specification, or work statement (or some combination) noting the nature of the work to be done. For products, this description is a performance or design specification or a combination of the two. For services, it is a work statement describing the nature of the service to be performed.

Prior to submitting a bid or proposal, contractors will thoroughly examine the engineering drawings, schedules, specifications, and standards to determine, as precisely as they can, exactly what is to be done. In many instances, they may perform a site visit to assess the impact of environment and terrain on their estimate.

Then they will set about the task of estimating the direct labor hours required to do the work. These direct labor hours are estimated for each labor category or skill (e.g., engineers, draftsmen, bricklayers, carpenters, plumbers) they believe will be deployed to perform the project. They know that work does not always go as rapidly as the original estimate might indicate, so they will figure in some extra hours to take care of any contingencies that might arise. This estimating is based on a combination of their past experience in similar work and their analysis of what this particular work will entail.

Next, they will convert direct labor hours to direct labor costs. Companies know the current hourly pay rates for different labor categories because they know what they pay their employees, the additional costs that go along with that salary payment, and the total number of working hours that they get from each person. The company will also take into account the possibility (or likelihood) that these current pay rates may be different (e.g., general cost-of-living pay increase) by the time the work is actually performed. Multiple pay raises are even possible—particularly if the project will be performed over multiple years. The estimator simply multiplies the hours for each labor category by the anticipated hourly pay rate. When all these figures are added together, the company has estimated the direct labor cost for the proposed project.

Work Breakdown Structures

One of the most widely used methods to estimate labor cost is the work breakdown structure (WBS).

A WBS is often used to estimate direct labor hours for a proposed project. The resulting estimated hours can then be multiplied by anticipated labor rates to determine the estimated labor costs. The WBS breaks a project down into its major parts, then each major part into its subparts, continuing until the entire project is broken down into the lowest level of detail. The entire project will then be divided into small enough segments to work with.

Let's say, for example, that Bricks & Mortar (B&M) General Contractors, Inc., receives a solicitation from a government agency to erect a warehouse, build an access road to the warehouse, and build an adjacent parking lot. The solicitation shows the location of the site and contains a complete set of drawings and specifications. The site is located in a heavily wooded area on the south side of a government installation. One of B&M's early steps in responding to the solicitation is to estimate the direct labor hours and the resulting direct labor cost.

B&M's chief estimator, Patrick O'Brien, prepares a WBS diagram (see Exhibit 6-1) showing the four major segments of the total construction project.

Exhibit 6-1
First-Level WBS for Total Construction Project

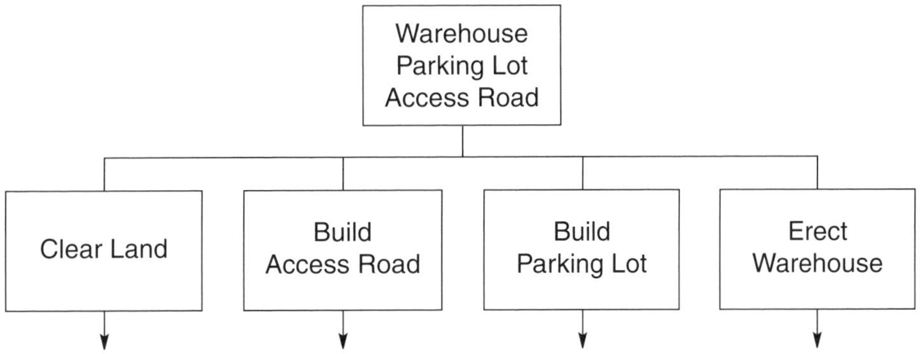

O'Brien needs more detail than that shown in Exhibit 6-1 to start estimating direct labor hours. He goes to the first level of detail, selecting the land clearing segment for further analysis. He then prepares another WBS diagram (see Exhibit 6-2) showing the four subsegments of labor to clear land.

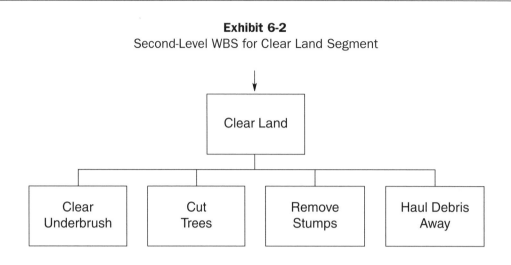

Exhibit 6-2
Second-Level WBS for Clear Land Segment

O'Brien knows he will have to develop a WBS for the access road, parking lot, and warehouse. He also knows that the WBS for each of these will be more difficult and complex than the "clear land" WBS. He will have to take all these other segments down to a much lower level to estimate the labor cost with reasonable accuracy. In addition to storage space, the proposed warehouse will contain an office, loading docks, elevators, and conveyors. O'Brien will probably go down four or more levels for the warehouse erection. But he also knows that land clearance must be accomplished before the other tasks. He decides to concentrate immediately on the "clear land" segment.

O'Brien shows the WBS to Mark Smith, a B&M foreman with previous experience on a similar construction project. Smith concurs with O'Brien's assessment of the work shown in the "clear land" WBS. O'Brien and Smith visit the proposed site. Upon arrival, Smith notices the standing trees and inquires about the disposition of the felled trees. O'Brien replies that the felled trees will be sawed into fireplace-size logs, then sold and delivered to a nearby retail merchant who will in turn sell the logs as firewood.

O'Brien then asks Smith to cruise the site "and get an idea of the hours needed to clear the land." Smith spends some time cruising the site, returns, and says:

> We'll need a brushhog for a couple of days to clear out all this underbrush so we can get at the big trees. We'd better bring in a small "dozer" to pile up all the stuff while the brushhog is cutting it off. I figure four men working three days can harvest the trees. It's going to take the crew another day to cut the trees into fireplace-sized logs so we can haul them off to the firewood dealer. The small "dozer" can dig up the tree stumps. I guess that'll likely take another day. I think we'd better bring in two of our big trucks the first two days and another one for the next day. We ought to be able to get it all cleaned up in a week. We'll need a front loader the whole time.

O'Brien records Smith's comments in a field estimator daily log. (Smith has also identified equipment needs, which O'Brien also records in the daily log for another part of the estimate.) O'Brien returns to corporate headquarters and translates Smith's observations into the following summary:

1 Heavy Equipment Operator (for brushhog)
  2 days x 1 person x 8 hours = 16 hours

1 Heavy Equipment Operator (for bulldozer)
  4 days x 1 person x 8 hours = 32 hours

1 Heavy Equipment Operator (for front loader)
  5 days x 1 person x 8 hours = 40 hours

3 Heavy Equipment Operators (for brushhog, bulldozer, and front loader)
                                                                      88 hours

2 Drivers (for heavy-duty trucks)
  5 days x 2 persons x 8 hours = 80 hours

1 Driver (for heavy-duty truck)
  3 days x 1 person x 8 hours = 24 hours

3 Drivers (for heavy-duty trucks)   104 hours

4 Laborers (to fell and cut trees, and help load trucks)
  5 days x 4 persons x 8 hours = 160 hours

4 Laborers (to fell and cut trees, and help load trucks)   160 hours

Direct Labor Hours to Clear Land (all three labor categories)   352 hours

The following day, O'Brien shows these labor time and labor mix estimates to Smith. Smith replies, "they look OK." But O'Brien raises Smith's estimates by 25%, because "Mark [Smith] thinks in terms of good weather, but it might be raining when we start." O'Brien now prepares the following labor time and labor mix estimates:

Heavy Equipment Operators (for brushhog, bulldozer, and front loader)
  88 hours + 22 hours (25% of 88) = 110 hours

Drivers (for heavy-duty truck)
  104 hours + 26 hours (25% of 104) = 130 hours

Laborers (to fell and cut trees, and help load trucks)
  160 hours + 40 hours (25% of 160) = 200 hours

Direct Labor Hours to Clear Land (all three labor categories)
  352 hours + 88 hours (25% of 352) = 440 hours

O'Brien contacts the B&M payroll office to determine the current hourly rate for each labor category. Payroll reports the following current hourly rates: heavy equipment operators, $42.08; drivers, $34.26; and laborers, $19.20. After consulting the latest economic indicators for the Washington metropolitan area (published every Monday in the *Business Maga-*

zine section of the *Washington Post*), O'Brien makes a judgment that these three labor categories will be paid 5% more during the contract performance period. He calculates the anticipated estimated hourly wages for each labor category as follows: heavy equipment operators, $44.18 ($42.08 x 105%); drivers, $35.97 ($34.26 x 105%); and laborers, $20.16 ($19.20 x 105 %). O'Brien then prepares the following labor cost estimates for clearing land:

> Heavy Equipment Operators (for brushhog, bulldozer, and front loader)
>   110 hours @ $44.18 = $4,859.80
>
> Drivers (for heavy-duty truck)
>   130 hours @ $35.97 = $4,676.10
>
> Laborers (to fell and cut trees, and help load trucks)
>   200 hours @ $20.16 = $3,840.00
>
> Direct Labor Hours to Clear Land (all three labor categories)
>   440 hours $13,375.90

O'Brien then follows the WBS procedure to estimate the labor cost for the access road construction at $583,698.43, the parking lot construction at $760,953.87, and the warehouse erection at $14,987,631.86. The total proposed labor cost for the entire construction project is $16,375,660.06 (($13,375.90 (detail shown) + $583,698.43 + $760,953.87 + $14,987,631.86)).

The WBS estimating method is a systematic way to demonstrate the basis of B&M's estimate for direct labor costs. Notice that O'Brien included contingencies in the direct labor cost, believing it would be otherwise too low should bad weather occur during contract performance. He also added a 5% escalation factor to current pay scales based on his judgment of future cost-of-living pay raises. A subsequent reviewer can not only check the accuracy of the estimate, but can also evaluate the facts and judgments used in making the estimate.

If the government places this contract by sealed bidding, no one in the government will ever see the details of B&M's direct labor cost estimate. With sealed bidding, the government makes a decision to award based on adequate price competition. Its total focus is on the price offered by a company and its competitors. The details of B&M's estimated costs are not the government's affair.

If the government awards the contract by negotiation, B&M is required to divulge its estimated costs. It is advisable not to go into any more detail than necessary. B&M should provide the government only the bulk figures for each type of labor that it will use for the total job, but if the government pushes hard, B&M can provide more detail. In the case of negotiation, it makes sense to start on the high side, preparing to come down so the government negotiator will think you are "reasonable to deal with." None of this approach is because a company is out to cheat the government. If you take a firm-fixed-price contract (as it likely will be), the government is totally unsympathetic if your costs are far above what you estimated. It is your job to take care of your company; it is the government negotiator's job to take care of the government's interests. One purpose of negotiation is to reach agreement so that both parties are reasonably protected.

Phase Diagrams

Phase diagrams are another method used by contractors to estimate costs. They are similar to the above approach, except that the details of the work are spread out over a time base. The chart in Exhibit 6-3 illustrates this technique for a negotiation to conduct a social study. The various phases shown on the chart illustrate the technical approach being taken.

Each phase of the chart is a work package. The offeror can make an estimate of the labor hours required to conduct each phase. It will probably be necessary to divide most of these phases into subphases, or perhaps even sub-subphases, to estimate the direct labor cost accurately.

Exhibit 6–3
Phase Diagram—Social Study

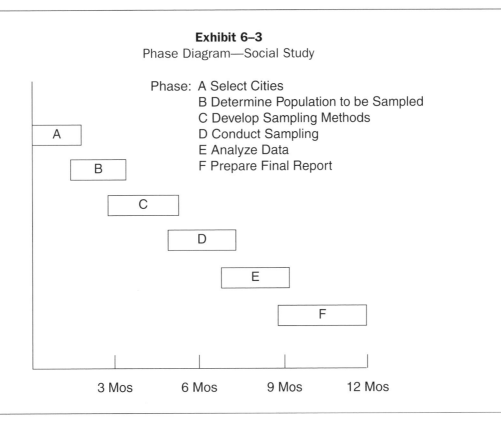

Phase: A Select Cities
B Determine Population to be Sampled
C Develop Sampling Methods
D Conduct Sampling
E Analyze Data
F Prepare Final Report

3 Mos   6 Mos   9 Mos   12 Mos

THE IMPORTANCE OF ANALYZING DIRECT LABOR COSTS

Fixed-Price Contracts

In fixed-price contracts, the detailed analysis of direct labor cost is extremely important when these costs are a significant part of total contract costs. There are two basic reasons:

1. *Finally agreed-upon direct labor costs are 100 percent allocable to the contract.* Direct labor cost estimates are a combination of factual data and certain judgments used to forecast the time needed for each labor skill to do the work, and the proper rates to apply, based on that factual data. The government's decision that the finally agreed-upon direct labor cost estimate is reasonable makes the government a party to the judgments used. It cannot make a case for price reduction after contract award if the contractor in good faith finds more economical ways to use direct labor to get the work done.

2. *Indirect costs are likely to be overstated if direct labor cost is too high.* Proposed indirect costs are commonly based on either direct labor or direct labor plus certain other costs. For example:

Total Direct Labor Cost	$567,000
Overhead Cost (85% of Direct Labor Cost)	481,950
Total Cost	$1,048,950

If the direct labor cost is overstated, the overhead is also overstated because the overhead depends on the amount of direct labor cost. The inclusion of excessive contingencies in this example could result in a $70,000 overstatement of direct labor cost (roughly 12 percent). A fairly simple calculation will show that this overstatement of $70,000 in direct labor cost will result in a total cost overstatement of $129,500.

Cost-Reimbursement Contracts

Highly precise analysis of direct labor costs is generally not feasible in cost-reimbursement contracting. Remember, we are using cost-reimbursement in the first place because the cost of performance is highly uncertain.

The government is protected in cost-reimbursement contracts because it will pay the actual cost of performance, not a pre-estimated amount. Nevertheless, the government has a responsibility to examine proposed direct labor costs, and to consider:

1. *Differences in labor rates.* The proposed labor rates tell us what the actual labor rates are likely to be. If one proposer has rates substantially higher than another for essentially the same skills, that fact has a bearing on the ultimate choice of the contractor.
2. *Level of the proposer's understanding of the work.* Here we are checking for cost realism. The proposer who comes in with direct labor costs obviously well below the likely requirement may not understand the work to be done.
3. *Fees.* The amount of the fee is partially dependent on the estimated total cost, and estimated direct labor cost is one part of that total. If the estimated direct labor cost is grossly overstated, some inflation of the fee could result. However, to keep this in perspective, fee is just one part of the final price actually paid to the contractor, and a small part at that. The government analyst should not become preoccupied with possible fee overstatement and lose sight of the primary objective: to select the offeror who is most likely to provide overall effective performance. That decision springs from a judgment based on technical factors, management competence, and the ultimate cost and fee.

FORMAT FOR SUBMITTING DIRECT LABOR COSTS

Table 15-2 in FAR 15.408 gives the directions for preparing a contract pricing proposal. Paragraph 1 of this table covers the submission of direct labor costs. These instructions are simple and straightforward, as quoted below:

Provide a time-phased (e.g., monthly, quarterly, etc.) breakdown of labor hours, rates and cost by appropriate categories, and furnish bases for estimates.

Exhibit 6-4 illustrates an example of a proper submission.

Exhibit 6-4
Example of a Proper Submission of Direct Labor Costs

Cost Element	Proposed Contract Estimate—Total Cost	Proposed Contract Estimate—Unit Cost	Reference
Direct Engineering Labor	$450,442	Optional (Unless required by CO)	Attachment 4

The cost information shown in Exhibit 6-4 is, by itself, totally inadequate. The instructions for submission of direct labor cost tell the proposer to "submit a time-phased (e.g. monthly, quarterly, etc.) breakdown of labor hours, rates and cost by appropriate categories, and furnish bases for estimates." Our proposer has complied with an Attachment 4, shown in Exhibit 6-5.

Exhibit 6-5
Sample Attachment to Submission of Direct Labor Costs

Attachment 4—Direct Engineering Labor

Design, test, and drafting hours:

Task 1	5,000 drawings @ 3 hours per drawing	15,000
Task 2	2,000 drawings @ 3 hours per drawing	6,000
Task 3	900 drawings @ 3 hours per drawing	2,700
Total		23,700

Hours per class of engineer:

Engineer	Task 1	Task 2	Task 3	Total
Design	4,500	1,800	810	7,110
Drafting	7,500	3,000	1,350	11,850
Aeronautical	3,000	1,200	540	4,740
Total	15,000	6,000	2,700	23,700

Computation of engineering labor costs:

Engineer	Total Hours	Labor Rate	Total Cost
Design	7,110	$21.47	$152,652
Drafting	11,850	16.75	198,487
Aeronautical	4,740	20.95	99,303
Total	23,700		$450,442

The number of direct engineering hours is based on the requirement for an estimated number of drawings for each task. Task 1 requirement is based on a contract that required 6,000 drawings for a similar design. Based on the previous experience and a slightly less complex item, it is estimated that 16 percent fewer hours will be required. The data to verify the number of drawings for the contract is in the files of the engineering department. Tasks 2 and 3 requirements are based on the actual drawings required for our commercial item, model X. It is estimated that the same number of drawings required on model X will be required on Tasks 2 and 3. Model X drawings dated between

February and May, 20X2 are located in the engineering department. The time required per drawing is the same as the average time experienced in 20X5. This can be identified by the cost summary figures in cost ledger Z.

The proposed labor rates are based on the actual average labor rates for the functional labor classifications, as shown in the monthly labor distribution tab run dated 31 October 20X2, our most previous monthly run. The actual rates were increased by two percent to cover half of the average yearly growth (years 20X3, 20X4, and 20X5) in the engineering department labor rate for the estimated period of performance under the proposed contract.

Note that the offeror has provided a full scale explanation of the source of the $450,442, including factual data (e.g., 6,000 drawings on previous contract) and judgment factors (e.g., "16 percent fewer hours"). The contractor does not provide the detailed data to support the 6,000 drawings used for the previous contract, but does tell us where to locate the data if we want to check. A government auditor could verify by checking the files at the engineering department, or the contracting officer could have the company bring in pertinent parts of the file for examination. It is unreasonable to expect an offeror to include in its proposal complete back-up documentation for every fact stated.

We might take issue with some of the judgments stated in the attachment at the time of cost and price discussion. It is unlikely that the basic verifiable data in the attachment is subject to any substantial challenge. Records of actual data are presumed to be accurate, and the burden of proof would be on the government to prove the data are wrong. Meeting that burden would be extremely difficult and generally not worth attempting. The company personnel, at the time they enter data into the files, have no motivation to change it; it is in the company's best interest to have accurate data on hand for estimating purposes.

We have gone into some detail to show one example of proper support of direct labor costs because we want to emphasize that bulk figures are rarely enough to substantiate estimated direct labor costs. The detailed breakout of these direct labor costs to show their derivation and justification is essential to a proper evaluation by the government.

GENERAL METHOD FOR ANALYZING DIRECT LABOR COST

FAR 15.408 requires the supporting documentation for estimated direct labor cost to show the breakdown of labor hours, rates, and cost by appropriate category. We will use the engineering direct labor cost to cover in broad terms how the analysis is made. (The example shown in Exhibit 6-6 will be referenced throughout the following sections on direct labor cost.)

Exhibit 6-6
Sample Engineering Direct Labor Costs

Engineer	Total Hours	Labor Rate	Total Cost
Design	7,110	$21.47	$152,652
Drafting	11,850	16.75	198,487
Aeronautical	4,740	20.95	99,303
Total Direct Labor	23,700		$450,442

The general approach is to examine each element of the proposed cost. First examine the skills proposed. If they appear to be reasonable, look at the hours proposed. If the hours are reasonable, check the labor rates. If all the individual elements look reasonable, we have established that the total estimated cost is reasonable. Any suspect element should be discussed with the proposer.

Analysis of Proposed Skills and Hours

Government technical personnel generally, cannot assess the reasonableness of bulk figures such as 11,850 hours of drafting time and $198,487. They need detailed information on the sources of these estimates. A highly reliable government estimate broken out into the cost elements the offeror used would give technical people a general idea of reasonableness, but it does not automatically verify the offeror's estimate.

The contracting officer should usually request a technical analysis of cost or pricing proposals by asking requirements, logistics, or other appropriate personnel to review and assess the need for the number and kinds of labor hours and the labor mix. Some care is necessary to ensure that these personnel do not perform this task in a perfunctory manner. The analysis works best if the reviewing personnel are instructed to review the proposed skills against the technical (and management, if applicable) proposals, the government estimate, and their own best judgment. These review personnel will need the detailed justification provided by the offeror, such as the contractor's cost breakdown structure described in Exhibit 6-5 and Exhibit 6-6. Some of the questions to be answered by these review personnel are:

- Do the proposed hours agree reasonably with the technical proposal? If not, discrepancies should be reported.
- Are the proposed skill levels in line with the work to be done? (We don't want to pay the professional-level rates for low-skill tasks.)
- Do excessive contingencies appear to be built into the estimate? If so, we need to know for discussion purposes.

Analysis of Proposed Rates

The final question to settle is whether the proposed rates per hour for each skill are reasonable. Cost Accounting Standard (CAS) 401 requires the contractor to use the same methods for estimating costs as it uses for cost accumulation and reporting. This CAS principle is mentioned here because it applies to the material covered in this section. Contractors often group homogeneous costs in their proposals. This grouping does not violate the idea of CAS 401. In its proposal, a firm may group all welding labor cost under the single title "Welding." It may arrive at this cost using an average labor rate for the entire operation. The welding department almost certainly contains several different job categories with different hourly rates. On the surface, it appears that the labor proposal should show each labor category, with hours and wage rates for each. Sometimes it should. Often it will not, and the grouping is perfectly acceptable.

Use of Average Rates
The offeror is very likely to propose average rates for each skill rather than exact rates. Like the government, private companies pay individual salaries, which vary even for the same type of work. The reasons include matters like length of service, merit increases, initial pay

provided at time of hiring, and educational qualifications. When the company makes its proposal, it generally is not certain about which particular persons will be assigned to the job. At this point, the company is not certain it will get the work, so it cannot forecast exactly which people will do the work. It may even hire additional people to work on the contract if they are awarded the work.

Variation with Geographical Area

Rates for the same work vary with geographical area. The Department of Labor (DOL) establishes prevailing wage rates for a wide variety of skills. Contractors are required to pay at least those prevailing wage rates under the Service Contract and Davis-Bacon Acts. It is government policy to ensure that even people not included in the DOL rate coverage will be paid at reasonable rates. The DOL rates help us establish the reasonableness of proposed rates.

Forecast for Time of Performance

The rate is a forecast of what the actual rate will be at the time the work is being done. Offerors may build in an increase in rate per hour depending on what wage rates they believe will be in effect at the time the work starts and for the duration of the work. In this case, the government expects them to divulge the current rate and the amount (or percentage) of increase that makes up the proposed rate.

Conditions in the Offeror's Work Force

The rate may vary with the size of the labor force. If a company is forced to let people go because of a fall-off in work, it will likely retain the most valuable people and let the marginal workers go. It is generally not practical to reduce the pay levels of these higher quality workers who remain. The overall effect will be to raise the average pay rate to a level above what might otherwise be expected, had the lower paid employees remained on the payroll. If the volume of business later improves, the company will hire additional people, generally at lower pay levels than long-term employees. This addition of people will gradually cause the average rate per hour to fall.

Payment of Usual Rates in the Area

Companies are likely to pay employees the usual rate in the area for people of like skills and experience. Some companies pay slightly higher wages, or incur somewhat higher wage-related costs (e.g., benefits) to reduce employee turnover. This practice is generally cheaper than incurring continuous training costs to orient new employees to the job.

Method of Calculating Rates Per Hour

Rates per hour may vary among companies for employees doing the same type work because of differences in the way rates per hour are calculated.

Some companies calculate rates per hour without including fringe benefits in the rate. If the company follows this approach, the fringe benefits appear as an indirect cost. Other companies include costs of fringe benefits with base pay when calculating the rate per hour. The two methods will produce very different results in rates per hour. There is no standard way to make this calculation, and government cost and price analysts will see both methods.

Many companies use 2,080 hours per year as the basis for calculating the rates per hour. This figure is based on 52 weeks per year and 40 hours per week. Aside from the fact that no one really works every day of the year, the 2,080 figure is not necessarily correct. For example, a recent calendar year, 20X1, had 104 weekend days and 261 work days, or 2,088 hours. A company may choose to be more precise by determining the actual days exclusive of weekends. The company may also exclude all federal holidays not worked. The year 20X1 contained 8 federal holidays within the work week. If the company actually observed those holidays by closing down as the government does, it left 253 work days in 20X1, or 2,024 hours.

Assessing Proposed Average Wage Rates

The preceding section discussed some of the general considerations involved in hourly wage rates. As a cost analyst, you will often need to perform a rather thorough assessment of these proposed rates. You must know how the offeror estimated the average wage rates so you can evaluate their reasonableness. How much assessment you do will depend on the proposed cost of the labor. A proposal with several million dollars of labor cost obviously should be scrutinized more closely than one with $100,000 of labor.

There are several ways to determine average wage rates. A few firms use a plantwide rate, which is a single hourly wage rate that applies to all manufacturing labor. Many firms use departmental rates, which are average wage rates established for each separate manufacturing department. Most firms with an engineering department use a labor category rate for that department. Individual labor rates are used in unusual circumstances. Each of these labor rate determination methods is covered in more detail below.

Plantwide Rate
Very few firms use this type of rate, but you may see it. It applies to firms that produce few products, and all of them pass through all the departments during manufacture. Exhibit 6-7 shows how this rate is calculated.

Exhibit 6-7
Calculation of Plantwide Rate

Labor Category	Work Force	Wage Rate Per Hour	Weighted Wage Rate
Parts Fabrication	200	$8.00	$1,600
Component Assembly (A)	400	6.00	2,400
Final Assembly (B)	300	5.50	1,650
Packaging (C)	100	5.00	500
Total (D)	1,000		$6,150

Weighted plantwide rate: $6,150/1000 = $6.15 per hour
Note: Letters in parentheses ( ) are Department Codes

The *simple* average hourly rate for this firm is $6.125 per hour. It is the total of all wage rates divided by four categories (($8.00 + 6.00 + 5.50 + 5.00)/4 = $6.125 per hour). This simple average rate is misleading and useless because it does not consider the fact that some departments are larger than others. If every employee worked on your contract for one hour, your labor charge would be $6,125 using the $6.125 simple average hourly rate. The last column of Exhibit 6-7 above shows that the cost should be $6,150. The simple average hourly rate would undercharge the contract by $25.

The *weighted* average rate does produce accurate results when a total of 1,000 hours is worked. The charge would be 1,000 hours x $6.15 per hour = $6,150, corresponding to the exhibit. The weighted average rate will produce reasonable results when your work gets a pro-rata share of the work available in all the departments. For example, the result will still be accurate if 20 persons in A, 40 in B, 30 in C, and 10 in D work one hour on your job. You will get 100 hours at a total labor cost of $615.

The plantwide rate of $6.15 per hour will not produce accurate results if your job does not get the same share of each department's labor. Assume that your job will get the effort shown in Exhibit 6-8, with one hour provided by each person.

Exhibit 6-8
Distortion Caused by Plant-Wide Rate

Labor Category	Persons on Your Job	Wage Rate Per Hour	Weighted Wage Rate
Parts Fabrication (A)	20	$8.00	$160
Component Assembly (B)	30	6.00	180
Final Assembly (C)	40	5.50	220
Packaging (D)	20	5.00	100
Total	110		$660

Weighted plantwide rate: $6,150/1000 = $6.15 per hour
Cost using plantwide rate: 110 hours x $6.15 per hour = $677
Note: Letters in parentheses ( ) are Department Codes

Compare the number of people on your job with the number of people in each department (see Exhibit 6-7). You are getting 1/10 of Department A, less than 1/10 of B, and more than 1/10 each of C and D. The labor cost per hour in the exhibit above is $660, using the proper rate for each category. This labor cost is correct. If the plantwide rate ($6.15 per hour) is used, the labor cost per hour is $677 (rounded) (110 hours x $6.15 per hour). The cost would be overstated by $17 per hour. You may not think this is very significant for one hour. It will be very significant if the 110 persons on your job use 200 hours each (110 x 200 x $17 = $374,000).

Departmental Rate

Departmental rates are much more common than the plantwide rate discussed above. Please refer to Exhibit 6-7 again. The individual wage rates per hour in this exhibit are departmental rates. For example, the departmental rate for parts fabrication is $8.00 per hour. The parts fabrication departmental rate may have been derived as shown in Exhibit 6-9.

Exhibit 6-9
Calculation of Departmental Rate

Labor Category	Persons on Your Job	Wage Rate Per Hour	Weighted Wage Rate
Machinists	70	$9.20	$644
Machine Operators	100	7.85	785
Machine Helpers	30	5.70	171
Total	200		$1,600

The departmental rate is calculated by dividing the $1,600 weighted wage rate for the department by its 200 employees. The result of that calculation is $8.00 per hour. Notice that this departmental wage rate corresponds to that in Exhibit 6-7 to calculate the plantwide rate.

In most cases, a departmental rate is superior to a plantwide rate. When departmental rates are used, the offeror determines the number of hours that each department will provide for the contract effort. The total labor cost is the sum of the labor costs for each department. Exhibit 6-10 below is an example.

Exhibit 6-10
Proposed Labor Costs, Using Departmental Rates

Parts Fabrication	2,100 hours	$8.00/hour	$16,800
Component Assembly	3,600 hours	6.00/hour	21,600
Final Assembly	1,300 hours	5.50/hour	7,150
Packaging	400 hours	5.00/hour	2,000
Total	7,400 hours		$47,550

If the plantwide rate of $6.15 per hour had been used for this proposal (see Exhibit 6-7), the proposed cost would have been $45,510 (7,400 hours x $6.15 per hour). This result again shows the general unreliability of plantwide rates. The contractor using a plantwide rate would have understated its own costs. You may believe this situation is attractive and that you should take advantage of it. Remember that you are required to tell the offeror if you suspect it has made a mistake. The problem, however, is not likely to arise. Few experienced contractors would use a plantwide rate in any case. The few who would are in situations where all their work flows through all departments in essentially the same way, but this type of work flow is very uncommon.

Departmental rates are fairly commonly used and are almost always better than plantwide rates. However, do not assume that they will work well in every case. Departmental rates work well when the skill mix for your work is very similar to the skill mix used to determine the departmental rate, but they will cause an overstatement of direct labor cost when your work gets a lower skill mix. Refer again to Exhibit 6-9. Notice that the machinists in the department account for a large share of departmental costs (close to 40 percent). Now look at Exhibit 6-11 below, which lists the skills and hours needed for your contract effort. Notice that your work requires a small amount of machinist time but large amounts of lower price machine operator and machine helper time.

Exhibit 6-11
Work Requirements for Parts Fabrication

Machinists	200 hours	$9.20/hour	$ 1,840
Machine Operator	1,300 hours	7.85/hour	10,205
Machine Helpers	600 hours	5.70/hour	3,420
Total	2,100 hours		$15,465

Notice that the direct labor cost is $15,465 when determined based on the actual skills needed for the work and the respective rates. These same rates are used to calculate the departmental rate for parts fabrication (Exhibit 6-9). The direct labor cost was $16,800 when the departmental rate was used for the proposal (Exhibit 6-10).

Companies often use departmental rates to predict manufacturing direct labor costs. They work well enough in most instances for several reasons. The skill mixes for most of the workers' individual outputs are reasonably close to the mix in the whole department. The spread of wage rates among the labor categories in a given manufacturing department is generally not large. You will need to know how the departmental rate was calculated. You must attempt to negotiate a cost adjustment if your contract work uses a skill mix very different from the overall department structure.

By now, you may be thinking that departmental rates are not very reliable either. You may believe offerors should propose direct labor costs based on the specific skills and hours they expect to use. This might be the best method in some circumstances; however, you will still have problems. One is that the proposed hours are an estimate. It does no good to have pinpoint accuracy on rates if it gets buried by inaccuracies in the hours. Second, the people within a given skill do not all have the same pay rate. Exhibits 6-9 and 6-11 show a rate of $7.85 per hour for the machine operators. There are 100 of them. Their actual wage rates will vary over a wide range, perhaps $6.70 per hour to $9.15 per hour. Their wage rate depends on factors such as time with the company, relative skills, and merit increases. Third, the rates may not be 100 percent accurate. Accurate average rates can be established for each labor category by using the present payroll. The problem is that the offeror will very likely propose future hourly rates. It will use the rates it believes will be in effect when the work is being performed. This estimate requires judgments that are never 100 percent accurate.

Rates by Labor Category
Exhibit 6-11 illustrates a labor cost calculation using labor category rates. It shows, for example, an average rate for machine operators at $7.85 per hour. That exhibit shows that labor category rates are likely to provide more precise estimates than departmental rates.

In manufacturing, rates by labor category are most commonly used to predict engineering direct labor costs because differences in wage rates are significant among draftsmen, project engineers, and project managers. All these labor categories, including project managers, are almost always direct costs. Rates by labor category are useful because each project generally requires a specific mix of skills rather than a pro-rata share of all of them. Rates by labor category are often used in other situations where there is wide variation in wage rates, but they are not as likely to be used in manufacturing departments where the spread of wage rates is usually not great.

Individual Rates

Individual rates are used when named individuals, generally highly paid, will be used for a contract effort. You will not see individual rates proposed very often. When they are used, the offeror will name the individuals to be assigned, estimate the hours required, and state their wage rates. Offerors prefer not to name specific individuals in most cases because it locks the offeror into using an individual who may be needed for other more important work. Also, employees can always exercise their right to go elsewhere, and the individual may not even be on the firm's payroll when the work must be done.

Projecting Wage Rates

The preceding discussion covered plantwide, departmental, labor category, and individual wage rates in considerable detail, with characteristics and computation method for each and emphasis on the unavoidable inaccuracies. You must understand that none of the methods is precise. However, you can find methods among them that are accurate enough for estimating purposes.

You are most likely to see departmental rates used for manufacturing and services and labor category rates used for engineering. You may find some manufacturers and service industries using labor category rates for all their estimates. The choices are largely up to the individual offeror. The government expects its offerors to use the same estimating methods for all their customers, government and private, and it expects consistency in rate development methods and applications.

Routine use of a carefully developed departmental rate will cause understatements of actual labor costs in some instances and overstatements in others. The contractor knows that, if departmental rates are used, some inaccuracies exist. These inaccuracies are not great, however, if the departmental rate is in fact the most practical. If the contractor believes the inaccuracies in a departmental rate will create major problems, he or she can move to a more precise labor category rate. It will cost more to implement the more precise system, and, even if adopted, it still is not 100 percent accurate.

It is not your job, as a cost analyst, to tell the offeror what system to use. It is your job to assess the results of the system actually being used. You need to be sure it is used across the board for all customers. You must understand that, no matter what system is used, it will not be 100 percent accurate, and you will have to use your judgment to determine whether it is accurate enough for your contract purposes. If you believe it is not, you must be prepared to negotiate the basis you believe is better.

THE HISTORICAL COST METHOD FOR ESTIMATING LABOR COSTS

The historical cost method for estimating direct labor hours is based on using actual experience in making the same or similar products. Most manufacturers maintain very precise historical data on the actual times used for each step in making their products. For example, the data will show the times used on past orders for steps such as cutting stock to length, performing each machining operation, grinding, and plating or painting. It will also have actual information on assembly, inspection, and packaging times. The data for prior work may be for single items or runs of tens or even hundreds of items.

In concept, it is simple to estimate the hours needed to build products for a new proposal if we have data on how long it took to make the products before. We simply adjust those previous actual times to the quantity needed for the current offer. For example, assume that 28 labor hours were used to assemble five Type 308 Transmitters in May 20X1. The firm is now (June, 20X2) preparing an offer for 17 Type 308 Transmitters. The calculation for the present quantity is:

May 20X1: $\dfrac{28 \text{ direct labor hours}}{5 \text{ transmitters}} = 5.6$ hours per transmitter

June 20X2:   17 transmitters $\times$ 5.6 hrs per unit = 95.2 direct labor hours

If the hourly rate for assembly is $21.66, the total cost is $2,062 (95.2 hours x $21.66 per hour). This is assembly cost and represents only one part of the total fabrication cost. This calculation is fairly simple. One reason is that the offer is for the same transmitter (Type 308) that the firm produced under contract last year.

We will now consider the advantages and disadvantages of this method when used for the same product. One advantage is that it is based on actual experience with the same item. The estimator calculated the 95.2 hours for the current 17 products without applying any judgments. It was a straight calculation. A disadvantage is that we do not know what inefficiencies, if any, are hidden in the experience figure of 5.6 hours per unit. You may detect another disadvantage. The 5.6 hours average time that applied to five units a year ago does not necessarily hold for 17 units this year. In the first place, the firm may have assembled the fifth unit in 20X1 in five hours because of experience gained. If they have been continuing to assemble similar transmitters for other customers, a more realistic *starting* time per unit could be five hours. It may also be that the firm would be using 4.6 hours by the time it reaches the 17th unit. The average time per unit, based on 17 units, might be more reasonable at 4.8 hours. The assembly cost would then be $1,767, not the $2,062 proposed by the firm.

The method becomes more complicated if the firm is comparing with a similar item, rather than the same item. Assume that the 20X2 proposal will be for 17 Type 314 Transmitters. This transmitter is similar to the Type 308 except that it has an additional amplifier stage. It also has a digital readout and a gasket to make it more watertight (for climates with heavy rainfall). Now a production planner, or engineer, at the offeror's plant must judge the time difference for assembly, although the firm has not assembled any such receiver before. Based on the 5.6 hours average time for the Type 308 in May 20X1, the estimator may judge that an additional 30 minutes (.5 hour) will be needed, raising the assembly time to 6.1 hours. The assembly cost would be $2,246 (6.1 hours x 17 units x 21.66). This calculation has the same advantages as the prior method. A disadvantage is that a judgment has been added to the calculation because the design is different. The judgment may or may not be valid. It also may not properly consider the learning curve. If you choose to challenge it, you will need good technical backup. If you do not challenge it, you may pay an unreasonable cost.

Negotiated contracts are generally awarded to companies with prior experience in manufacturing the same or similar items because these companies will usually have complete historical data on labor costs for prior contracts. The firm may not have experience in making an identical product, but many of the manufacturing steps for the other product will be the same as or similar to those for the new product. Consequently, the historical cost method is commonly used to estimate labor costs, even with its disadvantages. This method is especially useful for smaller contracts that do not justify using the more sophisticated (and expensive) methods described below. It is also commonly used by the smaller businesses that cannot afford highly sophisticated estimating systems. It is a usable and practical system, especially when the firm has recent experience in manufacturing the same or similar items.

When an offeror proposes labor costs based on historical experience, it is projecting direct labor hours and costs from prior recorded experience. Some manufactured components may be the same as those produced before. Others may be similar to prior items or they may be new items. You will need the precise historical data showing the starting point for the projection. You must also know what judgments the offeror used to go from the prior data to the current offer. Obtaining this information is the only way you have to assess the direct labor requirement stated in the offer.

You should use the following considerations in analyzing direct labor submissions based on historical data:

1. The offeror may use the same process hours that applied to a prior contract. Be sure that the manufacturing process has not changed to a more labor-efficient method. Make sure the offeror runs its production line as it did before. Find out if the offeror has installed new equipment that will reduce direct labor hours.
2. Do not let the offeror include additional time for personal needs, fatigue, rework, and such matters. The prior actual times should already include these times.
3. Determine whether the make-or-buy plan has changed since the last contract. The direct labor cost should decrease if the offeror plans to purchase some components that were previously manufactured in-house.
4. Determine whether the historical costs include the cost of contract changes. If so, examine them very carefully to be sure that you are not paying extra costs.

LABOR STANDARDS METHODS FOR ESTIMATING LABOR COSTS

Many manufacturers, especially those with long experience, have progressed beyond the historical cost method because they recognize that this method often masks and perpetuates labor inefficiencies. The labor standards method is an objective method for estimating labor hours that does not rely on prior experience. Many experienced manufacturers use labor standards and maintain a labor standards program, which is a file of objective labor standards showing a "standard" time for various manufacturing steps. It is based on standards developed within the company, data from other companies (often published by trade associations), and reference data on standards.

Meaning and Types of Labor Standards

Labor standards are expressed as output standards or time standards. An output standard states a production rate for a given unit for a specific manufacturing operation. For example, "installing three transformers every hour" is an output standard. A qualified workman working at a normal pace under proper supervision should be able to install three transformers every hour (60 minutes). A time standard is the time it should take to complete one operation. In the preceding example, the time standard is "20 minutes (.33 hours) to install one transformer." This time standard, as understood here, includes the basic time to do the work plus allowances for fatigue and personal needs.

Components of Standard Time

The standard time for an operation consists of the basic time required to complete the operation plus certain additional times. The formula below shows these time components:

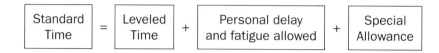

1. *Leveled time.* This is the time required to perform the operation by a worker with average skills under average conditions. It does not contain any allowances for delays like breaks or other personal needs. It is obtained by observing an average worker, or several, and timing performance on any number of operations. For example, the time study technician may time an average worker for ten successive transformer installations and find an average time of 15.1 minutes, with a minimum of 13.5 minutes and a maximum of 17.7 minutes. The technician adjusts the average time of 15.1 to a leveled time of 16.9 minutes using a conversion factor based on experience. The 16.9 minutes is the time for an average worker to install the transformers under average conditions. However, additional adjustments are made before this becomes a standard time.
2. *Personal delay and fatigue allowances.* These are additional time allowances for nonprocess needs. These include going to restrooms, getting a drink of water, waiting for materials, and rest periods. They are usually handled as percentages of the leveled time. They may be set at 5 percent each and rarely exceed 20 percent total. Assume that a total of 15 percent is used in your transformer installation example. This allowance will add 2.5 minutes (16.9 minutes x 15%), raising the total to 19.4 minutes so far.
3. *Special allowance.* The time study analyst may add special allowances to cover time periods that should not be included in the process time or personal allowances, such as time for machine and area cleaning. They are usually a historical percentage of the leveled time plus the personal time. Assume three percent for our transformer installation case. This adds another .6 minutes.

The total standard time (based on the calculations above) is 20 minutes to install one transformer.

How Labor Standards Are Used

The previous discussion covered the general concepts of developing standard times for manufacturing labor. Most companies that have been in operation for a considerable time have labor standards programs in use. Some have partial coverage and others have complete coverage of their labor processes. The purpose of the program is to establish how much labor time should be needed for each manufacturing process that a company has. The standard time to produce a finished product is the sum of the standard times for all its manufacturing steps. When properly developed, this standard time is much more reliable than historical data. However, it is a very complex and expensive program to carry out when the company tries to cover all its manufacturing processes. Despite the care taken in their development, standards are never 100 percent accurate, partly because judgments must be used in developing some parts of the standard time.

During manufacture, the firm records the actual time used for each process and compares it to the standard time. The difference is called "variance." Generally, no action is taken when the actual time does not significantly differ from the standard time. A small variance like 5 percent is not considered significant because the management knows that the standards are not 100 percent accurate.

The production managers will investigate when there is a significant variance between actual and standard time for a process. If the actual time is significantly greater than the standard, problems may exist. During early manufacture, a variance may indicate that the workers have not reached the planned skill levels. Additional training may be needed, or supervision may need improvement. Actual time that significantly exceeds the standard after considerable experience is gained is often an indication that labor time is not being efficiently used. This variance may be due to delays in material delivery, deficient worker training, or equipment problems. When the actuals exceed the standards, some supervisors will claim that the standard is incorrect and unreasonably tight, and they may be correct. Their claim may also be an excuse, when the real problem is something else. Actual times that are consistently lower than the standard are very likely and indication that the standard is improperly developed and should be redeveloped.

Estimating Labor Hours Based on Standards

The government would like to pay for manufacturing labor cost based on accurate standard times. However, this standard time may not be achievable, especially in the early stages of manufacture. The government will accept direct labor hours that exceed the firm's standard times when an adequate explanation exists. Bid times are projected by starting with standard times and adjusting them to reflect actual times. The offeror establishes the standard times and uses factors to convert the standard times into expected actual times for bid purposes. These factors are based on its experience in the relationships between standard and actual hours and are shown as follows:

- *Realization Factor:* The "realization factor" is the relationship between actual hours and standard hours. For example, the firm may have experience showing that its realization factor is 1.2. This means that the actual hours for a process are 1.2 times the standard hours. If the standard time for inserting a transformer is 20 minutes, the actual time will be 24 minutes (20 min. x 1.2). A realization factor of .95 means that the company expects a production time of 19 minutes.
- You should ask for an explanation, and be very skeptical, when the offeror proposes a realization factor greater than 1.0. A factor greater than 1.0 means that the firm does not expect ever to meet its own standard times.
- *Rework Time:* Rework time is the time needed to repair or correct a product in other ways because it is defective. Design changes may also cause rework in already completed items. Rework time is generally estimated as a percent of the leveled time in the standard time and is based on the firm's historical experience. Standard time itself does not include rework time because it is not a routine part of manufacturing the product. It happens only when defective work or design changes have occurred.
- *The Learning Curve:* The learning curve is another way of using standard times to predict labor hours and costs. The realization factor described above is not used when a firm uses the learning curve. The learning curve is covered below.

THE LEARNING CURVE (IMPROVEMENT CURVE)

As we have shown in Chapter 4, when you perform a repetitive operation, you almost always look for and find faster ways to do it. All of us have this experience in our private lives. The same thing happens in manufacturing when workers are making the same items repetitively. The learning curve is simply a graph that shows how this improvement can be measured and used and provides a way to predict labor hours and costs when we have beginning hours and costs. We could use the curve to predict the labor hours (and costs) needed for a 100th unit if we have the standard hours for a first or intermediate unit.

Early developers of the theory called it the learning curve because they believed that learning by workers caused most of the time saving. Later studies showed that other factors, such as equipment and set-up improvements, also help reduce unit production time. It is now called by various names such as "improvement curve," "experience curve," and "time reduction curve." Any of these titles are probably better than "learning curve." However, this text will continue using "learning curve" to maintain consistency with the prevailing vernacular.

When using learning curves, we use percentages to express improvement factors. A 90 percent learning curve means that a second unit takes 90 percent as long to make as the first unit. The 80 percent curve relates to an 80 percent improvement, etc. Exhibit 6-12 illustrates the method for applying the percentages and the importance of the concept in predicting labor hours.

Exhibit 6-12
Learning Curve Explanation

Unit	Hours Per Unit			Cumulative Total Hours		
	70%	80%	90%	70%	80%	90%
1	100	100	100	100	100	100
2	70	80	90	170	180	190
4	49	64	81	276	314	356
8	34	51	73	430	534	657
16	24	41	66	651	892	1,303
32	17	33	59	964	1,468	2,191
64	12	26	53	1,405	2,392	3,971
128	8	21	48	2,024	3,874	7,176
256	6	17	43	2,891	6,248	12,950

First, concentrate on the "Hours Per Unit" side of the exhibit. The left column shows successive production units from #1 through #256. Notice that the numbers double as you go from #1 to #256. Now look at the next column for a 70 percent learning curve. The 2nd unit requires 70 percent of the beginning hours (100), namely 70 hours. The 4th unit requires 70 percent of the preceding time, namely 49 hours (70% x 70 hours). The 8th unit requires 34 hours (70% x 49 = 34.3, rounded to 34).

Notice that the time per unit is decreasing as the serial number increases. The time for the 256th unit is 6 hours. (The time for #1,028 would be 4 hours and for #5,012 would be 2 hours. These figures are not in the exhibit.) Notice also that the difference in unit time is less as you go down the line; 4 hours are saved between #128 and #64 and only 2 hours between #256 and #128. The savings are much less dramatic as experience is gained.

The figures in the exhibit are rounded to the nearest whole unit. Remember that these calculations are based on the theory of learning curves. From a practical standpoint, other factors may set in, and the calculated 6 hours for the 256th unit may never happen. For example, the workers may rebel at the idea of going from 100 to 6 hours per unit. However, it is entirely possible that with a 70 percent learning curve these unit production times could fall to the order of 20 to 30 hours. This is a dramatic improvement over the original 100 hours and would result in major labor cost savings.

The second part of the exhibit shows cumulative total times for producing various quantities. For example, with a 70 percent learning curve, 964 total hours are required to produce 32 units. Contrast this with the 3,200 hours that result from multiplying 100 hours per unit (the starting hours) times 32 units. The saving is even more dramatic when you look at the cumulative time for 64 or more units.

The exhibit contains comparable information for the 80 percent and 90 percent learning curves. Notice that the savings in production hours are much less dramatic, especially for the 90 percent learning curve. Nevertheless, these learning curves would result in major labor cost savings if properly considered in estimating labor costs.

Learning Curve Tables

Some texts describe methods for plotting specific learning curves on "log-log" graph paper. If you do this plotting, you can use the graph to get approximate unit production hours for any intermediate quantity. This book does not cover this graphing method for predicting labor hours. Better and simpler ways exist to do the same thing. One method is using learning curve tables that are commercially available for these purposes. An even better method is to use commercially available computer programs designed to meet learning curve needs.

This book will briefly describe learning curve tables and their uses. Commercially printed tables are available covering the 51 percent, 52 percent 53 percent, etc., through 99 percent learning curves. There are two types of tables available: one is a unit progress curve table, used for projecting production units; the other is a cumulative progress curve table, used to project cumulative production totals.

Learning Curve Applications and Limitations

For simplicity, the preceding discussions have concentrated on using the learning curve for predicting labor hours, one of its major uses. Learning curves were originally developed using data for assembly labor in the aircraft industry, and they continue to find many uses in assembly operations in other industries as well as aircraft. Learning curve theory has expanded to uses in manpower analysis, space requirements, material analysis, estimating total costs, and purchasing. Learning curves do not generally apply well to engineering labor and almost never apply to scientific labor. They also do not work well with indirect cost analysis because indirect costs normally contain considerable fixed expenses.

The best source of data for learning curve analysis is the company itself. The learning curve that applies to one firm is not likely to apply to another, even in the same industry. Past studies show learning curves varying from 65 percent to 98 percent among large and well-known aircraft companies. At first glance, it might appear that a firm on the 75 percent learning curve is doing better than one on the 95 percent learning curve. This presumption is not necessarily correct. The firm with the 95 percent learning curve may have planned its production better from the beginning. The firm with the 75 percent curve may have a lot more to learn.

Because the learning curve applies primarily to continuous production, a break in production will invalidate strict application of learning curve analysis. It is difficult to predict the effect of a production break. The effect may not be great if production equipment is still in place, the break was recent, and the experienced work force is still available. If the break occurred six months or a year ago, much of the improvement may have been lost.

When examining labor estimates based on learning curve theory, be sure to check the offeror's arithmetic and rationale. Be especially careful about proposals that base projected labor on the hours and costs estimated for a first unit. The chances are that an offeror with any experience at all is further along the learning curve.

Do not be misled about learning curves. Proper application of the learning curve is much more complex than this brief overview shows. The concept is useful when mixed with good judgment and much deeper understanding than this overview provides. Although the mathematical tables show continually decreasing unit production times as the quantity increases, this reduction does not always happen in actual circumstances. Sometimes a point is reached where the unit production times start to climb, and there are various reasons for this occurrence. One of many is that workers may reach a point where they will not try to improve further. This concept is referred to as "a fair day's work for a fair day's pay."

ANALYSIS OF ENGINEERING LABOR

Many of the general considerations already discussed apply to engineering labor. However, there are some significant differences. Engineering labor is mostly involved in developing new approaches or in problem solving. This activity is not the same as the effort involved in manufacturing, much of which is process oriented rather than product oriented. By this we mean that manufacturing generally consists of workers doing a wide variety of repetitive processes, including cutting, grinding, machining, welding, soldering, assembling, etc. Soldering with a small soldering gun is basically the same, whether the work is being done for radio receivers or navigation equipment. Applying and securing nuts and bolts is basically the same, whether they are put in fixed equipment or vehicles. Engineering and scientific labor are far less transferable from one job to another.

Factors to Consider in Analyzing an Engineering Labor Proposal

When you analyze an engineering labor proposal, you need certain information, which should be included in the pricing or technical proposals, depending on its nature. If the information is not there, you must get it before you can hope to do an adequate job.

You must know the offeror's concept of operation for the engineering work. You must also understand the offeror's practices and definitions and the accounting classifications used for its engineering personnel. You need to know the offeror's time-phased plans for completing the work and the engineering categories and hours planned for each phase. You will definitely need government engineering assistance to analyze the proposal properly. Obviously, the proposed engineering labor must be consistent with the offeror's technical proposal.

Some engineering labor is very creative and requires highly trained individuals. Assessing the reasonableness of the proposed hours for the highly creative parts is often very hard. However, relatively few persons will be doing the highly creative engineering work. Most of the other engineering is of a support nature, and the time required will be more predicable. Some forms of engineering effort require very little creativity, such as preparing and correcting drawings, planning and setting up production lines, and planning production and plant layouts.

DIRECT AND INDIRECT LABOR IN MANUFACTURING

Manufacturers use direct and indirect labor to convert raw materials and purchased parts and components into finished goods. This conversion is accomplished through physical operations including cutting, grinding, drilling, machining, welding, soldering, fastening, and many others. Manufacturers often purchase some parts and components from outside vendors rather than making them in-house. Regardless of source, these parts and components are generally assembled into finished products within the factory.

Factory direct labor consists of people who are actually making parts from raw materials, installing parts into components, or assembling finished items. You can think of direct labor as the "hands-on" people. Most manufacturing plants have separate areas for various types of operations, such as storing raw stock, cutting, light and heavy machining, grinding, and plating. They install machines so that raw materials will flow down a processing line to become finished parts. Purchased parts and components will flow through separate receiving and inspection areas into temporary storage areas. These purchased items will be moved into final assembly areas when needed. Parts made within the factory will also flow to the final assembly areas. Final assembly is one of the very last steps, followed by final inspection and packaging.

A manufacturing plant also uses considerable numbers of indirect labor persons. The indirect labor category usually includes superintendents, maintenance and stockroom personnel, people in production planning and control operations, clerical personnel, and others not directly producing the physical products.

Some costs are borderline—they might be considered direct or indirect. Different companies have different practices for classifying these labor costs. For example, some companies classify all foremen as indirect labor. Others classify them as direct labor. Others classify only some foremen as direct and others as indirect. How they are classified depends on the number of persons they supervise, the number of cost objectives in their work area, and how the company keeps track of their time. If they supervise people working on only one cost objective, they are likely to be charged as direct. If they supervise several teams, each working on different cost objectives, they are likely to be indirect. Companies also vary in their classification of quality control personnel, sometimes called inspectors. These people are the technicians who check the work being done by workers who make parts and assemble final products, but they do not make products themselves. Some companies classify them as indirect labor, and others classify them as direct labor. Either method is acceptable as long as the company follows consistent practices.

A wide variety of processes and direct labor skills are at work in a factory at any given time. Each process has the direct labor people needed to get the work done. A welding department will have welders who are specialists in various welding methods. It will also have other labor categories such as foremen, helpers, laborers, and inspectors. Each labor category has its own job description and average hourly rate. The lowest skills may be laborers who work under close direction doing work such as sweeping floors, cleaning machines, moving materials, and removing scrap. The next higher levels may be apprentice workers and machine helpers. They have some skills but still need close supervision. Next you may find journeyman classifications. These are the workers who have completed formal training programs, often lasting several years. They have passed proficiency tests and do not require close supervision. Intermingled with all these labor categories, you will find other people such as quality control inspectors. Many of these people will be involved, one way or another and for various times, in making your product. Together they comprise the direct labor costs charged to your contract.

The mere fact that one company has a higher set of wage rates than another does not automatically make the higher wage rates unreasonable. In particular, the government analyst needs to know what costs are included in the wage rate and the number of days or hours used to calculate the wage rate per hour. There are numerous other factors that can affect the hourly rate.

When an audit of the cost or pricing proposal is conducted, the auditor will generally spot-check the calculation of wage rates to determine that the approach is reasonable and that the calculated rates agree with data quoted in the pricing proposal and in other government or private proposals.

Aside from verification by audit, wage rates may be checked for reasonableness by comparison to DOL prevailing rates for the area, comparison to rates proposed by other companies for similar skills, and comparison to government rates for similar skills. It is important to be sure that the we compare "apples to apples." Differences in the basic methods of calculating rates may cause comparisons to be very misleading.

CHAPTER 7
Analysis of Direct Material and Other Direct Costs

As has been previously stated, FAR 31.202 describes a direct cost as "any cost that can be identified specifically with a particular final cost objective." We have been using terms somewhat simpler than "final cost objective" and will continue to do so. For our purposes, the final cost objective is a term for proposed contract, task, or work. FAR 31.202, in a later paragraph, states the following:

> (b) For reasons of practicality, any direct cost of minor dollar amount may be treated as an indirect cost if the accounting treatment?
> (1) Is consistently applied to all cost objectives; and
> (2) Produces substantially the same results as treating the cost as a direct cost.

The above aspect of the FAR description has special application to material costs, as we will see shortly.

DIRECT MATERIAL COSTS

A direct material cost is the cost of significant materials that are used in the manufacture of a product or that are used up in providing a service. Direct material costs are specifically identifiable to the contract

They include items the offeror expects to buy specifically for the contract and an inventory on hand to be consumed in performing the contract. Because of the nature of direct material costs, accounting for them is practical only on a contract-by-contract basis. Examples are items of significant value, such as raw materials, parts, and assemblies that will be used to make final products.

Companies do not attempt to charge every item, no matter how small in cost, to a specific contract or job. Doing so is too much trouble, and the administrative cost of keeping up with all that detail would exceed the value gained by doing it. Consequently, it is customary to charge the direct material accounts with significant cost items conveniently identifiable to the work. The minor material costs are often changed to indirect expense. FAR 31.202 (b) provides authority for handling direct costs of minor dollar amounts as indirect, with certain restrictions. First, the indirect costs charged for the materials must be reasonably close to the costs if directly charged. Second, the contractor must follow a consistent procedure. We do not want the offeror to use one method for the government and another for its private customers.

A simple example may help clarify this idea. When I take my car to the garage for repairs, I get a copy of a job ticket when I pay the bill. The job ticket is really a sort of contract I signed in blank at the time I turned in the car for repairs. When I get my car back, the service people have filled in the details. Let's say that I got a tune-up, a grease job, and a repacking of the front wheel bearings. The upper left-hand corner of the ticket lists various items, like six spark plugs, five quarts of oil, and a new wheel bearing. Those items are direct material because they are specifically identifiable to my car. The total material cost may come to $50. It is convenient to charge them to my car because the stockroom clerk could easily record them on my job ticket when he gave them to the mechanic; perhaps the garage even ordered the parts from a nearby distributor specifically for the job.

I know that about a half-cup of grease is used to repack wheel bearings. The mechanic gets the grease from an overhead grease source or a can near his workbench. The mechanic does not rush over and tell the stockroom clerk that he used a half-cup of grease on my wheel bearings and he does not record it on the job ticket. If he did, it would probably be 20¢ or less. It isn't worth the bother to keep up with the exact usage of low-dollar value items. Short lengths of wire, cotter pins, connectors, and various other small items are handled the same way. The dealer has to pay for such items. The cost is charged to overhead for general supplies and is distributed to all customers.

Estimating Direct Material Costs

The concept of estimating direct materials costs is very straightforward. It consists of determining what is needed, how much is needed, and figuring the cost of the components. Then unit costs are applied to determine line item and total costs. The actual doing may be more complex than this simple concept suggests. The determinations of what material and how much material are generally done together.

Contractors consider several factors in deciding what materials to buy and how much is needed. These factors are described below.

Bill of Materials

When products are being bought to a design specification (a detailed set of drawings), a bill of materials is generally a part of the drawing package. The bill of materials is a list of all the items needed to make a product. Almost anything we buy, except for raw materials and very simple items which have no parts, consists of various parts that are put together in an assembly. For example, a lamp consists of the base, a column, a bulb socket, a harp for holding the shade, the shade itself, a length of insulated wiring, and a plug. The bulb socket contains various parts such as brass bottom and top halves, a cardboard insert, a switch, and several screws and other parts. A manufacturer producing lamps has, or develops, a list of parts needed to make each type of lamp it plans to sell. This information is essential to the manufacturer for determining, for example, which parts will be bought and which will be made from raw materials. A lamp manufacturer would be unlikely to make insulated electric wire or bulb sockets, but might well produce its own lamp shades.

If a company is producing products to meet performance specifications (which state what the product does but not exactly how to make it), it will first have to design the product and then, based on that design, develop a bill of materials needed to make the item.

The bill of materials states the exact number of each part needed to make the product. A bill of materials for, say a lamp socket, might state that one upper brass part and one lower brass part is needed for each socket. It would appear then that if we planned to manufacture 10,000 sockets, we would simply order 10,000 upper and 10,000 lower parts.

The Scrap Allowance

A scrap allowance is an extra amount of material or parts required to be sure that enough material will be available to make the final product. This allowance is usually stated as a percent of the basic quantity. The actual quantity of parts consumed in manufacturing or construction will almost always exceed the basic minimum quantity that is listed in the bill of materials.

Scrap is unavoidable. It occurs in normal manufacturing processes such as cutting, trimming, punching, boring, and machining. In the case of our lamp socket, it occurs because one part doesn't fit quite right into another. In construction, it occurs because we need a 2" x 4" x 5' length of pine lumber, and the boards come only in eight foot lengths minimum. So we saw off a three-foot piece, which is not needed anyplace?or if we do need it, it isn't handy so we get another eight-foot piece of lumber.

Spoilage also occurs. It is different from scrap because it is the direct result of someone making a mistake or a machine getting out of adjustment or a similar problem. The lamp socket assembler gets clumsy, or the construction worker cuts a board too short.

Shrinkage is another factor. This can be the result nature (e.g., evaporation), items being misplaced, or theft.

Defective materials sometimes are received and the defects overlooked until the materials are needed. It is then pretty late in the game to stop everything and try to get replacements.

So, for whatever reasons, contractors will generally add a scrap allowance to the basic quantity needed. For example, an order for 500 emergency lighting devices made to a special design may basically require ordering 500 specially made Ni-Cd 9 volt batteries. The producer may add a scrap allowance of five percent, ordering 525 Ni-Cd batteries rather than 500.

The government agent or the buyer must be aware that certain items are not subject to scrap at all. For example, when the government is making more expensive purchases such as 100 castings for 100 end items, if some of the products are unacceptable the government simply sends them back to the supplier for new ones. An overestimate of scrap allowance can be very expensive to the government.

Direct Materials for Services

When the government is soliciting services, it normally will not provide the offerors with a list of the specific quantities of various materials that are needed in addition to the labor. It is up to the offerors to determine that for themselves. We are not likely to try to tell custodial services firms, for example, how much detergent they will need to do the work. We tell them what cleaning services are required and let them determine the amount of materials needed. Similarly, in R&D, we will rarely try to tell offerors in advance what materials they will need. If we could do that, we might not need the R&D work in the first place.

Firms may use experience factors of various types to estimate the amount of material needed to perform a service. Experienced custodial service firms have a pretty good idea of the amount of cleaning, waxing, and polishing materials needed for the work they do. Maintenance contractors, who typically concentrate in well-defined areas such as heating and air conditioning, have experience records that enable them to predict materials cost with surprisingly high accuracy.

Estimating Unit Costs

Contractors predict unit costs using methods very similar to procedures the government and private companies use for price analysis. Contractors will use catalogs to get current prices. Calls to various vendors will be made and their quotations compared to see what the best price appears to be (cost to the contractor).

Contractors will provide offers to the government based on what they believe the unit cost of material will be at the time they are doing the work, or, at the earliest, the time when they are certain they will get the contract. Few, if any, firms are so foolhardy as to rush out and buy materials before they have the contract in hand. Instead, firms will attempt to predict unit costs based on current unit costs for each material item needed.

Firms will often get commitments from vendors (called current vender quotations) to furnish materials at preestablished costs to the firm, but contingent upon receipt of the government contract. This method is fairly effective in "locking in prices" and preventing vendors from raising their price once the government contract is actually awarded to the prime contractor. Some firms even go so far as to issue purchase orders in advance, contingent upon receipt of the government contract.

In some cases, the contractor who is proposing is in turn buying goods and services from suppliers in the absence of adequate price competition. Under these circumstances, the government expects the contractor to get cost and price breakdowns or data from their supplier, just as the government gets from primes in the absence of adequate price competition.

COST ANALYSIS FOR DIRECT MATERIALS—GENERAL RULES

FAR 31.205-26, Materials Costs, is the cost principle providing general guidance for the allowability of materials costs and related topics. The next paragraphs cover the major requirements of this cost principle. (Some of these requirements apply more closely to administration of cost-reimbursement contracts than to cost analysis of offers, but they are also used by government cost analysts to review proposed material costs.)

Material costs include the costs of items such as raw materials, parts, subassemblies, and manufacturing supplies, which may be purchased or manufactured by the offeror. These costs may sometimes include transportation and in-transit insurance. They may include reasonable amounts for overruns, spoilage, and defective work. These contingency costs are allowable, subject to certain requirements.

Material costs must be adjusted to reflect credits such as trade discounts, refunds, allowances, sale of scrap, or other actions that reduce their net cost. These credits can be taken as a reduction in the cost of the materials or as a credit to indirect costs.

Some companies stock materials in their inventories so they will be directly available when needed. Sometimes, a physical inventory shows a difference between the quantities on the stock records and the actual physical stocks. Any business has to accommodate these differences at times by making adjustments in costs as well as quantities in the inventory records. Reasonable adjustments may be made in the cost of materials charged to a contract when this difference in inventory occurs.

When materials are purchased specifically for a contract, the actual purchase price of the materials is charged to the contract. However, if the material is issued from stores, several possible methods are available for pricing the material, including last-in, first-out (LIFO), first-in, first-out (FIFO), lower of cost or market, and others. The offeror may price its inventory by any accepted accounting procedure, as long as the method employed is consistently applied to all of the contractor's operations.

The offeror may offer items that result from interorganizational transfers within the company, including subsidiaries. The next section will cover the rules for analyzing these transfers.

FAR 31.205-26, Material Costs, contains useful guidance. Its general content is stated below:

- Material costs include the cost of raw materials, parts, subassemblies, and manufacturing supplies and may include collateral cost such as transportation and intransit insurance. The costs of reasonable overruns, spoilage, and defective work (unless otherwise provided with respect to defective work) are allowable.
- Material costs shall be adjusted for items such as trade discounts, refunds, credits for scrap, salvage, and returns to vendors.
- When materials are bought specifically for a contract, their cost shall be charged to that contract. If material is issued from stores, the generally accepted methods for pricing are acceptable if they are consistently applied. (This is referring to inventory accounting methods like LIFO, FIFO, or weighted average inventory accounting.)

FAR SUBMISSION REQUIREMENTS FOR MATERIAL COSTS

FAR 15.403.5 contains the instructions for submitting a contract pricing proposal. The materials part requires a summary of the materials proposed for use in each task order, delivery order, or line item. The summary must show the proposed quantities and their prices. The offeror must show its basis for the proposed pricing (vendor quotes, invoice prices, etc.). The instructions elaborate on the general instruction by adding instructions for various material categories. The detailed categories are explained below.

1. Subcontracted Items: Subcontracted items are products that vendors will produce. They are not the same as "purchased items." The distinction is that the vendor will use specifications, drawings, or directions furnished by the offeror for subcontracted items. The offeror may have developed these specifications or drawings, or they might be government specifications or drawings that the offeror is passing on to the vendor. The offeror is buying the items specifically for the prime contract, not for general usage. The underlying point is that the vendor will make the product to meet *specific offeror requirements*. The offeror is not purchasing a standard off-the-shelf vendor item. The vendor furnishes a unit price and total price that the offeror shows on the contract pricing proposal. For example, a company offering to produce electronic equipment might subcontract the frames, chassis, and cabinets to a metal fabrication company.

The term "subcontracted items" also includes services that a vendor will provide based on a work statement developed by the offeror. For example, the electronics company might subcontract the preparation of parts manuals required as a part of the contract. The cost of preparing the manuals will be a subcontracted item.

If subcontracts are expected to exceed $550,000, the offeror must provide a listing showing the source, item, quantity, and price. It must also show the type of contract, degree of competition, and the basis for source selection. The offeror may have required potential subcontractors to submit certified cost or pricing data (FAR 15.408). If so, the offeror must explain the results of its analysis and review of the subcontractor proposals.

The subcontract material cost estimate example shown in Exhibit 7-1 illustrates the format and supporting documentation required by the instructions.

Exhibit 7-1
Subcontract Material Cost Estimate

Cost Element	Proposed Contract Estimate-Total Cost	Proposed Contract Estimate-Unit Cost	Reference
1.b. Subcontracted Items	$851,437.69	———	Sched. A

Here, as in the direct labor example in the last chapter, the government cannot assess the reasonableness of the proposed cost with the information in Exhibit 7-1 alone. It will require a detailed breakout of the subcontracted items, showing quantities, unit prices, and total prices for each line item.

The proposer attaches a schedule (see Exhibit 7-2) to justify the $851,437.69.

Exhibit 7-2
Sample Breakout of Subcontracted Items

Schedule A   See Bill Of Materials 12997, June 26, 19X3.
Basis of estimate: 450 units to be produced

Part No. and Nomenclature	Qty/ Item	Scrap factor	Total Qty	Unit Price	Total
9876543 Housing casting (Vendor-Pic Corp., P.O. issued 12/20/X2 to lowest of 3 proposals.)	1	4%	468	$84.72	$39,648.96
. . . .					
9876542 Bearing, X Design (Vendor, Sun Co., P.O. issued 12/5/X2 to only source approved by Gov't price analysis performed.)	2	4%	936	$14.89	$13,937.04
. . . .					
9876540 Cable Assembly (Vendor, Rockaway, Only proposal received. Completed SF 1411 attached.)	1	4%	468	$547.11	$556,047.48
. . . .					
9876536 Gear, drive (Eng. estimate, review of dwg.) (Estimate File, Eng-487.)	1	3%	464	$25.00	$11,600.00
Total Subcontracted Material					$851,437.69

The example above does not include every line item and therefore does not add up to $851,437.60 (the omission of line items is marked by the doted lines between line items). However, it does include enough items to illustrate proper disclosure methods. It is a full disclosure and any of the details could be checked. Note that the contractor has issued purchase orders (presumably contingent on getting the award) in two cases. Note also that the last item illustrated is costed based on an engineering estimate. The proposer likely intends to manufacture this gear in its own facility. The proposer has provided scrap factors that, of course, affect the total quantities of each line item needed.

Schedules similar to that in Exhibit 7-2 would be needed for other material items, such as standard commercial items and raw materials.

2. Standard Commercial Items: These items are normally produced and stocked by the offeror for sale to the public. When these items are included in the pricing proposal, the offeror must show the basis for their pricing. The prices may be the offeror's cost to produce the item, with no profit. If so, the offeror furnishes a cost breakdown. The prices quoted may be those used for sales to the public, with or without a special discount. The offeror must show that the proposed prices are reasonable, either by submitting cost or pricing data or by requesting an exception pursuant to FAR 15.403-1.

3. Interorganizational Transfers: Firms with several divisions or subsidiaries sometimes transfer products made by one division or subsidiary to another. These transactions are known as interorganizational transfers. For example, a corporation manufacturing vehicles might have three divisions making vehicles of various types. It could also have one division that produces engines and another producing transmissions. Vehicles are the corporation's primary output. The corporation could probably find outside sources for engines and transmissions, and may have in the beginning. However, it now has its own divisions making engines and transmissions, and the vehicle divisions will order all their requirements from them. This arrangement gives the corporation major economic advantages as well as tight control of engine and transmission design and performance.

The corporation has several possible ways to price products built by one division and used by another. One is simply to transfer at cost. When it transfers at cost, the component manufacturing division breaks even. The using division pays the cost for the item but does not pay a profit. Alternatively, the price charged by the component manufacturing division could cover its costs and some profit. The using division would treat this price, with included profit, as a cost. The final customer would pay a profit to the using division that makes the final product, but the final customer is also paying a "hidden" profit, which went to the division making the component.

Interorganizational transfers are not necessarily bad from the standpoint of the general customer, even if they include profits. The real question is whether the customer pays a reasonable final price. The final price may be as good as or better than it would have been if the corporation had bought the component outside the company. The using divisions themselves often resist paying prices to another division that are more than they would pay to an outside source for the same thing. They do not want to pay extra; it reduces their profits.

The government does not necessarily view interorganizational transfers as bad from a contracting standpoint. However, the offeror must identify any direct materials that it will provide by interorganizational transfer. The government may, under certain conditions, allow an interorganizational transfer of a proposed item at other than cost.

FAR 31.205-26(e) covers interorganizational transfers at other than cost. The government may allow a transfer at other than cost under limited conditions. The first is that the selling division must normally price its products at other than cost. This must be true whether they sell to another division or sell the products for use outside the company. If pricing at other than cost is normal, one of the following criteria must also be met:

a. The price of the component must be, or be based on, an established price for a commercial item sold in substantial quantities to the public. Additionally, the price must be as good as or better than that given to the offeror's most favored customers under similar conditions. If these conditions are met, it shows that the price is reasonable even though it does include a profit. It is reasonable because it is set by adequate commercial price competition and because the government is getting most favored customer treatment. (The alternative is next.)

b. The price must be the result of adequate price competition. The offeror must have obtained quotes from at least one outside source as well as the company division that makes the item. The price must be that quoted by the division and used for the actual award. The pricing proposal must show the quoted price on which the award was based. The price must be as good as or better than the price given to the firm's most favored customer.

4. *Interorganizational Transfer at Cost:* FAR 31.205-26(e), Material Costs, requires that interorganizational transfers be on the basis of cost incurred, but goes on to say that the government "may" allow prices for interorganizational transfers at other than cost, as discussed above. The government prefers transfers at cost only because they do not include profit. When the offeror proposes interorganizational transfers at cost, the government must be sure that the cost is reasonable. It requires the offeror to furnish a detailed cost breakdown by element for cost analysis.

5. *Raw Material:* Material that requires further processing is known as raw material. Examples include steel and aluminum plates and bars. The offeror is required to list the quantities to be used and their unit costs.

6. *Purchased Parts:* There are two categories of purchased parts. One is standard commercial items that the prime contractor does not make in its own plant. The other consists of parts and components that other companies make using their own design requirements. (When other companies make *subcontracted* items, they use the prime contractor's design requirements.) The instructions require the offeror to list the quantities and prices of purchased parts.

ANALYSIS OF PROPOSED ESTIMATED MATERIALS COSTS

The analysis of estimated costs for materials is done essentially the same way as for estimated direct labor costs. We examine the components of the cost and decide whether the total is reasonable. The examination breaks out into looking at each line item of material and the related quantity and looking at the unit and extended prices.

When you analyze direct material costs, you need to focus on the following major questions:

1. *Are the items, quantities, and unit costs correct?* From a quality standpoint, the items need to have adequate, but not excessively high, quality. In some cases, the quantities will contain allowances for scrap and spoilage; be sure they are not overstated. The offeror must provide the unit cost used and the basis for it. The government prefers to see competitive quotes serving as a price basis. Use caution when an offeror proposes an interorganizational transfer.
2. *Are the "make-or-buy" decisions appropriate?* When the offeror makes the component, you are paying its cost and a related profit. If the offeror purchases the component from a vendor, a profit for the vendor is built into the unit cost. The offeror earns a related profit on top. The offeror should earn a related profit if the item is subcontracted. The real question is, "should the offeror make the item or buy it?" A number of technical and management questions surround the "make-or-buy" decisions, involving availability of skills, equipment, space, and other factors. These issues extend well beyond the concerns of this manual. However, pricing is affected by the effectiveness of the "make-or-buy" decision.
3. *Is the material purchased efficiently and competitively?* This question addresses the quality of the offeror's procurement system. The government performs procurement system reviews for the larger government contractors. The knowledge that a contractor has an

effective and efficient procurement system helps the cost and price analyst because the probability is much higher that proposed quantities and prices will be reasonable.

If there are many line items of materials cost, we may find it impractical to check them all. In such cases, our energies can be concentrated on high-dollar items. Another approach is to take a sample and verify it. If the sample is carefully selected, we can pretty well tell how reliable the overall estimate is, based on that sample. We could randomly select samples from high- and medium-cost items for checking. Statistical sampling approaches can be used to enable us to reach conclusions about the entire submission based on what is found in the sample.

ANALYSIS OF PROPOSED MATERIALS AND QUANTITIES—ESTIMATING DIRECT MATERIAL COSTS

Estimating direct material costs can be done in various ways, either alone or in combination with each other. You can do a better job of analyzing direct materials costs if you have a general understanding of these estimating methods.

The Statistical Approach

This method is rarely used and will be covered only in this section of this text. It may be the only method an offeror can use when there is major uncertainty about what will be needed and how much. This uncertainty can occur in the very early stages of research and development of equipment never made before. When the offeror must use this method, both parties know that the actual costs will probably be very different from the estimate.

Imagine, for example, the need for a materials cost estimate for a new piece of equipment that has never been designed or built. The engineering staff estimates that it will weigh 10,000 pounds. All they have is some experience and weight and price relationships for several previously developed equipment items. They can make some very rough estimates based on this experience, as shown in Exhibit 7-3.

Exhibit 7-3
Rough Estimate Using Experience and Judgment

Raw stock (includes castings and forgings (60%)	6,000 lbs	@	$1.75	$10,500
A/N Standards (7%)	700 lbs	@	$3.25	2,275
Contractor-furnished equipment:				
Vendor designed (27%)	2,700 lbs	@	$9.40	25,380
Contractor designed (6%)	600 lbs	@	$7.75	4,650
	10,000 lbs			$42,805

The percentages in Exhibit 7-3 are an engineering estimate based on those for previously developed equipment. The estimators adjusted them to give a best judgement of what would apply to the new equipment. The unit prices are also a best estimate of what today's costs would average for each category.

How do you analyze this estimate? About all you can do is examine the starting data used by the contractor and assess the contractor's judgments. The saving grace for the gross inaccuracy is that it becomes a part of the estimated cost for a cost-reimbursement contract and probably will not cause any great harm. The government will pay actual costs only. (Some harm might occur if a cost incentive contract were used, but the government is not likely to use an incentive contract in a situation this uncertain.)

Offerors might use other estimating bases. Prior statistical data might show that, in some situations, direct material cost can be estimated as a percentage of direct labor cost. Other possibilities exist. None produce very reliable results, but they may be all we have.

Priced Bill of Materials

This method uses a detailed list of all materials needed to produce the required products. The offeror will usually use this method when the equipment design is well established, or when minor adjustments of a present design are required. The offeror goes through the drawings and determines what must be bought to make them. The bill of materials shows the items to be bought, the quantities, and the unit costs. The offeror's first task is to determine what to buy and how much. The second task is to determine the unit and total costs for each item needed. On the surface, this sounds like an easy task. Actually, it is likely to be very difficult and time consuming.

If a firm has made the product before, preparation of the priced bill of materials is fairly straightforward. The company should already have a detailed bill of materials from the prior manufacturing experience. If so, it will need to update that bill of materials to the present situation. The material quantities will almost certainly be different. The offeror must adjust items and quantities for any design changes that have occurred since the prior manufacture. The firm also must adjust the unit prices to reflect the current market conditions.

All this sounds very simple and in concept it is. In practice, however, even ordinary equipment items may have hundreds or thousands of parts, assemblies, etc. It is a major undertaking to revise a prior bill of materials unless the equipment covered is simple. It is an even greater task to develop a new bill of materials.

It is reasonable that the offeror will order some extra materials for contingencies that might arise. The cost of reasonable extra quantities is an allowable expense. For example, assume that the RFP calls for 100 equipment items, each with a locking assembly. The locking assembly has an outer case that the offeror will produce starting with a housing casting. In theory, the offeror needs 100 castings. In practice, it may need to order 105 or 110 to cover material and manufacturing problems that might occur. Experience is required to know how much extra, if any, to order.

The two reasons for the differences between quantities on a bill of material and those on the specifications are those we have already talked about: scrap and spoilage. These costs are allowable (see FAR 31.205-26 in Exhibit 4-11) if they are reasonable.

Projection of Average Unit Material Cost

Offerors usually have data on the unit material cost if they have made a product before. Assume that experience in producing 100 units of equipment shows a material cost of $5,600 per unit. The firm might then, by some analytical method, project a unit material cost of $5,400. You need to be very careful in assessing these projected unit material costs. Offerors may show a token reduction in unit material costs, but this token reduction is not likely to produce a good estimate. You should require the offeror to give you a lot more information than a mere unit material cost revision.

You may find it helpful to require the offeror to prove its case by using the learning curve. The learning curve will produce realistic estimates in some industries for some costs. Material improvement for some categories of direct material costs often are in the order of 95 percent. The range is usually from 90 percent to 100 percent. These improvements in materials usage occur because the firm develops better methods and employees become familiar with the work. The spoilage rate will decrease. The scrap rate is mostly unavoidable but may decrease some. Sometimes increases in unit costs of materials are enough to offset the improvements in their use due to the learning curve. In any case, the offeror may not be able to justify a single unit material cost by using the learning curve. But by applying a learning curve, the offeror might be able to justify single unit material prices for some categories.

It is important to segregate direct material costs when attempting to use the learning curve. Some material costs can be projected reasonably well with the learning curve. Others cannot be projected reliably with the curves. The firm buys raw materials and purchases standard items at market prices, which are generally affected only by quantity-price discounts and the general economic situation. Their unit prices are not predictable using the curves. However, the unit costs for subcontracted parts and assemblies are subject to learning curve cost improvement. In some circumstances, especially where a firm uses a high proportion of subcontracted parts and assemblies, projecting a reasonably valid, single unit material cost might be possible. In other instances, it is probably better to project based on material cost categories.

The average cost and price analyst is way out of his or her element in trying to decide whether the materials listed are proper and the quantities are reasonable. Making this assessment is again, as in direct labor analysis, a point where we need help from our technical people.

FAR 15.404-1 (e), Technical Analysis, states that the contracting officer should request technical assistance for evaluating:

- quantities and types of materials proposed;
- the reasonableness of proposed scrap and spoilage factors; and
- any other data that may be pertinent.

The analysis of proposed materials and quantities should consider several factors:

- Are the materials of the proper quality level and not overspecified? (Avoidance of "gold-plating")
- Are the proposed quantities reasonable? When products are being purchased, comparison of estimated quantities with the bill of materials is the most common, and reason-

able, approach. In service contracting, the bill of materials does not commonly exist. In this case, it is a matter of comparing the proposed quantity against government experience in similar work, if available, or assessing based on the best judgments of technical personnel.

- Are the scrap allowances reasonable? This aspect is actually a part of the quantity consideration above but is separated for emphasis. It is, of course, reasonable and realistic for offerors to plan on needing some extra materials over the basic amount expressed in a bill of materials. How much extra depends largely on the item, its complexity, and its durability. We would expect a small scrap allowance, or perhaps none, for very large and heavy metal objects that are the main frame of the product being ordered. On the other hand, we might have a large scrap allowance for parts made of glass or with rather fragile components. Excessive scrap allowances will unnecessarily inflate the estimated cost and lead to excessive pricing. This factor is especially important when negotiating a fixed-price contract.

UNIT PRICE OF MATERIAL

Proposed unit prices can be validated by price analysis techniques described in Chapter 3. Comparisons to unit prices paid by the government to purchase the same or similar items, and comparison to catalog prices are widely used methods.

The general tone of the offeror's cost submission and the thoroughness of support documentation often give strong evidence of its overall reliability. The government would be hard pressed to effectively challenge the unit price estimates in the submission example in Exhibit 7-2. The presentation of the information conveys the impression that this proposer knows what it is doing. The firms that send in shoddy support for their estimated materials costs, or that don't send in any, bear watching. In some cases, especially for the larger firms, the government has conducted reviews of their purchasing systems, and information is available to determine whether the firm follows competitive procedures and uses reliable purchasing systems.

Offerors may often have to estimate certain unit prices, generally because of insufficient time to submit a proposal by the deadline. The time available after proposal submission but prior to price discussions gives these firms an additional opportunity for further checking. Answers to questions that arise during the price discussions will further confirm, to the extent possible, that the material costs estimates are reasonable.

The accuracy of the estimate for type and quantity of material is one major component of the total cost. Unit cost for the items is the second. In many cases, the accuracy of the first component is likely to be more significant toward overall cost estimate reliability than the second, the unit costs. This factor places a serious responsibility on the technical personnel judging whether the material types and quantities are reasonable.

IMPORTANCE OF THE DIRECT MATERIAL COST ESTIMATE

Direct costs are totally allocable to the contract. When you agree to a cost proposed as direct, you are agreeing to pay 100 percent of it. So the first thing you need to do is decide whether it is a proper direct charge for your contract. If you decide that it is, you must then decide whether the cost is right. The cost depends on how much the offeror proposes to buy and the unit price. When you finally agree to some cost for some quantity, you have agreed that it is a proper part of the final price.

When you agree to a direct cost, you may also have agreed to a separate and related indirect cost. Indirect costs often depend on some or all of the direct costs, such as direct labor, direct material, or both. If so, your agreement to the direct charge also means that you agree to a related part of the indirect cost. In Chapter 6 we showed the compounding effect when indirect costs depend on direct labor costs that are overstated (see the section "The Importance of Analyzing Direct Labor Costs). This same effect can occur with other direct costs if indirect costs depend on them.

A good analysis is also important for other direct costs, such as travel and consultants. Your agreement to some cost for any of these items is a tacit agreement to pay for them 100 percent. These kinds of costs are not usually in the base for determining indirect costs. Consequently, overstatements of other direct costs are less likely to cause corresponding overstatements in indirect costs. Sometimes it is surprisingly difficult to analyze these direct cost categories. Travel is an example. Travel is often claimed as a direct cost, and it is proper if your contract is the only activity that it benefits. Sometimes, however, travel brings other benefits to the company, such as new business. The government should not pay the entire travel cost if the firm benefits in ways that do not relate to the contract. Use considerable judgment in analyzing costs such as travel and consulting.

Negotiating Fixed-Price Contracts

If the government agrees with the proposed costs in the direct materials estimate, it is saying that those costs are reasonable. The resulting cost is 100 percent allocable to the proposed contract, and we will pick it up totally as a part of the final cost. Every dollar saved in this examination is *at least* one dollar off the final price. Often the amount of overhead and G&A expense is directly related to the materials cost. Any overstatements in the direct materials figures will be reflected in such overhead and G&A costs that are also a part of the contract. This consideration applies if the method of determining overhead and G&A expense depends in part, or totally, on the amount of direct material cost.

Negotiating Cost-Reimbursement Contracts

We use cost-reimbursement contracts when the cost of performance is highly unpredictable. This factor can apply just as much to materials as to the more commonly considered direct labor costs. An offeror may be unable to accurately predict the type and quantities of materials that will be needed. Sometimes it will be possible to estimate unit costs fairly accurately if the type of material, rather than quantity, is known. In other cases, not even the type of material is known. Then about all the offeror can do is put in a best estimate.

Cost-reimbursement contracts are not as bad as they may sound on the surface. The government will pay for actual materials used, at cost, under the reimbursement terms of the contract. The government is in a position to exercise some degree of control on what is bought, as one part of the administration of the cost-reimbursement contract. In this one respect, the government may be better off than it would have been had a fixed-price contract been awarded. Once that fixed-price contract is awarded, the contractor may be in a position to effect unexpected economies and increase its profits. The possibility of doing so is enhanced if we in government have done a poor job of examining the direct materials estimate.

OTHER DIRECT COSTS

Numerous other costs, aside from direct labor and direct material, can be appropriately listed as direct costs by an offeror. Examples of such costs are listed in FAR 15.408, Table 15-2, Instructions for Submitting Cost/Price Proposals (see Exhibit 5-1). These costs may include special tooling, travel, computer and consultant services, preservation, packaging and packing, spoilage and rework, and federal excise taxes.

For costs that might be in either category, direct cost or indirect cost, you may require an explanation for designating them as direct. You must also be sure that the offeror handles these costs the same way in both private and government contracts.

This manual will not attempt to cover all the analysis methods and considerations involved in analyzing these various possible "other direct charges." The analysis methods are, in some ways, similar to those for direct labor and direct material. For example, how would we analyze a proposed travel cost of $37,500? The questions include:

- What is the purpose for the travel?
- How many trips are planned? What are the destinations? How many persons will go on each trip?
- What is the duration of each trip?
- What is the mode of travel?
- Are the per diem rates in accordance with FAR 31.205-46?

The offeror should answer these questions in its original pricing proposal. If it does not, you must get answers to these and other questions to do your cost analysis.

The submission and justification requirements for other direct costs are the same as for direct labor and direct material. The methods of analysis follow the same principles of breaking the overall proposed costs into their components and critically examining each. There is no need to repeat an explanation of these procedures.

CHAPTER 8
Analysis of Indirect Costs

Unlike direct costs, indirect costs cannot be conveniently or readily identified with one product or service. They are identified with multiple products or cost objectives. Therefore, they must be allocated to (or divided among) several cost objectives in a fair and equitable manner.

Every business has indirect costs; they are the firm's general operating expenses and are as much a cost of doing business as the cost of labor and material. The firm must recover indirect costs as well as direct costs to break even. Presumably, the price for each contract includes a full allocation of its own direct labor and material costs. The indirect costs are another matter. The firm collects its indirect costs into logical cost groupings, and then it allocates them among the various contracts.

WHAT ARE INDIRECT COSTS?

The government recognizes that businesses have indirect expenses. It is willing to pay its fair share of these expenses when it contracts with a firm, subject to certain requirements. The expenses must be reasonable, allowable, and allocable and the government must be certain that it is paying its fair share only. FAR 31.203, Indirect Costs, contains the following definitions and statements:

(a) An indirect cost is any cost not directly identified with a single, final cost objective, but identified with two or more cost objectives or an intermediate cost objective. It is not subject to treatment as a direct cost. After direct costs have been determined and charged directly to the contract or other work, indirect costs are those remaining to be charged to the several cost objectives. . . .

(b) Indirect costs shall be accumulated by logical cost groupings with due consideration of the reasons for incurring such costs. Each grouping should be determined so as to permit distribution on the basis of the benefits accruing to the several cost objectives. Commonly, manufacturing overhead, selling expenses, and general and administrative (G&A) expenses are separately grouped. . . . When substantially the same results can be obtained by less precise methods, the number and composition of cost groupings should be governed by practical considerations and should not unduly complicate the allocation.

(Note: FAR 31.001 defines a cost objective as "a function, organizational subdivision, contract, or other work unit for which cost data are required." For simplicity, this text will use the term "contract" rather than "cost objective.")

As FAR 31.203 says, we must first determine the direct costs for the contract before we look at indirect costs. Direct labor and materials, covered in Chapters 6 and 7 respectively, are common examples of direct costs. After we analyze the direct costs, we are left with the costs that cannot be specifically identified with the contract or conveniently charged to it; we are left with the indirect costs. Examples include higher level supervision, costs of equipment used for various contracts, and utilities expenses. FAR 31.203 requires that these indirect costs be gathered into logical cost groupings.

It would be logical, for example, to set up a cost grouping for the indirect costs of an engineering activity. It would not be logical to put indirect costs for manufacturing in the engineering indirect cost group. The engineering indirect cost group includes engineering-related costs that are not identifiable to specific contracts. Examples include higher level engineering supervision and costs for engineering equipment used for various contracts. These costs are then distributed to the various contracts by a method called allocation. The ideal allocation method will divide these indirect costs in proportion to the benefits that each contract gets.

FAR 31.203 states that manufacturing overhead, selling, and general and administrative (G&A) expenses are usually grouped separately. However, FAR quickly adds that it is not always necessary to make up separate groupings for each category. A firm may be able to achieve results that are essentially the same without going to this full length. Some larger firms have separate groupings for selling expense, general and administrative (G&A) expense, and various overhead accounts because they need the separations for their own information. They would have these groupings in any case, government contractor or not. Other, smaller, firms find by practical experience that they do not need so many indirect cost groupings. They achieve costing results that are essentially the same with fewer groupings. Some have only one indirect cost grouping.

Types of Indirect Costs

FAR 31.203, cited above, uses the terms "manufacturing overhead" and "general and administrative (G&A) expense." Overhead and G&A expense are two categories of indirect expense. The terms "overhead" and "indirect cost" are sometimes used interchangeably. Although we probably do no great harm by mixing the two terms, we are generally better off viewing overhead as one category of indirect cost, rather than using it as a substitute term.

Some small companies that operate from a single location and do only one type of work have only one indirect cost grouping, commonly called overhead. These companies have indirect costs that cannot be conveniently identified with their various contract jobs, government or private. Some of these indirect costs are technical in nature—the cost of excavating equipment used by a small construction firm for its various contracts is an example. Other costs are related to the general operations of the company, and still others are administrative. The firm could conceivably break out these various indirect costs into overhead and G&A groupings. Then it would need to find ways to subdivide these indirect cost groupings into their various contract efforts. This exercise is likely to be more trouble than it is worth. The government and the private sector agree that one overhead account is enough in such situations.

When businesses become larger, they often find that they need more information and better control than they can get with a single indirect cost pool. They now need two or more overhead accounts. They may start to operate in different areas. They may even be doing different types of work. One may entail a lot of indirect cost, and the other very little. Managing several different operations is extremely difficult if the costs are not segregated into each operating activity because each business sector in each area has its own peculiar indirect costs. The firm needs to establish separate cost accounts for each activity, including a separate overhead account for each.

Firms that use two or more overhead accounts eventually move to using a G&A expense pool. As the name implies, a G&A expense pool typically handles all general and administrative indirect costs for the entire firm. In the beginning, the overhead cost pools probably included some of these costs. Establishing a G&A expense pool usually results in pulling some of these administrative costs from the overhead pools and centralizing them in the corporate G&A expense accounts. The residual overhead cost pools in such situations contain indirect costs that are mostly operational. The practices vary from company to company.

OVERHEAD EXPENSE

Good management is properly concerned, among other things, with the close control of overhead costs. For obvious reasons, overhead costs should not become too large. However, there is another side to this coin. A company increases its overhead costs when it buys modern equipment and makes other technical advances, such as higher quality supervision. It can have low overhead costs by continuing to use outdated equipment and facilities, driving up direct costs in the process. The trick is to control the overhead to achieve effective and efficient operations.

It is important to understand that indirect costs are not some sort of inefficiency. They are a normal and necessary part of doing business and are very important because they are a large part of almost any contract.

Some people have preconceived (sometimes misconconceived) notions about what overhead rates should be. These people seem to view overhead as some sort of cost inefficiency, "burden," or "load." (Indeed, the terms "burden" and "load," unfortunately, are often used interchangeably with overhead and indirect cost.) The Armed Services Pricing Manual's discussion of this is still on point:

> Part of the prejudice against overhead is obvious in the common expression, "that rate is too high." This conclusion is often inane and can be outright dangerous. Because a rate represents the relationship between one number and another, it is relevant only to what is in those numbers. An overhead of 90 percent can be too high and another of 400 percent can be too low, depending on what's in the base and what's in the overhead. The 90 percent can describe a company that still depends on hand labor and hand tools with no automatic machines. As a result, its direct labor base, against which its overhead is measured, is high because of the greater amount of time needed to perform the tasks. At the same time, overhead is less than might otherwise be the case because it includes little or no cost for the depreciation of machinery. This is obviously a simplification but it is reasonable as far as it goes and it illustrates the point.

> The danger here is not that the rate is too low, but that the unit cost of a product from an unmechanized plant, or a plant that is old and filled with worn-out, fully depreciated machinery can be much higher than the unit cost from a modern plant with an overhead rate that is much, much higher.

To summarize, any given overhead rate can be too high or too low, depending on what costs are classified as direct, what costs are included in overhead, and the actual situation depicted by the nature of the costs in both categories. The rate is simply a device by which the costs are allocated.

Be very careful about comparing the company overhead rates and trying to draw conclusions about their relative cost efficiencies. The important figure is total cost, not percentages used to calculate overhead rates.

Controlling Overhead Costs

Unless well managed, overhead costs have a tendency to get out of control. The result, if the tendency continues unrestrained, is that the overhead costs increase. This increase in costs may well cause the overhead rate to increase beyond what it should be. The increase in the overhead rate in turn results in increasing the assigned costs for products, leading to price increases.

Well-managed companies regard overhead as a budget and handle it that way. Assume that Division A of a firm had general supplies expenses of $31,200 last year. This expense was a line item in Division A's overhead cost pool. When the firm develops this year's overhead cost pool, it will include a new estimate for general supplies expense. The people developing the amounts for the overhead accounts consider various factors to decide on this line item. The expected volume of work might justify setting $35,500 for general supplies for this year. General supplies represents one of many line items in the overhead account. The total estimate for this year might be $1,350,000 for all overhead. If we assume that business conditions remain as expected, the company expects the division manager to keep the overhead within the $1,350,000. He or she does so by watching the individual accounts. If, for example, the cost of general supplies is going out of control, the division manager will start actions to recover.

Normally, overhead rates will decrease as the volume of business increases, and increase when business volume falls off. When business is expanding rapidly, the allocation base is also expanding. The overhead cost will inevitably increase but typically not as fast as the base. One reason is that the company will not usually rush to buy new equipment and facilities. It will wait until it is sure the volume expansion will last. The overhead rate will usually decrease because the base has expanded faster than the overhead.

Experience shows that overhead rates rise when business volume falls off. It is true that some overhead costs decrease when the base decreases. However, some of the overhead costs are fixed or semi-variable and do not decrease a lot when the base falls off. Managers are often reluctant to cut out certain costs that really should go when there is a serious downturn in business.

The Composition of Overhead Costs

For purposes of illustration, this section will discuss factory overhead. The same general principles apply to other overhead costs, such as material and engineering overhead. Some of the major components of factory overhead include:

- *Indirect Labor:* This is the cost of supervisors, inspectors, and other people not charged directly to contract work.
- *Costs Associated with Labor:* These are costs such as the firm's contribution to Social Security (FICA), unemployment taxes (FUTA), vacation pay, overtime premiums, and group insurance.
- *Indirect Supplies:* This is the cost of items such as drill bits, solder, grinding wheels, small tools, etc.
- *Fixed Charges:* These are costs such as depreciation, rent, and property taxes.

When you analyze costs such as those above, you need to understand how these costs behave when the volume of business changes. The volume of business is reflected in the base, e.g., direct labor cost. One would expect the second and third categories above to vary directly with a base such as direct labor cost. The first category might vary some, and the fourth category will change little or none.

Methods of Allocating Overhead Cost

To make things a little simpler, we will focus this section on methods to allocate overhead cost. (Allocating G&A expense will be discussed later in this chapter.) Many ways are used to allocate overhead cost, but some basic principles apply to all these methods.

1. The overhead cost to be allocated is normally based on the total overhead cost for a year. The year used is the contractor's fiscal year, also called the accounting year. Some companies have fiscal years running January 1 through December 31; others are April 1 through March 31, etc. (The government's fiscal year is October 1 through September 30.) Companies decide on the fiscal year they use when they set up their financial accounting system. Their chosen fiscal year is reported to the Internal Revenue Service (IRS) for tax purposes. Prior permission of the IRS is normally required if the company desires to change its fiscal year.
2. The overhead cost to be allocated is an estimate of the total overhead costs for the present accounting year. These overhead costs are the total of all costs in the overhead pool, e.g., indirect labor, utilities, general supplies, rent, depreciation, etc. They are for the present accounting year because this is the year that the expenses are occurring. What the expenses were last year does not matter because the books have already been closed. Overhead costs are an estimate because most of them will not be known exactly until the year ends. (You will not know your heating cost for this year until the year is over and you have all the bills. But you can estimate it, based on last year's experience, if the weather is the same as it was last year.)
3. Estimated overhead cost is divided up by a factor called the "basis of allocation." The result of that division will tell us how much overhead to charge to each customer. The basis of allocation must be for the same time that is used for overhead costs. As explained above, this time period is normally the company's accounting year. The basis of allocation will almost always be an estimate. The examples in the next sections will help to clear up the full meaning of "basis of allocation."

The most common methods for allocating overhead are discussed below. You may encounter other methods, but they will be similar in principle to those shown below. All the examples are based on the allocation of an estimated overhead cost of $320,000. For simplicity, think of it as the estimated cost of all general operating expenses for a small company for a year.

Units of Production Method
This is one of the simplest methods used to allocate overhead. The formula is:

$$\frac{\text{Estimated overhead cost}}{\text{Estimated units to be produced}} = \text{Overhead cost per unit}$$

An example is:

$$\frac{\$320,000 \text{ overhead cost}}{8,000 \text{ units}} = \$40 \text{ per unit}$$

The company expects to have $320,000 of overhead costs during the year when it will produce 8,000 units. Each unit produced will have $40 of overhead cost in it. This is in addition to its direct costs. If a customer buys 40 units of the 8,000 output, we will charge that customer:

$1,200	Direct labor cost (assume $30 direct labor per unit x 40 units)
$800	Direct material cost (assume $20 direct material per unit x 40 units)
$1,600	Overhead (40 units bought x $40 per unit)
$3,600	Total cost ($90 per unit)

This method is useful when a company makes only one product and each product gets about the same amount of attention. For example, it would work well for a small company that makes only one model of a stereo speaker. It would not work well if the company makes two different stereo speakers, one requiring three hours of labor ($30) and $20 of material and the other requiring five hours of labor ($50) and $30 of material. If the customer buying the $50 direct cost speaker pays the same overhead as another customer buying the $80 direct cost speaker, it is an inequitable (unfair) allocation of overhead.

Direct Labor Hour Method
This is a fairly common method of allocating overhead when labor costs are the major part of the work and material costs are insignificant. The formula is:

$$\frac{\text{Estimated overhead cost}}{\text{Estimated direct labor hours}} = \text{Rate per direct labor hour}$$

A calculation is:

$$\frac{\$320,000 \text{ overhead cost}}{20,000 \text{ direct labor hours}} = \$16 \text{ per direct labor hour}$$

This equation shows that the company expects to have $320,000 of overhead cost during the period when it will produce an estimated 20,000 direct hours of labor. The rate of accumulating overhead cost is $16 per direct labor hour. If a customer gets 1,000 hours of direct labor at $10 per hour, it will have the following costs:

$10,000	Direct labor cost (1,000 direct labor hours x $10 per direct labor hour)
$16,000	Overhead (1,000 direct labor hours x $16 per direct labor hour)
$26,000	Total cost

This method works well when most of the direct labor employees make about the same rate per hour, as in a custodial service company. It can produce very inequitable results if a wide range of pay rates exists. In the latter case, for example, the customer would pay the same overhead cost ($16,000) whether it got 1,000 hours of engineering time or of laborer time. Many companies have a fairly wide range of pay rates and find this method unsatisfactory. Moreover, the direct labor hour method may not work well when material costs are a significant part of the direct costs.

Direct Labor Cost Method

This method is widely used and is much better than a base of direct labor hours when there is a wide range of direct labor pay rates. The formula is:

$$\frac{\text{Estimated overhead cost}}{\text{Estimated direct labor cost}} \times 100 = \text{Percent of direct labor cost}$$

A calculation based on the above formula is shown here:

$$\frac{\$320,000 \text{ overhead}}{\$200,000 \text{ direct labor cost}} \times 100 = 160\% \text{ of direct labor cost}$$

During the year, when overhead cost is expected to be $320,000, the company expects to produce direct labor worth $200,000. The overhead rate is therefore 160 percent of direct labor cost. We will use two examples to illustrate the effect of this type of rate.

First, suppose we have a customer who gets a lot of engineering time (100 hours) and a small amount of drafting time (20 hours), as shown below:

$2,500	100 engineering direct labor hours at $25 per direct labor hour
300	20 drafting hours at $15 per direct labor hour
$2,800	Total direct labor cost
$4,480	Overhead ($2,800 direct labor cost x 160% of direct labor cost)
$7,280	Total cost

Now suppose we have a second customer who gets 20 engineering hours and 100 hours of drafting time:

$ 500	20 engineering direct labor hours at $25 per direct labor hour
1,500	100 drafting direct labor hours at $15 per direct labor hour
$2,000	Total direct labor cost
$3,200	Overhead ($2,000 direct labor cost x 160% of direct labor cost)
$5,200	Total cost

The second customer gets 120 hours of labor like the first, but gets fewer engineering hours. The second customer is getting less skilled labor than the first customer and therefore pays considerably less overhead. Unlike the direct labor hour method, the direct labor cost method bases the overhead charge on the hours *and* the labor content. As a result, the direct labor cost method is generally more equitable than the direct labor hour method when there is wide variance in labor rates, as in the cases shown above.

Direct Material Cost Method

Sometimes it is better to allocate overhead cost based on material cost rather than labor cost. This premise may be true in a highly mechanized production operation where material cost is the major part and labor costs are minor, or in a warehousing operation where material is sold as is, and the overhead expense is in the handling of the material. The formula is:

$$\frac{\text{Estimated overhead cost}}{\text{Estimated materials cost}} \times 100 = \text{Percent of direct material cost}$$

A simple calculation based on the above formula is:

$$\frac{\$320,000 \text{ overhead}}{\$1,000,000 \text{ direct material}} \times 100 = \text{32\% of direct material cost}$$

Now suppose we have a customer who gets $100,000 of direct material. The calculation of this customer's total cost is:

$100,000	Direct material cost
32,000	Overhead ($100,000 of direct material cost x 32%)
$132,000	Total cost

Prime Cost Method

Prime costs are the sum of direct labor and direct material costs. As most products contain substantial amounts of both labor and material, allocating overhead based on the two costs may make more sense than allocating it based solely on labor or on material cost. The formula is:

$$\frac{\text{Estimated overhead cost}}{\text{Direct labor cost (D / L)} + \text{Direct material cost (D / M)}} \times 100 = \text{Percent of prime cost}$$

A calculation is:

$$\frac{\$320,000 \text{ overhead}}{\$1,000,000 \text{ D / L} + \$300,000 \text{ D / M}} \times 100 = \text{80\% of prime cost}$$

The calculation for a customer who gets $10,000 of direct material and $20,000 of direct labor is:

$30,000	Prime cost (direct material cost + direct labor cost)
$24,000	Overhead (80% of prime cost)
$54,000	Total cost

Machine Hour Method

Sometimes, as may occur in data processing, a machine is doing practically all the work. The costs for labor and material may be insignificant. The formula for allocation by machine hours is:

$$\frac{\text{Estimated overhead cost}}{\text{Estimated machine hours}} = \text{Rate per machine hour}$$

A sample calculation is:

$$\frac{\$320,000 \text{ overhead}}{20,000 \text{ machine hours}} = \$16 \text{ per machine hour}$$

If a customer gets 1,000 hours of machine time at $40 per hour, the total cost calculation is:

$40,000	Direct cost of machine time ($40 per hour x 1,000 hours)
$16,000	Overhead (1,000 machine hours x $16 per machine hour)
$56,000	Total cost

Summary of Allocation

Allocation of overhead is nothing more than a way to divide overhead cost. The examples that we have used are common methods of allocating overhead cost; you may encounter others. We have given you formulas for all the examples. In every case, the overhead cost ($320,000 in these examples) is at the top of the fraction because that is the figure being divided. The figure at the bottom of the fraction is a basis of allocation. For example, the use of a direct labor cost basis (see "Direct Labor Cost Method" above) tells us that the overhead is 160 percent of the direct labor cost. All this percentage means is that for every dollar of direct labor spent, we will simultaneously be spending 160 percent of that, or $1.60, for overhead expense.

The allocation rate, e.g., 160 percent of direct labor cost, gives us a simple means for calculating the overhead for any job that arises. If we estimate that a particular job will use $1,000 of direct labor cost, we know that the associated overhead will be $1,600 ($1,000 of direct labor cost x 160% of that direct labor cost). If a job requires $16,457 of direct labor cost, we can calculate that the overhead will be $26,331.20 ($16,457 x 160%).

All the other allocation methods work the same way. If we choose to use direct labor hours for the allocation method, we know that the overhead rate is $16 per direct labor hour, meaning that for every hour of direct labor used, the associated overhead is $16. If, then, we are estimating for a job that will require 1,000 hours of effort, we know that the overhead cost for the job will be $16,000 ($16 per direct labor hour x 1,000 hours of direct labor).

Keeping units of measure straight in calculating overhead rates is very important. If we have an overhead rate of $14 per ton for a materials handling situation, it is important to multiply that rate by the number of tons handled to calculate the total overhead cost. If it is multiplied by some figure that does not apply, such as the dollar cost of the material, the result is meaningless.

Effect of Different Allocation Bases

Each allocation method shown in this chapter will give different answers for the overhead cost in the same situation. We will illustrate these differences using a fairly simple example. The data in the following table is for a small company that makes only two products, A and B.

	Product A	Product B	Total Cost
Direct Cost	$10,000	$6,000	$16,000
Units Produced	50	25	75
Overhead Cost	?	?	$12,000

The company must decide what each product costs in order to price it for sale, so it must decide how much of the overhead goes with A and how much with B. There are several possible ways, as shown in the following examples:

1. *Divide overhead equally between the two products.* If the company chooses this method, the results come out as follows:

	Product A	Product B	Total Cost
Direct Cost	$10,000	$ 6,000	$16,000
Overhead Cost	6,000	6,000	12,000
Total Cost	$16,000	$12,000	$28,000
Unit Cost	$320	$480	

Now the company knows that it must charge at least $320 each for product A and $480 each for product B just to break even. But customers (including the government) may say: "That doesn't make sense. You have a lot more money invested in A than you do in B. You ought to divide the overhead based on the direct cost in each product." This method is described in the next example.

2. *Allocate overhead based on direct costs.*

	Product A	Product B	Total Cost
Direct Cost	$10,000	$ 6,000	$16,000
Overhead Cost	7,500	4,500	12,000
Total Cost	$17,500	$10,500	$28,000
Unit Cost	$350	$420	

Product A has 62.5 percent of the total direct cost. Product A gets $7,500 of the overhead ($12,000 x 62.5%). Product B has 37.5 percent of the total direct cost. Product B gets $4,500 of the overhead ($12,000 x 37.5%). We have accounted for all the overhead. We get new total costs for products A and B, which are different from those in the first table. The unit costs for A and B (total cost for each product divided by number of units produced) are also different. Now the company has to charge $350 for product A and $420 for product B to break even.

3. *Allocate overhead based on production quantity.* Overhead cost can also be allocated based on the number of units produced. For example:

	Product A	Product B	Total Cost
Direct cost	$10,000	$ 6,000	$16,000
Overhead cost	8,000	4,000	12,000
Total cost	$18,000	$10,000	$28,000
Unit cost	$360	$400	

There are 50 units of product A in a total of 75 units, so A gets two-thirds (2/3) of the overhead cost, or $8,000. There are 25 units of product B, so it gets one-third (1/3) of the overhead, or $4,000. Now we have new total and unit costs.

These examples show that total and unit costs can be changed by changing the method of allocation. A case could perhaps be made for any one of the three methods above, depending on the circumstances. A company will decide on an allocation method that produces the most reasonable results. It continues with that method unless the results distort total and unit costs for their products and services and create problems in estimating costs. Some judgment is involved in choosing the method to be used. Cost accountants used by companies are highly trained in these matters. You will find that companies in the same lines of business tend to use pretty much the same concepts in their choice of allocation methods.

Typical Example of Overhead Allocation

The ACME Company is a small business that is primarily engaged in service work. Their overhead expense, direct labor cost, and overhead rate are displayed in Exhibit 8-1.

Exhibit 8-1
ACME Company Overhead Pool for the Current Year

THE ACME COMPANY
Overhead Pool for Current Year

Indirect Labor	$1,594,835
FICA Expense	421,862
Unemployment Tax	70,266
Group Health Insurance	515,611
Disability and Life Insurance	144,684
Equipment Rental	32,614
General Supplies	33,575
Utilities (except telephone)	36,050
Telephone	82,220
Building Maintenance	7,680
Depreciation	171,614
Property Insurance	85,147
Travel Expense	50,711
Interest Expense	480,855
Legal Expense	8,000
Security Costs	51,075
Entertainment Expense	31,410
Advertising Expense	152,708
Training Expense	14,950
Property Taxes	41,760
Total Overhead Expense	$4,027,627
Direct Labor Cost for Current Year	$4,235,565

$$\text{Overhead rate} = \frac{\$4,027,627 \text{ (overhead)}}{\$4,235,565 \text{ (D/L cost)}} \times 100 = 95.1\% \text{ of D/L cost}$$

Discussion of Overhead Pool Statement

The Overhead Cost Is an Estimate: The overhead pool statement in Exhibit 8-1 says that the overhead cost for this year is $4,027,627. This figure, although stated precisely, is an estimate. It is actually the sum of 20 individual estimates. For example, the table shows that the company estimates utility costs at $36,050 for this year. The company will not know the exact utilities cost until the end of the year. The figure used is an estimate, based on prior experience. The table states that the FICA expense for this year will be $421,862. The company pays FICA tax on the salaries of its employees. This particular figure happens to be based on 239 employees, using a tax rate of 7.05 percent on the first $39,600 of pay. It is fairly precise if the company will really employ these 239 people throughout the year. The number of people it will actually employ depends on how much business volume it has. It could have more or fewer employees, and the actual FICA expense will change accordingly.

The Basis of Allocation Is an Estimate: In the overhead pool in Exhibit 8-1, The ACME Company uses direct labor cost as its basis of allocation of overhead costs. The table above says that ACME's direct labor cost for this year will be $4,235,565. How does it know what its labor cost will be for this year? It depends on its sales volume, which cannot be precisely predicted. It is an estimate based on the company's belief that it will get enough work this year to support 197 direct labor employees whose total direct cost to the company is estimated to be $4,235,565. The prediction of the amount of work it will get (its business volume) is uncertain at the beginning of the accounting year. As the year progresses, the company will be able to predict the business volume more accurately, but it will not know the exact amount of direct labor cost until the year is ended.

The Overhead Rate Is an Estimate: ACME states that its overhead rate is 95.1% of direct labor cost. This rate was obtained by dividing the overhead cost of $4,027,627 (an estimate) by the direct labor cost of $4,235,565 (an estimate). Because the overhead rate is obtained by dividing one estimate by another, it is itself an estimate. If ACME has a customer who gets 1,000 hours of direct labor at an average rate of $15 per hour, the cost charged to the customer will be:

$15,000	Direct labor cost (1,000 hours x $15 per hour)
14,265	Overhead (95.1% of the direct labor cost)
$29,265	Total cost

The $14,265 is an estimate because it is based on an estimated overhead rate and an estimate of the direct labor cost for the job.

Why an Exact Overhead Rate Is Not Used: The company could conceivably use an exact rate. The solution appears to be very simple. As each customer's job is completed, ACME could bill the customer first for direct cost alone, a figure fairly easy to establish. Then, after all the bills for the month come in, perhaps 30 days after the end of the month, it could calculate the exact overhead rate for the month and send a supplemental bill to each customer saying, "By the way, you also owe us $____ for your part of our overhead cost last month." However, ACME would have to go without the money it needs to pay overhead bills as they appear. This approach would be ridiculous. Among other drawbacks, the monthly overhead rate would vary depending on the actual overhead costs and the amount of work it gets each month. It would even vary somewhat depending on the time of the year.

Normal Practice for Overhead Rates: Most companies calculate the overhead rate for their accounting year. An overhead rate based on a year of operation will smooth out fluctuations and result in an overall average that is workable. Prior to the start of the new year, the company will predict what its volume of business is likely to be. Business volume is expressed in terms of direct labor cost, or direct labor hours, or whatever base is used for allocating overhead. The company predicts what its overhead is likely to be, based on past experience with the various expenses within its overhead, and uses that rate for the work that comes early in the year. Then, as the year proceeds, it may make some adjustments in the rate. The adjustments depend on how the overhead expenses are actually running and the business volume that the company believes will actually happen.

Underabsorption and Overabsorption of Overhead Costs

A proper overhead rate is essential for a company to determine its costs and, ultimately, the price to charge for each of its products or services. If the overhead rate is not correct, the company may fail to cover its actual overhead, or it may recover too much overhead cost.

Underabsorption

If the overhead rate is set too low, the company will not get enough money from its customers to meet its actual overhead cost. This shortfall can happen because the estimate of overhead costs is lower than the actual overhead. It can also happen because the company predicted more business volume than actually occurs (that is, the base was too high), causing the estimated overhead rate to be too low. By the time the company discovers that it is not charging enough overhead, it is generally too late to go back to customers to get more money from them. The work has often already been done and paid for, or the customers have been given a fixed price for work and would get upset if the company demanded a higher price. The overall result is that the company takes a loss. Companies will tend to set their overhead rates on the high side to avoid this problem.

Overabsorption

If the overhead rate is set too high, the company will include more for overhead in its charges than is needed to meet the actual overhead costs. The extra money received during the course of the year adds to the company's profit. Given a choice between underabsorption and overabsorption of overhead, the company prefers to overabsorb the overhead because overabsorption adds to profits. It also gives a safety margin for estimating costs. However, the company may take that method too far. The overhead cost is a part of the total cost, and ultimately the price. If the company's costs become excessive, it can price itself out of the market.

Exact absorption

The chances of absorbing the exact actual amount of overhead by a series of many customer billings throughout the year are nil. The overhead rate charged to each customer is an estimate. Although the overhead rate used may be very close to actuality during the company's operating year, it is difficult to estimate with total accuracy. The actual rate will not be known for one to two months after year's end. By then all the overhead-type expenses are precisely known, and a precise overhead rate for the past year can be calculated.

Cost Analysis of Overhead Rates

Suppose that the ACME Company provides the government with a cost and pricing proposal as shown in Exhibit 8-2.

Exhibit 8-2
ACME Company Cost and Pricing Proposal

Direct Labor Cost:

Maintenance Technician, Gr 1	9,415 hours @ 17.41 per hour	$163,915
Maintenance Technician, Gr 2	11,195 hours @ 12.97 per hour	145,199
. . . .	. . . .	. . . . .
. . . .	. . . .	. . . . .
Laborers	9,088 hours @ 7.29 per hour	66,252
Total direct labor cost		$451,497
Direct Material Cost		$ 43,199
Overhead @ 95.1% of direct labor cost		
(based on the calculation in Exhibit 8-1)		$429,374
Total Estimated Cost		$924,070

We have already established a cost objective for direct labor and material cost. Our present concern is the proposed overhead rate of 95.1 percent of direct labor cost.

If ACME states the overhead rate alone, with no supporting information, we have no idea what the basis of the 95.1 percent of direct labor cost is. The government cannot assume, without supporting data, that the 95.1 percent figure is correct and then blindly apply it to the direct labor cost objective; it needs more information.

Now suppose ACME provides the following information:

$$\text{Overhead rate} = \frac{\$4,027,627 \text{ (overhead)}}{\$4,235,565 \text{ (D / L cost)}} \times 100 = 95.1\% \text{ of D / L cost}$$

Supplying this equation is better, but it is not nearly enough information. Our principal concern is whether the "95.1 percent of direct labor cost" is a proper rate for applying overhead cost. We must know what is in the overhead cost and where the direct labor cost came from. We will be able to rely on the 95.1 percent figure only if the two figures that make it up are reasonable. The FAR requires offerors to submit indirect cost support information in a way that will make it possible to evaluate proposed indirect costs intelligently.

FAR (15.408 Table 15-2) Requirements for Submission of Indirect Costs

The FAR instructions for submission of indirect costs follow the same format that we have already seen for direct costs. The FAR requires:

> Indirect Costs. Indicate how you have computed and applied your indirect costs, including cost breakdowns. Show trends and budgetary data to provide a basis for evaluating the reasonableness of proposed rates. Indicate the rates used and provide an appropriate explanation.

A sample overhead pricing submission for the ACME Company, based on the FAR instructions above and examples, is shown in Exhibit 8-3.

Exhibit 8-3
ACME Company Overhead Pricing Submission

Cost Element	Proposed Contract Estimate–Total Cost	Proposed Contract Estimate–Unit Cost	Reference
Overhead	$429,374	——	Exh. 7

Exhibit 7   Overhead Cost Submission, March 1, 20X3

The estimated overhead costs for the year ending December 31, 20X2 were computed by our accountant, James V. Ogilvie, CPA, 59 W. Farragut Street, Glenheim, MA (ZIP). In accordance with standard practice for the last five years, our overhead is allocated to individual contracts in proportion to the amount of direct labor cost charged to each contract. The attached breakdowns of overhead costs for last year and the year before represent the ending balances in those accounts for the years stated. Our overhead rate has steadily decreased during each of the preceding two years and is expected to decrease for this current accounting year. The details supporting our estimated overhead costs for 20X3, by element, and the direct labor forecast, are available in our main office, 59 Peachbottom Street, Room 15, Glenheim, MA. These figures are supporting documentation to our 20X3 budget. The company treasurer, Joanne Smith, has been directed to reveal their contents to the government auditor and answer any questions you have. We request, if possible, at least a two-day advance notice so that Mr. Ogilvie may also be present to assist you.

Acct. Title	2nd Yr. Prior	Last Year	Current Yr.
Indirect Labor	$1,182,483	$1,398,994	$1,594,835
FICA Expense	252,133	342,073	421,862
Unemployment Ins.	46,207	67,200	70,266
Group Health Ins.	372,220	427,190	515,611
Disab. & Life Insurance	111,666	121,615	144,684
Equipment Rental	26,500	29,415	32,614
General Supplies	25,700	31,050	33,575
Utilities	32,916	34,098	36,050
Telephone	64,175	74,202	82,220
Bldg. Maintenance	5,813	6,419	7,680
Depreciation	155,611	161,744	171,614
Property Ins.	81,792	83,672	85,147
Travel Expense	44,180	48,790	50,711
Interest Expense	439,714	460,071	480,855
Legal Expense	6,174	7,714	8,000
Security Costs	48,630	49,144	51,075
Entertainment Exp.	24,610	26,740	31,410
Advertising Expense	39,382	70,417	152,708
Training Expense	10,114	12,369	14,950
Property Taxes	39,645	39,980	41,760
Total Overhead	$3,009,665	$3,492,897	$4,027,627
Direct Labor Cost	$2,483,725	$3,289,062	$4,235,565
Overhead Rate as percentage of Direct Labor Cost	121.2%	106.2%	95.1%

The schedule in Exhibit 8-3 is complete, showing trend and budgetary data as required by the FAR instructions and making it possible for the government analyst to analyze the reasonableness of the proposed overhead rate with very little additional information.

Analysis of the Overhead Rate

The government analyst must consider the following factors in assessing the reasonableness of the proposed overhead rate:

1. *Does the allocation method used divide overhead costs in an equitable manner?* The ACME Company allocates overhead based on direct labor cost. If we assume that the company is labor intensive, without heavy direct material inputs, this allocation method is commonly used.
2. *Are the costs in the overhead cost pool reasonable, allowable, and allocable?* The definition of allocability is so broad that most common costs are allocable. The real tests are reasonableness and allowability. If any costs fail to meet these tests, you would discuss them with the offeror during the discussion stage. If the negotiation is for a cost-reimbursement contract, the contractor must understand that the government will not pay unallowable costs. If it is for a firm-fixed-price contract, the rules are somewhat different. You would still try to get unallowable costs removed; however, you could conceivably award a contract even though the contractor refuses to remove all unallowable costs.
3. *Does the allocation base reflect a reasonable forecast of the expected business volume?* You should require the offeror to give you a complete justification for this figure. An understatement will cause the overhead rate to be higher than it should be. If undetected, this understatement could cause the government to pay more than it should in a fixed-price contracting situation. The government may have done an excellent job in finding all the unallowable and unreasonable costs in the overhead pool, but it can still lose very badly if the allocation base is seriously understated.

You need to understand the fixed and variable components of the overhead pool to analyze its line item costs. Some expenses, such as indirect labor, rent, and property insurance, are usually fairly fixed. Other costs, such as social security and unemployment taxes, will vary with the direct labor cost. Factory supplies will vary in the same way. First, look at the fixed-type expenses to see if they are in line with past costs. Then, look at those costs that vary with volume changes. The information on past trends will help, but will not substitute for your understanding of how various overhead costs behave with volume changes.

The volume figure (allocation base) should represent all the business of the company or plant. It is more than just the government business. A firm might do all its government work in a separate area, and desire that the allocation base represent government work only. If so, you must require that the overhead allocated be solely for the government work.

The business volume in the allocation base depends on the firm's expected sales. The expected sales in turn depend on several factors, including the general economic outlook for the nation, the industry, and the firm. The political situation also might affect sales in some cases. The competitiveness within the industry and the firm's own aggressiveness in selling its products affect sales volume.

When a firm is in a highly competitive business, with a low ratio of sales to the government, you are not likely to gain much by a detailed review of its overhead expense items. Its competitive industry forces it to be economical in overhead expenses. However, do not trap yourself with a discovery that one firm has a much higher overhead rate than another. The firm may be able to produce at a much lower unit cost because it is much more automated.

You need to take special care when you are dealing with a firm that does a heavy volume of government business. This company may very well be different from a company in a highly competitive business. First, you must be sure that the costs are appropriate for your contract; that is, the costs must provide adequate, but not excessive, quality. Next, you must be sure that the projections are realistic. And, if they are realistic based on past history, it merely means that the projection is well done. The firm may be projecting from past inefficiencies and perpetuating them. You need to develop a capability to judge what these costs should be.

You may get some rough insights by comparing overhead rates. Be careful with this practice. Do not jump to a conclusion that one firm is more efficient than another because it has a lower overhead rate. It may merely have an old, outmoded plant with fully depreciated equipment and a much larger direct labor force.

The Location of Certain Labor-Related Expenses

There is often a question about the proper location for labor-related expenses such as social security taxes and unemployment taxes. (These are taxes paid by the company, based on employee pay. For social security, the company adds to the employee's own payment by payroll deduction.) The question can also extend to other expenses that are based on labor costs, including company contributions to health plans, disability and life insurance coverage, and retirement programs.

Many companies place labor-related expenses in the overhead cost pool. The direct labor cost rate does not contain any share of these expenses when they are in the overhead pool. Some companies increase the basic hourly rate to include its share of these labor-related expenses. This rate is sometimes referred to as "loaded," to distinguish it from a rate without fringe benefits. If a company takes this approach, none of these labor-related costs for the direct labor employees should appear in the overhead. However, the overhead will still contain some labor-related expenses, which represent the corresponding expenses for indirect labor employees. Such expenses might be inside the total indirect labor cost line item, or they might be separately listed.

Which is the better way? Some authorities argue that employee-related expenses should always be included in the hourly wage rate. Others argue just as vehemently that these expenses should be in the indirect cost accounts. The arguments are mostly academic. As a practical matter, it does not make much difference as long as the company follows a consistent practice. You must be aware that the two possibilities exist because you may see widely different wage rates in the same locality.

Vacation, Holiday, and Sick Pay

Overhead accounts often show line items for the cost of holidays, vacation time, and sick time. Cost Accounting Standard (CAS) 408 refers to these costs as compensated personal absences. It requires that they be segregated into an indirect cost account and allocated to all cost objectives. This procedure follows normal commercial practice for firms with more sophisticated cost accounting systems.

An employee who is absent for any reason is not producing anything for the company, yet the company pays for the employee's time. If the employee's hourly rate is $20 (based on a 2,080-hour year), an 8-hour absence costs the company $160. This cost is not properly chargeable to any contract as direct labor. Since these expenses are not direct costs, they are automatically indirect costs. They are allocated like other indirect costs in the same pool.

The procedure described above does not cause double charging. When a direct labor employee is out sick, the sick time is charged to the sick pay overhead account. When he or she returns, say after a 4-hour absence, the remaining 4 hours are charged to direct labor cost. The end-of-the-day balance is $80 charged to sick pay and $80 to direct labor cost (for a rate of $20 per hour).

When a firm projects overhead costs for the current year, it estimates the hours that employees will be out for holidays, paid vacations, and sick leave. Holidays are easy to predict. Few employees do not take their full vacation time; the firm estimates this cost based on the full vacation entitlement. It is an expense for the current accounting period even if the vacation time is not taken until later. The company estimates the sick time for employees using its developed experience factors. For overhead, it can project the hours for each type of absence. It converts the hours to costs using the employee hourly rate and subtracts the estimated hours for these absences from the total available hours in the year. The result is the estimated *productive* labor hours for the year. The firm determines the estimated cost of the productive labor hours by using employee hourly rates. The productive direct labor hours are used for doing contract work.

(Note: As discussed in Chapter 6, we are accustomed to thinking of a year as having 2,080 hours. This figure is the number of weekday hours in a year that has 52 weeks (52 weeks x 40 hours per week). Some years have 2,088 hours, and few people actually work 2,080 hours of straight time. The actual productive time is the 2,080 (or 2,088) less time for holidays, sick leave, and vacations.)

The company that does not have overhead accounts for these compensated personal absences is burying them in its direct labor costs. When you deal with such a firm, be aware that some of the direct labor hours quoted for your fixed-price contract will actually include absences. This practice might be tolerable for small contracts with smaller firms who do not come under the cost accounting standards. It is intolerable in a cost-reimbursement contract, because the government would pay the full cost of an employee on vacation. This type of overhead expense should be allocated to all contracts.

Proper Handling of Overtime Premium Costs

Hourly paid employees and certain other employees are paid time-and-a-half for the overtime hours they work. Assume the case of a direct labor employee, John Doe, who works 12 hours today on your contract. He works overtime because the company is behind on the job. John's wage rate is $20 per hour. His base pay for the 12 hour day is $240 (12 hours x $20 per hour). Your contract got the full benefit of the 12 hours and should pay for 12 hours by $240 of direct labor cost.

What about the overtime premium that John gets? This additional $40 (4 hours x $20 per hour x 1/2) is a cost that the company must recover. One way to recover this cost is for you to pay it as a direct charge. In this case, you are paying more than the proper labor rate for the 12 hours you got. You are paying $280 for 12 hours ($23.33 per hour). You would have paid $240 if the company had put another employee on the job for 4 hours of regular time. In other words, your contract is picking up an extra $40 because the company had a scheduling problem. It could have given you 12 hours of straight time from 2 employees and let some other contract get the overtime.

The proper way to handle the situation is for you to pay $20 per hour for the 12 hours of effort you received. The premium cost of that effort should be placed in the overhead and allocated to all contracts like other overhead costs.

You will often see overtime premium cost in the overhead accounts of well-managed firms. They use it, among other things, to monitor and control overtime usage. Do not jump to the conclusion that a firm is inefficient merely because they use overtime. Overtime is not an indication of inefficiency unless it is excessively used. In fact, the firm that never has any overtime is probably overstaffed.

(Note: Directing the use of overtime on your contract is another matter. In that case, the entire cost, including overtime premium, is directly associated with your contract and is a direct charge.)

Forward Pricing Rate Agreements

FAR 15.407-3 provides for reaching forward pricing rate agreements (FPRAs) with selected contractors for specified periods. You can use these agreements to set indirect cost rates, labor hour rates, material handling rates, and a variety of other cost arrangements. Negotiate these various rates in advance of specific contract actions. They are then available for use when contract situations arise.

Contractors who do a lot of contract work for the government develop various factors and rates to use in new proposals, change orders, and other contract pricing actions. They negotiate the rates with the government and reach final agreements on a case-by-case basis. When many such actions occur, the government and the company can save a lot of time and effort by negotiating factors and rates that will apply on a continuing basis.

Several considerations apply to these agreements. The government and the contractor must be involved in a relatively high volume of contracting actions. All government agencies who deal with the contractor significantly should agree to the rates, factors, and conditions established by the negotiations. The period for the agreement should be long enough to be worthwhile, but not so long that a major risk is created for either party.

The first step in the process is to determine, for a given contractor, whether an agreement is feasible and necessary. If the government decides to proceed, the contractor submits cost or pricing data. The government agency invites participation by other government agencies doing significant business with the company. The government determines its negotiation objectives and conducts negotiations with the firm. If the negotiations are successful, both parties sign the forward pricing rate agreement. Contracting officers use the agreed-upon rates for all contracts, modifications, and other contract actions during the period of the agreement. The conditions applying to the original agreement might change significantly during its term, but if they change so much that the factors and rates are no longer useful, the agreement is invalidated.

Analysis of Overhead Cost

The government is willing to help support a total overhead cost *provided it is reasonable, allowable, and allocable*. In the proposal in Exhibit 8-2, ACME proposes that we pay an overhead charge of $429,374. This amount is actually our contribution to the total estimated overhead cost of $4,027,627 for the year. In a similar way, the other customers of the company will each make a contribution to the company's total overhead cost.

The government's first concern is what cost elements are in the overhead cost pool. ACME has provided a listing of the cost elements in Exhibit 7 to their pricing proposal (see Exhibit 8-3). Note that the listing shows the elements of the current overhead cost and the prior cost history for each element through the past two years. This information helps us see how those costs have varied over the past two years and how they compare to those predicted for the current accounting year. Our judgment tells us which elements are likely to vary with the volume of business (direct labor cost) and which are relatively fixed.

In general terms, if the total overhead cost for the year ($4,027,627) is supportable by government rules, then the government is willing to contribute a fair share of that total overhead. If it disagrees with elements of the total overhead (unreasonable, unallowable, or unallocable), then it is willing to contribute a fair share to whatever overhead is left after any objectionable elements have been eliminated. For example, if the government were to disagree with a total amount of $100,000 within the total overhead cost for any such reasons, it would be willing to share in support of the remaining $3,927,627 (i.e., $4,027,627 – $100,000).

(Note: Government cost analysts should not try to be management analysts. They should be primarily concerned with costs as they exist within the company, not with determining whether the company is operating efficiently and effectively.)

The first question to be asked is whether a cost element is allowable under FAR Part 31. If it is allowable, the next question is whether it is allocable. Remember, a cost is allocable if a direct or an indirect benefit is received from it, and if it can be apportioned to the contract in an equitable manner. The vast majority of costs pass the test for allocability. We may at times see proposed cost elements that, although allowable and allocable, appear to be unreasonable. We need to exercise some caution at this point. Does it make sense that a company would incur expense for no good reason? One presumption is that an expense will tend to be reasonable merely because it is pointless to incur needless expense. This premise is especially true when a company is in a highly competitive atmosphere; it may apply somewhat less if the company is a sole source.

This section has been concerned with methods used to determine whether the government is *willing* to share in the support of the total annual overhead cost for the company. The next section will cover *how much* of a share the government will support.

Analysis of the Basis of Allocation

The two primary questions used to analyze the basis of allocation are:

1. *Does the basis of allocation produce reasonably equitable results?* Put another way, does it result in the government's paying its fair share of the total overhead? Most of the commonly used allocation methods have been explained earlier in this chapter, along with their advantages and disadvantages. Every basis of allocation has imperfections. The ideal basis would be one in which variations in the basis would produce proportional variations in the indirect cost that is being allocated. As a practical matter, this perfection is almost never attained. As general rules, when labor is a predominant factor, bases such as direct labor hours or direct labor costs are generally used. When both labor and material are major components, using a basis that considers both labor and material is generally better. The basis should also reflect data that is reasonably accessible in company records. Labor hours and labor costs fit that criterion, as do all the other bases discussed in this chapter.

2. *Is the figure used reasonably accurate?* The base figure is almost always a prediction of the company's business volume. For ACME, the prediction was that $4,235,565 direct labor cost would be generated during the year for all customers. Like all other predictions, ACME's projection could be over or short of the actual. The company has no positive way to know because business volume is affected by multiple factors. It is to the company's advantage to understate this figure somewhat. An understatement of the figure results in a higher overhead rate, making the absorption of actual overhead costs more certain. We have to take some care in the examination of the overhead to ensure that the figure is a realistic projection of company business. In the final analysis, the government may be very hard pressed to demonstrate in a credible way that it knows more about the company's future business volume than the company knows.

The Importance of Overhead Rate Analysis

Obviously it is important to do a good job of overhead rate analysis because the rate determines what the government's fair payment will be for overhead. Additional points to be covered regarding overhead rate analysis and type of contract are as follows.

Firm-Fixed-Price Contracts

Once the government awards a firm-fixed-price contract, it is committed to pay that price. Because overhead cost is a part of the price, the government analysis of the overhead rate must be as precise as is possible under the circumstances. Absolute accuracy is not attainable because, at the time of price discussions, the overhead cost, the basis of allocation, and the overhead rate are estimates. However, to keep this concept in perspective, we must recognize that all the other costs in the cost or pricing proposal are also estimates. The purpose of the analysis is to come up with a "bottom line" price that is reasonable, remembering that we can never predict future costs with total accuracy. On the other hand, we must also remember that "there are no second chances." Once we have negotiated a price and a contract is awarded, the government is "locked-in" to paying that price. The only possible chance for reconsideration arises from the submission of defective cost or pricing data, a rather uncommon occurrence.

Another aspect of negotiating fixed-price contracts is that the application of the cost principles may differ somewhat from their application to cost-reimbursement agreements. FAR 31.102 points out that there is no positive requirement to reach agreement on every element of cost when negotiating a fixed-price contract. The primary purpose in using the cost principles in fixed-price contracting is to help reach agreement on a total price that is reasonable.

Cost-Reimbursement

We use a cost-reimbursement contract because the costs of performance cannot be predicted with high accuracy. The government is protected by cost-reimbursement contracts because they are finally settled based on actual costs incurred. In the case of overhead costs, the government waits until the end of the accounting year and negotiates a final overhead rate. The negotiated rate is based on actual costs that meet the criteria of reasonableness, allowability, and allocability. In the meantime, the contractor is paid based on billing or provisional rates. The negotiated overhead rate is then used to adjust the final payment to the contractor. This built-in protection does not mean that we can ignore analysis of overhead rates during the cost discussions. The rate gives us an idea of the likely overhead rate that will finally apply and could be one of the considerations in final selection of a contractor. The rate also establishes the estimated overhead cost, one part of the estimated total cost. This estimated total cost is one of the considerations in determining the fee.

GENERAL AND ADMINISTRATIVE (G&A) EXPENSE

The majority of this chapter has been concerned with overhead expense. We will now focus our discussion on another type of indirect cost: general and administrative expense, or G&A. Cost Accounting Standard 410 defines general and administrative expense as:

> Any management, financial and other expense which is incurred by, or allocated to, a business unit and which is for the general management and administration of the business unit as a whole.

This CAS 410 definition is written for accountants. Those of us who are not accountants may need more explanation.

G&A expenses are a type of indirect cost you will probably see any time you get a pricing proposal from a company with several operating divisions. They are the indirect costs incurred at the top level of a larger company. Such a company will have overhead cost pools (indirect costs) for each of its operating divisions. In addition, the company will have top level costs for operating its corporate headquarters. These top level costs are "G&A" and represent a layer of indirect costs in addition to overhead.

(Note: Many companies, especially smaller businesses, perform one basic type of activity and operate from one location. Such companies will normally have only one indirect cost pool because that is all they need. It contains all their general operating expenses, or the costs that are not direct. Most companies refer to this single indirect cost pool as their "overhead." Occasionally, you will find a small company calling this single cost pool their "G&A expense." In either case, you will analyze it like the overhead discussed earlier in this chapter. This text uses the term "general and administrative expense" to define top level expenses of a multidivision company.)

Consider, for example, a fictitious company, the Wyandotte Corporation, which has three operating divisions. Two divisions of the Wyandotte Corporation are located in Arlington and Alexandria, Virginia. The Arlington division does electronic maintenance for commercial customers; the Alexandria division does mechanical maintenance, mostly on heating and air conditioning equipment. The third division is in Rockville, Maryland. It performs security guard services and is a recent acquisition. The corporate headquarters may be co-located with one of the divisions or separately located. For this discussion, we will assume that it is located in a separate office suite in Arlington.

Each operating division has its own set of overhead costs. They include costs such as indirect labor, rents, depreciation, utilities, and telephone service for the division. Divisions usually operate as "profit centers," i.e., the corporate president expects each division manager to control his or her own costs so the division will make a profit on the work it does. This profit is a part of the corporate profit for the year. The division manager controls his or her own direct labor and material costs. The overhead expenses for each division are usually only those costs directly controllable by the division manager, including its own indirect labor cost, depreciation for the buildings and equipment it uses, utilities, telephone service, and similar costs. The overhead expenses differ among the divisions because they are in different places and do different work.

In addition to division overhead costs, the Wyandotte Corporation has general and administrative (G&A) expenses. They are "general" expenses because they apply to the overall operation of the company. The word "administrative" is used because the expenses are mostly administrative rather than operational in nature. The company assigns most or all of the operational costs to the divisions doing the actual work. G&A expenses include a wide variety of costs for the entire company, including indirect labor costs for corporate officers and clerical personnel, as well as accountants, personnel administrators, purchasing agents, and attorneys. G&A expense also includes depreciation for corporate level equipment (furniture, copiers, etc.), and may include many other costs such as office supplies, utilities, interest expense, legal costs, and others.

As mentioned earlier, the division overhead expenses usually contain only those expenses that the division manager can control. The G&A expenses contain all the top level company expenses and indirect costs that the division managers cannot control. No rules exist for these cost distributions. Each company has its own ideas about how best to divide them. For example, interest costs are not often found in division overhead, even if money was borrowed to buy equipment for the division. The division manager usually has no voice in whether to borrow money or use equity capital to purchase equipment. If the firm borrows the money, the division manager cannot control the interest rate paid or rate of repayment to reduce the interest. By the same token, costs like property taxes and property insurance are in the G&A expense pool.

The cost for fringe benefits is another example. The fringe benefits for G&A indirect labor are themselves a G&A expense. They are clearly a top-level expense. Now consider the fringe benefits for the direct and indirect labor in the divisions. The division manager has no control over the rates that set the amounts of various fringe benefits. For example, federal law sets the FICA tax rate, and the manager cannot control this rate. On the other hand, fringe benefits for division employees are part of the division direct or overhead costs. The division manager does control the number or employees and their wage rates. Hence, he or she indirectly controls the amount of fringe benefit expenses. Viewed another way, the fringe benefits are actually part of the total employee cost that the division manager must control for his or her division.

The Government View of G&A Expense

The government views G&A expense as it does overhead and direct costs associated with a contract effort—they are a cost of doing business. The government is willing to pay a fair share of the firm's G&A expense, subject to certain rules. The firm must allocate G&A expense by acceptable methods, and the allocation base must be the same as that used for other customers. The costs must be reasonable, allowable, and allocable as defined by FAR Part 31.

The Allowability of G&A Expense

G&A expenses are a cost to the firm. In concept, they are like any other costs, such as labor, material, and overhead. The firm must recover these costs, as well as all other costs, to break even. Unlike other costs, however, G&A expenses have certain peculiarities.

You are much more likely to find unallowable costs in the G&A expense pool than in the subordinate overhead accounts. Most division overhead costs pertain primarily to operations of the division itself. Companies with a corporate headquarters usually move activities into the corporate staff if these activities are not directly needed for manufacturing operations. For example, it is usually not efficient for each division to do its own payroll accounting; the company can do payroll accounting more efficiently at the corporate level. Using a single, specialized payroll staff is almost always better than having each division do this work. The total manpower requirement is lower, and division managers prefer not to be bothered by purely administrative tasks. Similarly, the central corporate staff usually handles company functions such as purchasing, selling, personnel administration, money management, insurance, and taxes.

The relatively few unallowable costs in FAR Part 31 are very often of a G&A nature. Interest, contributions, and advertising are examples.

You may also find that certain G&A expenses, although basically allowable, are unreasonable. Indirect labor costs are often the largest single component of G&A expense. The reasonableness of total executive pay may be a critical area. This pay includes every amount that is paid currently or accrued. Current pay includes salary, bonuses, incentive awards, stock options, fringe benefits, and any other payments during the contract period. Deferred pay includes personal payments to be made later, such as an annuity after retirement. These future payments have a present value, and their present value is part of the present pay.

The cost principle dealing with compensation (FAR 31.205-6) is rather complex; you will probably need help from the auditor to apply it if a major question about reasonableness of executive pay arises. The basic rule has always been that personal compensation is allowable if it is reasonable for the services done. Reasonableness for the services used to be measured several ways. One was the total pay for a position must not exceed the cost allowed by the Internal Revenue Code. Another was the total pay must be comparable to that for a similar position in a similar company with similar responsibilities. The emphasis used to be on *total* pay. But FAR 31.205-6 requires examination of each component of the compensation. Each part of the total (including, for example, deferred pay) must be comparable to that for similar positions in similar industries doing the same sales volume. Some offsets are allowed but they must be among components of one pay package. You cannot allow excessive compensation for a bonus even if the company claims it is offset by lower-than-usual pay for an executive secretary.

Special consideration and possible limitations may be required for:

1. Payment and salaries to owners of closely held corporations, partners, sole proprietors, or members of immediate families;
2. Changes in pay policy that cause substantial increases in compensation levels; and
3. Executive pay in businesses that are not highly competitive.

Problems in the Allocation of G&A Expense

The accounting profession considers allocation of G&A expense to be a very difficult area. Even though it is a category of indirect cost, it does not behave in the same way as overhead costs. For overhead, changes in the allocation base will cause proportional changes in many of the overhead pool accounts. For example, a significant increase in a direct labor cost base will cause increases in labor-related expenses, such as operating supplies, in the overhead. As a general rule, most overhead accounts increase when the work force goes up and decrease when the work force goes down. (Note: Sometimes expenses in overhead accounts are comparatively fixed. An example is top level supervision within the indirect labor account.)

G&A expenses are different from other indirect costs. Many of them are more fixed in nature than overhead costs. They do not vary as much with changes in business volume. Sometimes, they do not vary at all. For example, the corporate staff will stay about the same unless there is a drastic rise or fall in company business volume. Since many G&A expenses stay about the same, it is difficult to find an allocation base on which G&A expenses actually depend.

Allocation Methods for G&A Expense

FAR 31.203, Indirect Costs, states:

(b) . . . The base should be selected so as to permit allocation of the grouping (of costs) on the basis of the benefits accruing to the several cost objectives. When substantially the same results can be achieved through less precise methods, the number and composition of price groupings should be governed by practical considerations and should not unduly complicate the allocation.

(c) Once an appropriate base for distributing indirect costs has been accepted, it should not be fragmented by removing individual elements. All items properly includable in an individual cost base should bear a pro-rata share of indirect costs irrespective of their acceptance as government contract costs. For example, when a cost input is used for the distribution of G&A costs, all items that would properly be a part of the cost input base, whether allowable or unallowable, shall be included in the base and bear their pro-rata share of G&A costs.

(d) The contractor's method of allocating indirect costs shall be in accordance with the standards promulgated by the CAS Board, if applicable to the contract; otherwise the method shall be in accordance with generally accepted accounting practices which are consistently applied. . . .

You can easily overlook one important statement in (c) above: that a basis of allocation must not be fragmented by removing some of its cost elements. G&A allocation is then used as an example to explain that the allocation base must contain all its normal cost parts, no matter whether allowable or unallowable. In plain English: *Never remove an unallowable cost from an allocation base.*

This rule applies only to the allocation base. It remains proper to challenge and remove unallowable costs that are in the G&A expenses being allocated. In other words, the numerator may be reduced but the denominator contains all costs, allowable or not. At first glance, this rule appears to contradict itself. Actually, it makes certain that contractors allocate indirect costs, including G&A, to the government in the same way as they do for other customers. The government takes an added step by restricting the types of costs it will help support.

CAS 310 describes three methods for allocating G&A costs. These methods are listed below.

Total Cost Input

The total cost input base should include all significant costs representing the total business activity. It will include all direct and indirect costs at the operating levels of the company. The G&A rate is a percent of the total input costs. The G&A expense for a given contract is the product of its own input costs (direct labor, materials, and overhead) and the G&A allocation rate.

Value Added

A company may use this base if inclusion of material and subcontract cost would significantly distort allocation of the G&A expense pool. The rationale is that material and subcontract costs, when large in amount, do not significantly affect the firm's internal G&A costs. Hence, G&A should be allocated based on value added by the firm.

Single Element Cost Input

A single element allocation base, such as direct labor cost, may be appropriate for a company that primarily produces labor intensive services, with very small material and subcontracted expenses.

The G&A Portion of a Pricing Submission

Assume that the Wyandotte Corporation has submitted a pricing proposal in response to an RFP. The firm has proposed that its Arlington division perform the work. The pricing proposal appears in Exhibit 8-4 in summary form:

Exhibit 8-4

Summary of Wyandotte Corporation Pricing Proposal

Direct Labor	$141,650
Direct Material	111,600
Overhead (50.4% of prime cost)	127,638
Total Input Cost	$380,888
G&A (10.7% of Total Input Cost)	40,755
Total Proposed Cost	$421,643

The instructions accompanying FAR 15.408, Table 15-2, Requirements for Submission of Indirect Cost require the offeror to show how it computed indirect costs and to include trends and budgetary data. Assume that the Wyandotte Corporation provides an Attachment 7 to its pricing proposal to support its G&A rate, 10.7 percent of total input costs. This attachment is shown in Exhibit 8-5.

Exhibit 8-5

Attachment 7 to Wyandotte Corporation Pricing Proposal

Attachment 7   G&A Expense $40,755

This corporation allocates general and administration expense based on a total input base. Our method complies with CAS 410. Exhibit 1 to this attachment shows the method used to calculate the G&A rate. It also shows trends and budgetary data as required by the FAR (15.408 Table 15-2) instructions. These narrative comments supplement and further explain the information on Exhibit 1.

The G&A expenses are for our corporate headquarters located in Arlington, VA. They do not include operating costs for our divisions located in Arlington and Alexandria, VA, and Rockville, MD.

Salaries and wages category: This is for the indirect labor people in our corporate headquarters. Each operating division has an indirect labor account for its own purposes. The G&A indirect labor cost shown is for actual productive hours. The productive hours include regular hours actually on the job and overtime hours at the standard hourly rate. They exclude holiday, vacation, and sick time which are separately costed and listed. We separately account for the overtime premium cost and list it separately.

Personnel expense: This firm authorizes all suggestion awards at the corporate level. It does not provide suggestion award funds in division overhead accounts for discretionary use by division chiefs. We also centrally control all relocation funds, recruiting funds, and educational scholarship and loan funds. All other costs in the personal expense category (e.g., FICA) apply to corporate headquarters personnel only. Division costs include these type expenses for their assigned personnel.

Operating expenses: These expenses are for corporate headquarters only. There are no advertising or printing costs at the division level. Division overhead costs include depreciation for their own equipment, equipment rental (if applicable), general supplies, maintenance, postage, and shipping.

Public utilities: These expenses are for the headquarters only. Division overhead accounts include similar expenses for their own needs.

Miscellaneous expense: These expenses are for the corporate headquarters only and have no counterparts in division overhead. We sometime authorize division personnel to use the corporate courtesy meal expense for special guests. If so, the charges are made directly to the corporate level account, never to an overhead account.

Bid and proposal costs: These costs are exclusively at the corporate level and have no division counterparts.

EXHIBIT 1   General and Administrative Expense

Account Title	2nd Yr Pr.	Last Year	This Year
Salaries and Wages			
Indirect Labor	$1,732,107	$1,938,419	$2,121,056
Overtime Premium	14,157	17,785	17,887
Sick Pay	42,862	49,259	56,225
Holiday Pay	57,704	56,472	80,459
Vacation Expense	78,241	97,019	111,333
Personnel Expenses			
Social Security Tax (FICA)	82,387	94,096	108,992
Unemployment Insurance (FUTA)	12,992	13,475	11,396
Group Health Insurance	54,963	63,304	72,102
Disability and Life Insurance	38,646	43,945	88,665
Pension Plan	81,109	97,590	107,628
Suggestion Awards	15,434	18,690	21,000
Travel Expenses	71,555	75,464	80,500
Training and Technical Conferences	11,223	13,665	15,600
Recruiting	11,575	13,778	15,500
Relocation-Transferees	7,556	8,887	10,280
Educational Loans, Scholarships	5,666	6,110	6,780
Operating Expenses			
Advertising	467,889	543,667	630,000
Depreciation	38,778	54,366	57,800
Equipment Rental	4,340	4,700	6,700
Supplies, Printing	41,333	43,233	45,600
Maintenance	5,678	6,889	7,550
Postage and Shipping	9,651	11,234	23,400

Public Utilities

Telephone	89,887	91,676	93,500
Heat, Light, and Power	97,160	102,498	112,300

Miscellaneous Expenses

Interest	97,878	116,766	123,400
Legal and Auditing	5,332	6,578	6,900
Professional Services	4,897	6,426	6,700
Patent Expense	15,567	18,777	19,800
Public Relations	16,777	17,999	18,700
Property Insurance	26,334	28,778	29,800
Inventory Insurance	14,532	15,888	17,650
Courtesy Meal Expense	9,745	11,234	18,400

Bid and Proposal Costs	998,677	1,244,300	1,556,700
TOTAL G&A EXPENSE	$4,262,632	$4,932,967	$5,700,303
TOTAL INPUT COST	$37,357,899	$44,301,780	$53,509,215
G&A RATE (% of Total Input Cost)	11.4%	11.1%	10.7%

COMPOSITION OF TOTAL INPUT COST

Account	Arlington Division	Alexandria Division	Rockville Division	Total
Direct Labor	$10,665,800	$11,161,560	$8,914,610	$30,741,970
Direct Material	3,676,490	2,614,970	340,900	6,632,360
Overhead	7,224,620	4,921,565	3,988,700	16,134,885
Total Costs	$21,566,910	$18,698,095	$13,244,210	$53,509,215
TOTAL INPUT COSTS (Total for Divisions A, B, and C)				$53,509,215

Overhead Rate for Arlington Division: 50.4% of Prime

Cost Overhead Rate for Alexandria Division: 35.7% of Prime

Cost Overhead Rate for Rockville Division: 44.7% of Direct Labor Cost

Analysis of the G&A Rate

Analyze G&A rates using the same basic method used for analyzing overhead costs. The method consists of these steps:

1. Analyze the G&A Expense Pool: In the Wyandotte case, or any other, you will review each line item to determine whether it is reasonable, allowable, and allocable. You have already learned that G&A accounts are more likely to contain unallowable costs than the overhead accounts. Certain other costs, such as executive pay, may require close scrutiny for reasonableness. You should record all instances where you believe the G&A expense pool contains questionable costs. You will need this detailed record when you conduct price negotiations with the offeror.

It is important to separate significant issues from trivia when preparing for price negotiations. You must, of course, prepare fully to discuss any costs that are clearly unallowable or unreasonable. Once prepared, you must remember that all these costs are *estimates* for the current year. The estimates involve judgments, and the contractor's judgments are based on experience. Although the contractor is likely to know much more about its costs than you do, you should not blindly accept anything the contractor says. If you believe a cost is unreasonably high, you should challenge it. The burden of proof is on the offeror to show that the cost is reasonable. However, do not challenge merely to be challenging.

You may challenge the amount of a cost that is allowable. When you do, be sure that your challenge is significant enough to have an impact on your own cost proposal. For example, the Wyandotte G&A account shows a $6,900 estimate for legal and auditing expenses. These expenses are basically allowable; a few minor categories of legal expense are not. You could conceivably raise a major issue about the legal part of the $6,900. Assume that Wyandotte finally concedes $3,000 to get you off the point. The effect is to reduce the G&A rate from 10.7 percent to about 10.65 percent. This adjustment will reduce the G&A charge in the pricing proposal from $40,755 to $40,565, a $190 change in over $40,000 of estimated cost. This adjustment is not worth making, especially if it creates a lot of argument. By concentrating your efforts where the payoffs are worth the time invested, you will keep the offeror's respect. You can lose respect by bringing up trivial items.

2. Analyze the Base: The Wyandotte example shows a total input base, or an estimate of its sales volume. The input base consists of all input costs at the operating level (direct labor, direct material, and overhead). The cardinal rule is: Never remove an unallowable cost from the base. So you are not looking for unallowables in this cost input base. Your concern is whether it is an accurate estimate of the sales volume. If the input base is too low, the G&A rate will be overstated. An overstated G&A rate will cause an overstatement in the G&A expense for your proposal.

The government is not in a strong position to judge the accuracy of the firm's sales volume. The firm estimates its sales volume by estimating the total of all work it will get from commercial and government sources. The sales department is usually responsible for preparing the estimate, starting with general guidance from top management of the firm. Most firms have a long range estimate for three to five years and a short range estimate for the current year. The current year projection is often stratified into segments known as firm, near-firm, anticipated, and potential business.

Firm business is the business already on hand, based on firm contracts and commitments. Sometimes called "backlog," firm business has a 100 percent probability of actually occurring. *Near-firm business* is the category that is very likely to happen. Examples are requirements for spare parts and work that repeat customers are likely to order. The firm might assess its probability at 90 percent.

Anticipated volume is the work that is likely to arise from the various bids and proposals the company makes. The firm usually has historical data on its success rate in this category. Its experience may show that it gets awards for around 50 percent of its bids, based on dollar value. *Potential volume* is a highly uncertain area, representing business that might result from major programs that the company might attempt. The firm might estimate the probability for potential work at 10 percent.

A firm might use the probability figures above to forecast likely sales volume and then determine the total cost input of material, labor, overhead, and G&A costs needed to produce the anticipated sales volume.

Such a projection for the Wyandotte Corporation might be as shown in Exhibit 8-6.

Exhibit 8-6
Wyandotte Corporation Projected Sales Volume

Category	Sales	Probability	Weighted Sales
Firm	$51,500,000	100%	$51,500,000
Near-firm	4,000,000	90%	3,600,000
Anticipated	10,000,000	50%	5,000,000
Potential	40,000,000	10%	4,000,000
Projected Sales Volume			$64,100,000

The firm will use the $64,100,000 in Exhibit 8-6 to determine the labor, material, and overhead requirements. For example, the firm may feel that in order to produce $64,100,00 of sales, it would have to incur a total cost of $59,209,518, which would yield a profit of $4,890,482. The calculation is shown in Exhibit 8-7.

Exhibit 8-7
Wyandotte Corporation Projected Profit

Project Sales Volume	$64,100,000
Projected	
Input Cost	$53,509,215
G&A	$5,700,303
Total Cost	$59,209,518
Projected Profit (before taxes)	$4,890,482

No one expects this method to be precise, but it is a logical approach to estimating the sales volume and the inputs needed.

Not only must the cost analyst review the G&A expense pool for reasonableness, allowability, and allocability, but also he or she must ask the appropriate questions to assess the firm's method of predicting sales volume and the ensuing total cost input bases.

CHAPTER 9
Facilities Capital Cost of Money

"Facilities capital cost of money" refers to a special means developed by the government to reward firms for the deployment of fixed assets to government contract work. Some government contracting people are familiar with this system because they see it used frequently; however, many government contracting personnel are not familiar with it. Even if they have heard of it, some contracting people may regard it as something that will never arise in their own work. They are probably wrong. It is likely to appear, sooner or later.

Commercial offerors have a right to request facilities capital cost of money in most situations when negotiation is used. You will also know how to review the request and where it fits in price negotiation.

THE CONCEPT OF FACILITIES CAPITAL COST OF MONEY

When a contractor does work on a government contract, the government gets benefits from the facilities that the contractor uses. The Cost Accounting Standards Board (CASB) developed Cost Accounting Standard 414, Cost of Money as an Element of the Cost of Facilities Capital, to meet the need for paying contractors properly for the use of their facilities. The Board issued the standard on June 2, 1976, and made the following statement:

> Performance under negotiated contracts usually requires the use of facilities which represent significant contractor investments. Accounting principles applicable to financial reporting do not provide any explicit recognition of the cost of capital committed to facilities. The Board has long been interested in identifying, as a capital cost, a part of the contractor total cost of capital. . . .

Facilities capital cost of money is an "imputed" cost. By imputed, we mean a cost that can be inferred from the contractor's use of capital funds to buy the facilities. It is not the type cost that normally appears in accounting records.

One can say that the contractor does get a return on facilities cost because depreciation is an allowable expense. Depreciation is a way to charge off a part of facilities costs each year, and because depreciation is allowable, the government is paying for the facilities devoted to its contract. However, depreciation does not really cover all the expense. Depreciation is based on the actual paid-out cost of facilities, including installation, and does not recognize that the capital funds used to purchase the facilities have their own expense. If the firm uses borrowed funds, it pays interest for use of the money. If it uses its own funds (equity capital), it still incurs a cost for using the funds. The cost is the interest lost by using the funds rather than leaving them in an interest-bearing account.

The basic idea of facilities capital cost of money is straightforward (instructions are in CAS 414). Using a form (CASB-CMF) developed specifically to determine the facilities capital cost, the contractor first computes the cost of the facilities devoted to contract work during the accounting period. This value is the facilities capital. It is determined only for actual tangible assets or intangible assets that are subject to amortization. It does not, for example, apply to cash working capital. Once this value is determined, an interest (cost of money) rate is applied to it. The result is an imputed cost of the facilities capital devoted to contract work for the period. Then the contractor can, by allocation methods, determine the cost of facilities capital for a specific contract.

For example, suppose the facilities capital devoted to a contract is $1,000,000. Assume also that the cost-of-money rate used is eight percent. The imputed cost of the facilities capital is $1,000,000 x 8% = $80,000. This $80,000 can be viewed as the cost to borrow money for one year to deploy these facilities.

The Allowability of Facilities Capital Cost of Money

Facilities capital cost of money is an allowable cost under the FAR Part 31 cost principles (FAR 31.205-10), even though it is an imputed cost. FAR 31.205-10 defines it as a cost that is imputed uniformly to all contractors, and directs use of the cost-of-money rate specified by the Secretary of the Treasury. Whether or not the source of the capital involved is equity or borrowed capital, FAR 31.205-10 specifically states that this imputed cost is not a form of interest on borrowing. If it were, it would be unallowable under FAR 31.205-20.

Facilities cost of capital may be allowed as an actual incurred cost even if the Cost Accounting Standards (CAS) are not applied to the contract. As an actual cost, it is payable under cost-reimbursement contracts and in the progress payments of a fixed-price contract. Facilities cost of capital is allowable if:

1. The contractor's capital investment is measured, allocated to contracts, and costed as required by CAS 414;
2. The contractor has adequate records to show compliance with CAS 414; and
3. The estimated facilities capital cost of money is specifically proposed for the contract under which it is claimed.

Contract Provisions and Clauses

Certain provisions and clauses regarding facilities capital cost of money should be included in your contracts, as specified below.

FAR 52.215-16 Facilities Capital Cost of Money (Provision)
FAR 15.408 (h) requires you to insert this provision in all solicitations that will result in contracts subject to the cost principles for commercial organizations (FAR 31.2). It notifies offerors that facilities capital cost of money will be an allowable cost if required criteria are

met (the criteria are summarized above). It states that the offeror must claim facilities capital cost of money as a part of its proposal and adds that failure to request facilities capital cost of money will be considered a waiver of the right.

FAR 52.215-17 Waiver of Facilities Capital Cost of Money (Clause)

Use this clause in the contract if the offeror did not request facilities capital cost of money in its proposal. The clause states that the contractor did not request facilities capital cost of money, and it is therefore not an allowable cost.

THE PROCEDURE FOR DETERMINING FACILITIES COST OF MONEY

CAS 414 provides the instructions for the offeror to use in submitting its request for facilities capital cost of money. It requires the contractor to make its calculations on a form CASB-CMF. The next discussion covers the detailed preparation of the form. Whether you will be reviewing the submission or preparing it, you can do a better job if you know how to prepare a submission.

Step 1: Determine the Current Cost-of-Money Rate

Determine the current cost-of-money rate and enter it in Column 1. This rate is the most recent rate set by the Secretary of the Treasury. The rate changes every January 1 and July 1 and is published in the Federal Register. (It is usually the same rate used to pay interest under the Prompt Payments Act.) This example uses 8.0 percent.

Step 2: Record Net Book Value of Property

Column 2, at the top of the form, has space for recording the net book value of property. This data is for the particular business unit submitting a proposal. The offeror must use the average net book value of its facilities for the accounting period. (Net book value is the acquisition cost of the facility minus the accumulated depreciation.) Average net book value is the average of the beginning and year-end net book values.

This particular example shows $9,000,000 for the average net book value of recorded facilities, which are the facilities recorded in the asset records of the business unit. However, the business unit has other facilities it expects to use, including $1,000,000 of leased property. Constructive cost of ownership is allowed for these items rather than leasing costs. Finally, the business unit has an allocated share of corporate facilities valued at $500,000. The total business unit facilities capital is $10,500,000. All this data comes from the firm's financial accounting records, not cost accounting records.

Step 3: Allocate the Average Net Book Value of Property

This step divides the total $10,500,000 average net book value among the overhead and G&A accounts. The first step is to divide the $10,500,000 into the distributed and undistributed facilities.

- *Distributed facilities* are those that are clearly and directly assigned to specific overhead or G&A accounts. In our example, the firm has directly distributed $6,000,000 of business unit facilities to the engineering and manufacturing overhead pools and to the G&A expense pool. These organizations are the sole users of the equipment represented by the $6,000,000. Engineering overhead has $4,500,000 for its use, and manufacturing overhead has $1,000,000. The G&A Expense pool has the remaining $500,000. We still have to account for $4,500,000, shown as undistributed.
- *Undistributed facilities* are facilities capital costs incurred for more than one indirect cost pool. The cost of these facilities must be allocated to the indirect cost pools that benefit from them. The firm may use any allocation method that divides the cost so each indirect cost pool receives its fair and proper share. For example, it might be reasonable to divide the net book value of a building based on the square footage occupied by each organizational segment. This method assumes that the occupancy rate is about the same regardless of where each segment works. Alternatively, the firm might place the entire amount for the building in the G&A expense pool.

In the example we are using, the firm allocated the undistributed $4,500,000 so that engineering gets $3,000,000, manufacturing gets $1,000,000, and technical computer gets $500,000. Column 3 shows this allocation.

Step 4: Record Total Net Book Value by Organization Segment

The firm completes Column 4. It is the sum of the costs in Columns 2 and 3. It shows the total net book values by organizational segment.

Step 5: Calculate the Imputed Cost of Capital

This step calculates the imputed cost of capital allocated to each cost pool. The firm multiplies the cost of money rate (8%) by the total net book value figures in Column 4. This calculation gives the figures in Column 5. The total imputed cost of capital is $840,000, broken out by the indirect cost pools. This $840,000 is the *total imputed cost* for all the facilities for the accounting year and represents the cost of borrowing the $10,500,000 devoted to facilities capital. This $840,000 would be allocated to all contracts for the accounting year. The next problem is to determine how much of this $840,000 goes with each contract effort.

Step 6: Allocate the Total Imputed Cost for All Facilities

The $840,000 is the total for all indirect cost pools. The form has broken it out to $600,000 for engineering, $160,000 for manufacturing, $40,000 for technical computer, and $40,000 for the G&A pool. These costs can be handled like any other costs included in indirect cost pools. For example, $600,000 is the annual facilities capital cost for the engineering division. The firm can allocate this cost to various contracts by the same allocation base it uses for other engineering overhead expenses.

The firm allocates engineering overhead by an engineering direct labor cost base. This allocation base is $2,000,000 of direct labor cost. It is entered in Column 6. The engineering overhead cost of money (Column 5) divided by the $2,000,000 allocation base gives the factor .3000. This factor is entered in Column 7. (Note: The instructions call for factors. If percentages were used, this one would be 30 percent of engineering direct labor cost.) Column 7 shows the other factors. In each case, the firm uses its normal allocation base for the indirect cost. For example, 2,250 hours is used to allocate overhead for the technical computer pool. Note that this rate is $17.7778 per hour.

Facilities Capital Cost of Money Factors (Column 7)

What is the meaning of the calculated factors in Column 7, and what are they good for? The engineering factor is .3000, meaning that the engineering overhead type facilities capital cost is 3/10 of the direct labor cost, or .30 times the labor cost. You can also look at it as $.30 for each dollar of direct engineering labor cost, or approximately 30 percent of the labor cost. If you know how much engineering direct labor cost applies to the contract, you can calculate the contract amount for facilities capital cost for engineering. You can use the other factors to calculate the other types of facilities capital cost.

Final Calculation of Facilities Capital Cost of Money

The sample calculations above, using the CASB-CMF form, resulted in the following facilities capital cost of money factors:

Engineering	.30000 (based on engineering direct labor cost)
Manufacturing	.26667 (based on manufacturing direct labor cost)
Technical Computer	17.77780 (based on computer hours)
G&A Expense	.00133 (based on total cost input)

The firm can multiply the contract costs for each category by its factor to calculate the facilities capital cost of money for that category. Then it adds the individual costs of money to get the total cost of money for a particular proposal. Assume a proposal with the costs shown in Exhibit 9-1.

Exhibit 9-1
Sample Proposal of Facilities Cost of Money

Facilities Capital	Proposed Cost	Factor	Cost of Money
Engineering Direct Labor	$330,000	.30000	$99,000
Manufacturing Direct Labor	$102,000	.26667	27,200
Technical Computer	50 hrs	17.77780	889
G&A Expense	$39,000	.00133	52
Contract Facilities Capital Cost of Money			$127,141

This firm will propose $127,141 as its facilities capital cost of money. Do not lose your perspective about this $127,141. The factors for engineering and manufacturing in the example in Exhibit 9-2 are rather high. These factors show that the firm has heavy costs for capital facilities in the engineering and manufacturing departments. These costs are high compared to their labor costs. This firm appears to be highly mechanized and would probably propose substantially fewer labor hours for a contract effort than a firm not as highly mechanized. The tradeoff is that it proposes a charge for facilities capital cost of money that will offset the cost savings that the government will see in direct labor.

You might want to know the facilities capital represented by the $127,141 facilities capital cost of money. If you divide the $127,141 by 8 percent, you will get $1,589,263. This is the facilities capital devoted to your contract.

Most agencies use a DD Form 1861 for the calculations above. A completed DD 1861, showing these calculations, is shown in Exhibit 9-3. Please note the section called "Distribution of Facilities Capital Employed."

Exhibit 9-2
Form CASB-CMF

Form CASB-CMF							
			FACILITIES CAPITAL COST OF MONEY FACTORS COMPUTATION				
CONTRACTOR:				ADDRESS:			
BUSINESS UNIT:							
COST ACCOUNTING PERIOD:	1. APPLICABLE COST OF MONEY RATE ____%	2. ACCUMULATION & DIRECT DISTRIBUTION OF M.B.V.	3. ALLOCATION OF UNDISTRIBUTED	4. TOTAL NET BOOK VALUE	5. COST OF MONEY FOR THE COST ACCOUNTING PERIOD	6. ALLOCATION BASE FOR THE PERIOD	7. FACILITIES CAPITAL COST OF MONEY FACTORS
BUSINESS UNIT FACILITIES CAPITAL	RECORDED	9,000,000	BASIS OF ALLOCATION	COLUMNS 2+3	COLUMNS 1×4	IN UNIT(S) OF MEASURE	COLUMNS 5÷6
	LEASED PROPERTY	1,000,000					
	CORPORATE OR GROUP	500,000					
	TOTAL	10,500,000					
	UNDISTRIBUTED	4,500,000					
	DISTRIBUTED	6,000,000					
OVERHEAD POOLS	Engineering	4,500,000	3,000,000	7,500,000	600,000	2,000,000	.30000
	Manufacturing	1,000,000	1,000,000	2,000,000	100,000	600,000	.26667
	Technical Computer		500,000	500,000	40,000	2,250 hrs.	$17.7778
G & A EXPENSE POOLS	G & A Expense	500,000		500,000	40,000	30,000,000	.00133
TOTAL		6,000,000	4,500,000	10,500,000	840,000	//////////	//////////

Exhibit 9-3
DD Form 1861

CONTRACT FACILITIES CAPITAL COST OF MONEY		Form Approved OMB No. 0704-0267 Expires Oct. 31, 1989
CONTRACTOR NAME	2. CONTRACTOR ADDRESS	
BUSINESS UNIT		
RFP / CONTRACT PIIN NUMBER	5. PERFORMANCE PERIOD	

DISTRIBUTION OF FACILITIES CAPITAL COST OF MONEY

POOL	ALLOCATION BASE	FACILITIES CAPITAL COST OF MONEY	
		FACTOR	AMOUNT
Engineering (DL $)	$330,000	.30000	$99,000
Manufacturing (DL $)	$102,000	.26667	$27,200
Technical Computer (Hours)	50 Hours	$17.7778/hr	889
G&A Expense (Total Input)	39,000	.001333	52
TOTAL			$127,141
TREASURY RATE			8 %
FACILITIES CAPITAL EMPLOYED (TOTAL DIVIDED BY TREASURY RATE)			$1,589,263

DISTRIBUTION OF FACILITIES CAPITAL EMPLOYED

	PERCENTAGE	AMOUNT
LAND	9 %	$143,034
BUILDINGS	21 %	$333,745
EQUIPMENT	70 %	$1,112,484
FACILITIES CAPITAL EMPLOYED	100 %	$1,589,263

CHAPTER 10
Profit or Fee Determination

Reduced to its simplest terms, profit is whatever is left after all the costs of doing business are paid. Profit is often described as the reward for taking risks.

The profits that a company earns are the sum of its total revenues for the operating year less its total operating expenses. The company will try to make some profit on every job it does; if it is successful, the overall profits are higher. In many cases it will earn a profit on some jobs and take losses on others. The company will stay afloat if its profits on some jobs exceed its losses on others; in the long run, it will "go under" if the reverse is true.

Well-run companies have cost accounting systems that enable them to estimate costs likely to be incurred for each job. If they get a job, they use the same system to measure what the job actually costs and to control its costs. The ultimate benefit of the system is that it enables companies to determine the profit or loss taken on each job. As a company gains experience, it uses its cost accounting system to determine which lines of work are profitable and which are not.

HOW ARE PROFITS SET BY A COMPANY?

A company will set profits based on whatever it believes it can get after considering the cost of doing the work. This practice is the same as what is done by private individuals when selling property they no longer need or when working on the side for various customers. Who among us who would sell a house or car for less than the market says it is worth, or work for less than we think we can earn simply because it would not be "fair"?

If the market is highly competitive, the company will set an initial price based largely on what it believes its competitors would charge. It will then examine its own costs to do the job and decide whether the profit that would result is worth the effort. It will trim its estimated costs very closely and may set very narrow profit aspirations. It will then set an asking price intended to be just under its competition and designed to get the job by undercutting the competition. The degree to which it will go depends very heavily on how much it needs the business. If there is plenty of business available, the chances are that the company and its competitors are setting prices (including profit levels) on the high side. If bad times prevail, a company may even forego profit and try to recover its costs only. In extreme cases, the company may seek only to recover its variable costs and some part of its fixed cost. When a company goes to this extreme, it is losing money. There is a limit to how long the company can continue this practice and still manage to survive. Eventually, the creditors will force it to close.

If the market is not highly competitive and the demand is high, the seller is motivated to get high profits. The only significant deterrent is that the buyers may choose to do without, seek substitutes, or aggressively develop competition.

No magic formula exists for profit determination. Some companies set profit goals, like 20 percent of costs or a specific rate of return on investment, and set prices accordingly. Meanwhile, they monitor what the competitive marketplace charges for similar products or services. If a company does not make the profit it expected on one customer's work, the company will try to make it up on other work.

BROAD GOVERNMENT POLICIES REGARDING PROFIT

FAR 15.404-4, Profit, states the general policies and procedures that apply to profit considerations. The principle underlying government policy is that contractors should receive a reasonable profit for the work they do. The problem is, of course, to decide what a reasonable profit is for each case. A better way of expressing government policy is that the government is willing to pay a fair and reasonable price, as we have discussed in Chapter 1. Then the exact amount of profit that a contractor will make depends on the contractor's own initiative in controlling its costs.

Misconceptions about Profit and Fee

FAR 15.404-4(1) points out a consideration sometimes misunderstood by government people who are negotiating cost, profit, and price. This misconception is that the negotiated profit or fee is what the contractor will actually get.

It is reasonable, and required, for government negotiators to set prenegotiation objectives for the elements of cost and profit. The offeror enters the price discussion session with its own goals for cost and profit. Now let's say that under a fixed-price contract, agreement is reached on the following price:

Estimated Total Costs (labor, materials, and indirect costs)	$534,197
Profit	69,400
Total Negotiated Price	$603,597

Negotiating a profit of $69,400 as a part of the total price does not guarantee that the offeror will actually make a $69,400 profit. The entire negotiation is based on *estimates* of future costs and a reasonable profit to go with those costs. The actual costs will rise or fall depending on factors that neither party can anticipate. The chances of the actual costs coinciding exactly with the estimate are remote.

The same general principle applies in cost-reimbursement contracts. When we negotiate a cost-plus-fixed fee contract, we typically think of that fee as a firm figure. And it is, in that the government will definitely pay the fixed-fee in addition to the allowable costs. However, if the contractor incurs some costs that are disallowed, it takes a loss on those costs. In effect, those losses reduce their profit for that work. When we negotiate other types of cost-reimbursement contracts, such as cost-plus-award-fee, the exact amount of the total fee that we will pay is not necessarily the total fee that we negotiated. Here, as in the fixed-price situation, it is not accurate to think of negotiated fees as absolutely "locked in concrete."

The lesson in the above discussion is: We should do the best job we can to determine what the reasonable cost is likely to be. Once we do that, we should determine a reasonable profit to go with the costs. But once we set that profit or fee, it is not absolutely the profit the offeror will get; the actual profit realized by the contractor depends on the many variables that affect contract performance. Moreover, the profit or fee is a small percentage of the total price that will ultimately be paid. Many people have preconceived notions of what a "proper" profit is, in terms of a percentage of cost, based on "what somebody told them." There is no "proper" profit percentage; do not artificially focus on one small part of the ultimate total price.

Adequate Profit Is in the Government's Best Interest

FAR 15.404-4 points out that it is in the government's best interest to offer contractors reasonable rewards for doing government work. There are other possible rewards, but profit is certainly a major one. FAR 15.901(b), 15.404-4 (a) (2), and 15.404-4 (a) (3) add some considerations:

- Contractors who have an opportunity to earn reasonable profits on a government contract are motivated to turn in a good job because they can afford to do so. If we, for whatever reason, have set the price too low, the contractor is forced to find cheaper ways to get by. Too often this results in shoddy work and increased costs to the government in contract administration.
- Agencies with a reputation for paying reasonable prices attract the better offerors from among both small and large businesses. The better firms are already well established with their private work. Why should a firm, already doing well in the private sector, take up its time and resources doing government work that does not pay enough profit to make it worth the risk? The government negotiator who wins a first "victory" by beating the price down to some unreasonably low level may have "won a battle and lost the war." If that contract winds up costing the government excessive dollars just to administer it, that cost does not show up on the contract itself but it certainly appears in the total government cost.
- The wise use of government contracting, including reasonable profits, expands the general industrial base of the nation. Government contracting accounts for many billions of dollars annually. When more and more businesses are attracted to government contracting by the prospect of reasonable rewards, the industrial base for use by the government is expanded, competition is improved, and the nation and its citizens benefit.

DETAILED GOVERNMENT POLICIES REGARDING PROFIT

FAR 15.404 (a) (3) states:

> . . . Negotiation of extremely low profits, use of historical averages, or automatic application of predetermined percentages to total estimated costs do not provide proper motivation for optimum contract performance.

The quotation above should leave no doubt that government policy is strictly against the use of arbitrary factors such as "nine percent of cost." Contracting activities who persist in violating the intent of this regulation (it may be done in various subtle ways) are inviting offerors to come in with inflated cost estimates that may be very difficult to detect.

FAR 15.404-4 (b)(1), Profit Policy, states that agencies with noncompetitive contract awards over $100,000 totaling $50,000,000 or more per year:

1. Shall use a *structured approach* for determining the profit or fee objective in those acquisitions that require cost analysis; and
2. May prescribe specific exemptions for situations in which the mandatory use of a structured approach would be clearly inappropriate.

The FAR adds that agencies may use another agency's structured approach. (A typical structured profit system will be covered later in this chapter.)

When price negotiation is not based on cost analysis, there is no requirement to analyze profit. This principle applies when bid prices are received as a result of sealed bidding, adequate price competition, or any situation where price analysis alone is used to determine a price.

Contracting Officer Responsibilities (FAR 15.404-4 (c))

Government contracting officers must adhere to certain requirements in the following areas:

* *Profit (Fee) Prenegotiation Objective:* Contracting officers are required to use the government prenegotiation cost objective amounts as the basis for calculating the prenegotiation profit objective. As previously mentioned, the government enters pricing discussions with a prenegotiation objective for what it believes the proper estimated costs should be. These objectives are, of course, based on its assessment of the proposed estimated costs. These individual cost objectives are used to calculate the profit or fee objective. The word "calculate" means that a systematic method (structured profit approach) is used. If the structured profit system is not applicable to the acquisition at hand, the contracting officer establishes the prenegotiation profit objective by other means.
* *Facilities Capital Cost of Money:* When calculating the profit or fee objective, the contracting officer is required to *exclude* any facilities capital cost of money that was included in the prenegotiation cost objective. Cost of money is described in FAR 31.205-10 and Chapter 9 of this text.
* *Statutory Limitations on Prices or Fees:* The following price or profit ceilings are required by statute (10 U.S.C. 2306(d) and 41 U.S.C. 254(b)):
  1. For experimental, developmental, or research work under a cost-plus-fixed-fee contract, the fee must not exceed 15 percent of the estimated cost, excluding the fee.
  2. For other work under a cost-plus-fixed-fee contract, the fee must not exceed 10 percent of the estimated costs, excluding the fee.
  3. For architect-engineer contracts, the contract price or the estimated cost plus fee must not exceed 6 percent of the expected cost of the public work, exclusive of the architect-engineer fee.

Factors Bearing on Profit Levels for Government Contracts

FAR 15.404-4 (d) lists six major factors, and a number of subfactors, to be used by agencies in developing their structured profit approaches. Agencies may use other factors besides those specifically listed. Most of the structured profit guidelines that have been developed at the time of this writing have contained these factors in pretty much the same order. The major factors and subfactors listed in FAR 15.404-4 (d) are:

1. *Contractor Effort:* The cost the contractor will incur in doing the work is a measure of the contractor effort consisting of the direct costs and indirect costs associated with that effort. Because the contractor incurs risks and brings management skills to bear in the application and control of these costs, a related level of reward (profit) is appropriate. Greater profit should be provided for contracts that require higher amounts of technical and management skill. This level of profit takes both direct costs and general management expenses (overhead and G&A) into consideration. Subfactors of contractor effort are:
   - Material acquisition—Managerial and technical skills are required to obtain the materials, parts, and subcontracted items to do the contract work. Profit considerations should consider the management and technical effort involved. The degree of effort depends on the complexity of the items, the volume of purchase orders and subcontracts, whether new or existing sources are used, and whether the materials can be bought by routine effort or require the development of complex specifications.
   - Conversion direct labor—This element is the cost of direct engineering, manufacturing, or other direct labor needed to actually provide the finished products or services. Some of the profit considerations include the complexity of the effort, the skill levels that will be applied, and the amount of supervision and coordination that must be employed.
   - Conversion-related indirect costs—Indirect cost elements make a contribution to the contract effort, and some profit can properly be related to them. Supervision in the indirect cost should be given the same weight for profit purposes as it would be if direct labor.
   - General management—This profit element is related to the other indirect costs (such as G&A) and the general management effort to be expended by the prospective contractor. The profit factors include how the indirect labor would be treated in profit terms if it were direct labor, the overall contribution of the general management costs to the contract effort, and any special management skills that need to be applied to the effort.
2. *Contract Cost Risk:* Some contract work carries more risk than other work. For example, a contractor carries almost no cost risk in a cost-reimbursement contract and all the cost risk in a firm-fixed-price contract. Contractor risk increases as we go across the spectrum from a cost-plus-fixed-fee contract through the incentive types until we finally reach the firm-fixed-price type. Other risks need also to be considered. For example, difficulty of the contract task also has a bearing on contractor risk. The government is willing to pay a higher profit to prospective contractors with higher risks.
3. *Federal Socioeconomic Programs:* Government policy favors subcontracting to small and small disadvantaged business concerns and to labor surplus area concerns. It is reasonable to reward those prime contractors who conscientiously pursue these government policies by adjusting their profit upward. It also is appropriate to adjust profits downward for those with a consistent pattern of failure to pursue these goals.
4. *Capital Investments:* Some prospective contractors provide everything needed to do the work. Others may receive government furnished material or facilities. Some may re-

ceive advance payments. Some, for working capital reasons, may receive payments more frequently than normal. Whatever the reasons may be, it is reasonable to give a prospective contractor who is self-supporting a somewhat higher level of profit than others who need government assistance.

5. *Cost Control and Other Past Accomplishments:* Contractors who control costs and perform work well benefit the government and taxpayers. This factor provides the opportunity to award additional profits to contractors who have performed well in the past.

6. *Independent Development:* This factor may be used to provide some additional profit to prospective contractors who have, without government assistance, independently developed concepts or products useful to the contract effort.

THE STRUCTURED PROFIT APPROACH

All the structured profit guidelines systems take the same general approach. They establish a total profit objective by adding profit increments for various major cost inputs and for other contract factors. Mandatory percentage ranges are used for each major factor. The General Services Administration (GSA) structured profit method is illustrated below. This method is almost identical to those used by the National Aeronautics and Space Administration (NASA) and the Department of the Interior. A summary description of the GSA system appears in the following pages.

GSA Structured Profit Guidelines

The GSA structured profit guidelines are illustrated in Exhibit 10-1 below.

Exhibit 10-1
GSA Structured Profit Guidelines

Profit Factors	*Weight Range (%)*
1. Contractor Effort	
Material Acquisition	1 to 4
Direct Labor	4 to 12
Overhead	3 to 8
Other Costs	1 to 3
General Management	4 to 8
2. Other Factors	
Cost Risk	0 to 7
Investment	−2 to +2
Cost Control, Other Past Accomplishments	−2 to +2
Federal Socioeconomic Programs	−.5 to +.5
Special Situations	−2 to +2

Profit Factors

The profit factors specified in the GSA profit guidelines are as follows.

Contractor Effort

This section assigns profit increments for the individual cost categories involved in the contract effort. A percentage *within the allowable limits* must be used for assigning profit for each element.

Material Acquisition (1 to 4%)—Determination of the percentage to be used is based on the managerial effort and general difficulty entailed in acquiring the needed supplies, equipment, or components involved. Simple off-the-shelf materials would be worth about one percent, more complex items on the higher side. When the cost of materials is a significant element, with some difficult and others simple to procure, using a systematic determination of the proper profit is better than simply choosing a percentage factor by intuitive methods. Break the material acquisition costs into categories of simple, fairly complex, and very difficult to purchase and assign a percent to each, as illustrated in Exhibit 10-2.

Exhibit 10-2
Profit Determination—Material

Complexity	Cost	Profit %	Profit
Complex specs. and inspection	$ 40,000	4%	$1,600
Medium complex, some inspection	30,000	2.5%	750
Off-the-shelf, minor inspection	80,000	1%	800
Total Material Cost	$150,000	Total profit	$3,150

The above calculation results in a profit of 2.1 percent. This calculation is far more systematic than looking at the overall cost of $150,000 and attempting to estimate a proper percentage based on a gross examination of the types of material to be purchased.

Direct Labor (4 to 12%)—The profit percentage to be applied is based on an evaluation of the skill levels and costs for each type of direct labor applied to the contract. Highly skilled engineering or professional costs might be assessed at 12 percent, and support personnel such as draftsmen at 6 percent. Because most proposals are a mix of skill levels and associated costs, it is desirable to assign a percent factor to each level of labor cost and calculate profit by that means. Exhibit 10-3 illustrates this point.

Exhibit 10-3
Profit Determination—Direct Labor

Skill Level	Cost	Profit %	Profit
Highly complex	$100,000	11%	$11,000
Medium complex	80,000	8%	6,400
Lower levels	40,000	4%	1,600
Total Labor cost	$220,000	Total Profit	$19,000

The calculation above results in a profit of 8.64 percent—slightly above the midpoint of the allowable range.

Overhead (3 to 8%)—This factor requires an analysis of the overhead cost elements to determine the contribution each makes to the contract effort. The approach is to consider the subcategories and assign percentages to the subcategory costs. Indirect labor is analyzed as if it were a direct labor charge at comparable skill levels (e.g., highly skilled engineering supervision might be assessed at 12 percent and clerical at 4 percent). Profit levels for factors such as depreciation of highly complex equipment might be assessed at fairly high percentages, and depreciation of ordinary equipment (e.g., office furniture) at lower percentages. Percentages on the low side would likely be proper for routine indirect costs like utilities and administration of fringe benefits. Note that percentages used for the subelements in this approach may be higher or lower than the percentage range for the total group. The only restriction is that the final overall profit percentage for overhead must fall within the 3 to 8 percent range.

A simplified example of the approach described above is shown in Exhibit 10-4.

Exhibit 10-4
Profit Determination—Overhead

Categories	O/H Costs	Profit %	Profit
High skill supervision	$ 90,000	12%	$10,800
Clerical and support	80,000	4%	3,200
Depreciation or rent (complex)	80,000	6%	4,800
Depreciation or rent (routine)	40,000	3%	1,200
Fringe benefits (administrative)	170,000	3%	5,100
Routine expense	90,000	1%	900
Total overhead cost	$550,000		$26,000

The profit on overhead in the above calculation represents 4.7 percent of overhead ($26,000 ($550,000 = 4.7 %). This final overhead profit percentage falls within the 3-8 percent range. Accordingly, the 4.7 percent profit calculated can then be applied to the overhead cost objective of the proposal. If the overhead cost objective for our proposal is $200,000, the resulting profit for overhead is $9,400.

Other Costs (1 to 3%)—These are direct costs such as travel and use of consultants. If, for example, the contractor expects to incur $10,000 of travel, assignment of a 1 percent factor would give a $100 profit.

General Management (4 to 8%)—This factor applies profit for overall management of a business. In some cases, firms may have an overhead cost pool only. In such cases, it is often appropriate to separate G&A type expenses from the overhead and assign profit to them using general management factors. When a G&A cost pool exists, it is generally best to break out cost categories and apply individual profit rates as described above. Use of this procedure might result in a 6.1 percent profit rate. Application to a hypothetical G&A cost objective of $150,000 results in $9,150 profit.

A summary of the calculations to this point is shown in Exhibit 10-5.

Exhibit 10-5
Recapitulation of Profit—Contractor Effort Only

Factor	Cost	Profit Range	% Used	Profit
Material Acquisition	$150,000	1–4%	2.1%	$ 3,150
Direct Labor	220,000	4–12%	8.64%	19,000
Overhead	200,000	3–8%	4.7%	9,400
Other Costs	10,000	1–3%	1.0%	100
General Management	150,000	4–8%	6.1%	9,150
Total Cost Objective	$730,000		Total	$40,800

Note that on the basis of the numerical examples covered in Exhibits 10-2 through 10-4 and summarized in Exhibit 10-5, a profit of $40,800 based on a total cost of $730,000 has already been calculated (5.59 percent so far). Additional factors must be considered to establish the *final* profit objective.

Other Factors

This group of factors adjusts the profit obtained above. The percentage figures in this section apply to the total estimated cost of the contract.

Cost Risk (0 to 7%)—The largest single determinant in this factor is the type of contract. The GSA instructions call for 0 to 3 percent for cost-reimbursement and 3 to 7 percent for fixed-price types. Other factors to consider are the reliability of the cost estimate and the difficulty of the contract task. If, for example, a firm fixed-price contract is being considered, the likely range is 5 to 7 percent which, after consideration of the other factors, might give a value of 6.5 percent. In our hypothetical case above, with total costs at $730,000, this factor would add $47,450 profit to the figure already obtained. (Note that a cost-reimbursement contract has an upper limit of 3 percent. The GSA instructions indicate that a cost plus fixed fee contract might well merit 0 percent.)

Investment (–2 to +2%)—This factor considers the extent to which the contractor is providing needed facilities and materials and the frequency of payments to the contractor. Normally payments made more frequently than monthly merit a negative percent figure. If we assume in the hypothetical case we have shown above that the contractor is providing all facilities and material with very reasonable payment requirements, we might add 1 percent for an added profit of $7,300.

Cost Control and Other Past Accomplishments (–2 to +2%)—This factor requires evaluation of the contractor's past and present performance in areas of quality, meeting performance schedules, efficiency in cost control, accuracy and reliability of past cost estimates, timely processing of changes, and other general performance aspects. We will assume for our numerical example that no percentage is to be added or taken away.

Federal Socioeconomic Programs (–0.5 to +0.5%)—This factor refers to the contractor's successful participation in programs for small business, small disadvantaged business, labor surplus area, and energy conservation. Like the two preceding factors, it provides for reduction or addition to profits. We will assume for our hypothetical case that an additional 0.2 percent profit is appropriate, adding $1,460 to the profit objective.

Special Situations and Independent Development (–2 to +2%)—This factor provides an opportunity to grant additional profit in unusual situations, including rewards for contractor-initiated and financed programs that promote the agency's interests. Also included are situations in which the contractor agrees to share in contract cost or accept lower-than-normal fee or profit adjustments for modifications or changes within certain ranges. A negative weight may be appropriate when the contractor is expected to get some spin-off benefits, such as products with commercial applications. Assume, for the hypothetical case we have followed above, that a contracting officer decides it would be appropriate to add 0.1 percent profit for this portion (such situations are uncommon). This adjustment results in added profit of $730.

The brief explanation above illustrates the rudimentary principles of structured profit guidelines. Our hypothetical case for a firm-fixed-price contract has resulted in a profit objective of $97,740 against an estimated cost of $730,000 (13.4% of cost, or 11.8% of total price). Exhibit 10-6 summarizes the illustrative example used in the preceding discussion.

Exhibit 10-6
Profit Guidelines Determination, General Services Administration Procedure

Profit Factors	Cost Obj.	Profit Range	% Used	Profit
CONTRACTOR EFFORT				
Material Acquisition	$150,000	1 to 4%	2.1%	$3,150
Direct Labor	220,000	4 to 12%	8.64%	19,000
Overhead	200,000	3 to 8%	4.7%	9,400
Other Costs	10,000	1 to 3%	1.0%	100
General Management	150,000	4 to 8%	6.1%	9,150
Total Cost Objective	$730,000			
OTHER FACTORS				
Cost Risk		0 to 7%	6.5%	47,450
Investment		–2 to +2%	+1.0%	7,300
Performance		–1 to +1%	- - -	- - -
Federal Socioeconomic Programs		–.5 to +.5%	+0.2%	1,460
Special Situations		–2 to +2%	+0.1%	730
Total Profit Objective				$97,740

SUMMARY

Structured profit guidelines give a measure of orderliness and system to profit determination. The guidelines are designed to:

- Reward contractors who take on the more difficult tasks requiring higher skills;
- Encourage contractors to accept greater cost responsibility by establishing substantially different profit levels for different types of contracts;

- Encourage contractors to make cost-effective capital investments;
- Encourage contractors to utilize nongovernment resources in the financing and performance of federal contracts;
- Reward contractors for implementing socioeconomic programs; and
- Reward contractors for self-initiated endeavors that further the buying agency's interests.

Admittedly, the calculated result of a structured profit approach is itself the application of judgments and percentages, but that application is systematic.

Occasionally we encounter people who set a profit percentage in advance and then manipulate the structured profit guidelines until they get that figure or something close to it. Aside from being a somewhat ridiculous effort, this practice is a clear violation of FAR principles dealing with profit determination.

CHAPTER 11
Pricing Equitable Adjustments for Contract Changes

Sometimes the government may have to change a contract because situations arise that it did not anticipate at the time of award. Government contracts contain various clauses that require written changes to the contract when new situations arise.

The courts and the boards of contract appeals (BCAs) have developed a number of basic concepts for determining equitable price adjustments. Unfortunately, there are no hard-and-fast rules that will always ensure agreement between contractors and the government. There are not even any rules that will always ensure success before the courts and the BCAs. The guidance and materials do, however, offer a framework to consider in pricing equitable adjustments.

The need for equitable adjustments arises when the government changes a contract, usually through a change order accompanied by a written modification to the contract that affects the contract price. In most cases, the change order is pursuant to one of the following clauses:

FAR 52.242-14, Suspension of Work: Used for architect-engineer and construction contracts.

FAR 52.242-15, Stop Work Order: May be used for negotiated contracts for supplies, services, or research and development (R&D).

FAR 52.242-16, Stop Work Order—Facilities.

FAR 52.242-17, Government Delay of Work.

FAR 52.243-1, Changes—Fixed-price: The basic clause is for supply contracts. There are alternates for services, supplies with services, architect-engineer, transportation, and R&D contracts.

FAR 52.243-2, Changes—Cost-reimbursement: The basic clause is for supplies contracts. There are alternates for services, supplies with services, construction, facilities, and R&D contracts.

FAR 52.243-3, Changes—Time-and-materials or Labor Hours.

FAR 52.243-4, Changes: Used for fixed-price contracts for construction and for dismantling, demolition, or removal of improvements.

187

FAR 52.243-5, Changes and Changed Conditions (Construction).

FAR 52.245-2, Government Property—Fixed-price Contracts.

FAR 52.245-5, Government Property—Cost-reimbursement, Time-and-material or Labor-hour Contracts.

All these clauses provide for equitable adjustments if the change causes an increase or decrease in the contractor's costs. The adjustment may be a price increase if the government change causes the contractor to incur added costs or necessitates an extension of the contract performance period. Conversely, the adjustment may be a price decrease if the change could cause a decrease in the cost of performance or make earlier delivery possible.

Occasionally changes may materialize without a written modification to the contract. These *constructive* (from the verb "to construe," *not* "to construct") changes materialize as a result of some action or inaction by a government representative. For example, a government representative takes overt actions that cause a contractor to incur costs for work not covered by the contract. Or the government causes extra work by failing to issue a change order that was actually needed.

Equitable adjustments for constructive changes follow the same basic rules as those for written changes directed by a contracting officer. When a contracting officer (or a BCA or court) establishes that a change has occurred, how the change happened is not important in determining the price adjustment. This is much better than having two sets of rules—one for written changes and another for constructive changes.

REASONABLE COST APPROACH: PREFERRED MEASURE OF EQUITABLE ADJUSTMENT

Two general principles prevail in measuring equitable adjustments.

First, some cost impact must result from the contract change. All the clauses state terms essentially as follows: "Equitable adjustment shall be made if the change *causes an increase or decrease in the contractor's costs or time of performance.*" (Emphasis added.) The clauses say nothing about the estimates the contractor used in preparing its bid or proposal. Instead, the clauses refer to the specific cost incurred or to be incurred at the time of the change. The clauses do not in any way consider what the cost might have been for another contractor or for contractors at large, or an unsupported concept of a "reasonable" cost. A contracting officer can question the reasonableness of costs, but not based on what some hypothetical contractor might have paid.

Second, both parties—the contractor and the government—are to "remain whole." The equitable adjustment for the change should be based on the difference between the reasonable cost of performing the contract *with* and *without* the change. The "wholeness" concept provides that neither the contractor nor the government should be in a better or worse position as a result of the change. Contractors should not use the equitable adjustment as a means of overcoming a loss (often referred to as the practice of "getting well"). Indeed, any losses sustained or accruing to the contractor at the time of the change should not be mitigated. Conversely, any profits earned or accruing to the contractor at the time of the change should not be eroded.

Using the contractor's original cost estimate as the base for determining an equitable adjustment does *not* leave both parties whole. To demonstrate the impact of an improper base in calculating an equitable adjustment, let's look at two examples (see Exhibits 11-1 and 11-2).

Consider the following example, where the contractor is in a profitable situation at the time of the change:

In anticipation of preparing a price proposal for a government solicitation, Acme Enterprise sought competitive bids from vendors for component part Gamma. Vendor A tendered a competitive price of $20,000. Acme included $20,000 as part of its price proposal, and was awarded the contract. After the contract award, Acme found an alternate supplier willing to sell component part Gamma for $15,000—$5,000 less than Vendor A. Needless to say, Acme was pleased, since the $5,000 price savings would enhance its profitability on the contract. Acme placed orders with the alternate supplier at the reduced unit price of $15,000. Later the government issued a change order modifying the design requirements and replacing component part Gamma with component part Kappa. Acme sought competitive bids from vendors for component part Kappa, and learned (from the competitive vendor quotations) that the best price would be $21,000.

Exhibit 11-1
Improper Base for Equitable Adjustment Erodes Contractor's Profit

	Improper	Proper
Cost of Component Part Kappa as Changed	$21,000	$21,000
Cost in Original Price for Component Part Gamma	$20,000	
Actual Cost of Component Part Gamma		$15,000
Equitable Adjustment	$ 1,000	$ 6,000

Notice in Exhibit 11-1 how the improper use of the cost estimate in the original price proposal results in a price increase of only $1,000 despite the fact that the contractor will have to spend $6,000 more for the replacement component. By denying Acme the benefit of the $5,000 price savings accruing prior to the change, the government would effectively erode Acme's existing profitability. Acme remains "whole" if the equitable adjustment is $6,000.

Now let's consider the following example, where, conversely, the contractor is in an unprofitable situation at the time of the change:

In anticipation of preparing a price proposal for a government solicitation, Belmont, Inc., sought competitive bids for component part Omega from multiple suppliers. Supplier A tendered a competitive price of $25,000. But in preparing its price proposal, Belmont misread Supplier A's price as $20,000—creating a $5,000 understatement in its submitted price proposal. Belmont was awarded the contract, and soon after discovered its $5,000 error. Needless to say, Belmont was unhappy, since the $5,000 error would reduce its profitability on the contract. Nevertheless, Belmont "soldiered on," deciding that it would have to sustain its $5,000 mistake. Later the government issued a change order modifying the design requirements and replacing component part Omega with component part Sigma. Belmont sought competitive bids from suppliers for component part Sigma, and learned (from the competitive supplier quotations) that the best price would be $21,000.

Exhibit 11-2
Improper Base for Equitable Adjustment Enables Contractor to "Get Well"

	Improper	Proper
Cost of Component Part Sigma as Changed	$21,000	$21,000
Cost in Original Price for Component Part Omega	$20,000	
Actual Cost of Component Part Omega	$25,000	
Equitable Adjustment	$ 1,000	$ 4,000 -

Notice in Exhibit 11-2 how the improper use of the cost estimate in the original price proposal results in a price increase of $1,000–$5,000 for the mistake in Belmont's originally proposed price less the $4,000 difference in the prices between component parts Sigma and Omega. The government would effectively finance the $5,000 for the mistake in Belmont's originally proposed price. The government remains "whole" if the equitable adjustment is a price reduction of $4,000.

In both examples, the improper base is advantageous to one party (the government in Exhibit 11-1 and the contractor in Exhibit 11-2), and disadvantageous to the other (the contractor in Exhibit 11-1 and the government in Exhibit 11-2). If the proper base is used, neither party is in a better or worse position as a result of the change.

For both parties to remain whole, courts and BCAs have ruled over the years that the proper base for determining an equitable adjustment is the cost incurred or to be incurred at the time of the change—*not the estimated cost included in the original price*. Courts and BCAs have consistently based their decisions on the following measure of equitable adjustment:

Reasonable Cost to Perform the Work as Changed
Less: Reasonable Cost to Perform the Work Originally Required
Plus: Profit

Equals: Equitable Adjustment

We will see later in this chapter that the Instructions for Submitting Cost/Price Proposals, especially Part III B, which provides instructions for calculating equitable adjustments for change orders, modifications, and claims, are consistent with the reasonable cost approach.

Indirect Costs in Equitable Adjustment

Overhead and general and administrative (G&A) expenses are normally indirect costs associated with contractor work. Normal allocation rules cover the application of indirect costs to the equitable adjustment for a contract change.

An equitable adjustment is based on the changes in the contractor's actual costs created by the contract change. Some indirect costs are relatively fixed. They are partly (and sometimes totally) unaffected by increases or decreases in direct costs. If these fixed costs are significant, they could have a material impact on the amount of the equitable adjustment. Under these circumstances, the government contracting officer might very well want the contractor to eliminate such fixed costs from the indirect cost pools.

Profit in Equitable Adjustment

The Supreme Court, lower courts, and the BCAs have endorsed profit as a proper part of an equitable adjustment. If the contractor did not get a profit, the equitable adjustment would consist only of reimbursement for extra costs incurred. The contractor would not get any consideration for its management skills, investment, or added risks. Equitable adjustments favoring the government result if the change lowers performance costs. If the equitable adjustment favoring the government did not include some profit, the contractor would get the original profit with less work.

Profit is specifically excluded from equitable adjustments resulting from suspension of work. All other equitable adjustments include profit as a long-standing practice.

Various BCA decisions have refused to let the government take profit away when it was established that the deleted work would have been performed at a loss. The BCAs say that removing this profit unfairly adds to the contractor's loss.

How much profit to allow for an equitable adjustment requires careful consideration. If the change requires work more complex than the original requirement, the profit percentage for the changed work is normally increased. Conversely, it is proper to reduce the profit percentage when the work required by the change is less complex. The profit rate is often reduced if the costs of the work as changed are known precisely in advance. The risk is lower in this case.

PROCESSING OF EQUITABLE ADJUSTMENTS

Ideally, the contracting officer and the contractor will work together to negotiate the price for the equitable adjustment—without resorting to the courts and BCAs. Fortunately, this approach is effective for most claims for equitable adjustment.

The changes clause requires that the contractor submit its claim for equitable adjustment within 30 days after receipt of the change. The contracting officer can extend this period if the circumstances justify doing so.

FAR 33.207 (c) requires that the following certification accompany any claim in excess of $100,000:

> I certify that the claim is made in good faith; that the supporting data are accurate and complete to the best of my knowledge and belief; that the amount requested accurately reflects the contract adjustment for which the contractor believes the Government is liable; and that I am duly authorized to certify the claim on behalf of the contractor.

FAR 15.403-4 (a) iii requires that the contractor submit certified cost or pricing data if the expected value of a contract modification exceeds $550,000. This $550,000 is exceeded if the sum of the expected costs for the additions and deletions exceeds $550,000. (For example, deleting $400,000 and adding $200,000 requires submission of the data.) In submitting certified cost and pricing data, the contractor must follow the procedures delineated in FAR 15.408, Table 15-2, Instructions for Submitting Cost/Price Proposals. This formal procedure is a methodical way to document the calculation of the equitable adjustment.

If the contracting officer and the contractor are unable to agree on the price, the disputes clause comes into play. In this case, the contracting officer issues a written decision. This decision is binding unless the contractor appeals to a court or BCA.

TIMELINESS OF EQUITABLE ADJUSTMENTS

It is important to negotiate and settle change orders as soon as possible. Change orders can be settled more quickly when their frequency is kept to a minimum. Failure to negotiate and settle equitable adjustments soon after the directed changes has several negative effects. First, if several changes affect the same parts of the work, it may be very difficult to keep the costs for each change separated. This makes it harder to price each change properly. Second, long delays in settling these claims make it more difficult to recall the specific circumstances that existed. Third, excessive delay can seriously affect the contractor's cash flow position. Almost always, the contractor has paid for the work but must wait for the claim settlement to be repaid.

It is better to negotiate the price of a change before the changed work begins. For one thing, the government may decide not to order the change if the price is too high. Nevertheless, many contract modifications are priced after the work is underway or even completed. This is especially true when multiple changes are necessary. There is generally not enough time to delay the work so each change can be priced in advance. It is therefore important to keep the number of changes to a minimum. This requires both the government and the contractor to exercise restraint in controlling change orders.

EQUITABLE ADJUSTMENT BASED ON SEGREGATED COSTS

Experienced contractors will try to segregate the costs for performing changed work. They usually accomplish this by assigning special accounting codes to those transactions attributed to the changed work. The contractor has a very strong case when it has actual cost records clearly identifying direct costs to the changed work. Also, actual costs are far easier to validate than estimates.

For example, the government may direct a sewer line change to "dig up, change pipe from a 30 inch diameter to 24 inch diameter, and refill beginning at Location 23 and ending at Location 39." The contractor could give this a special job title such as "Change Sewer Line, #20." The contractor's foremen and timekeepers can use this job order title to report all labor and materials usage for the change. The associated cost records are very convincing to a contracting officer or to a BCA or court.

FAR 52.243-6, Change Order Accounting, may be used in research and development and supply contracts if numerous changes are likely. This clause requires the contractor to maintain separate accounts for all segregable direct costs of work for each change.

APPROACHES TO EQUITABLE ADJUSTMENT

Over the years, the courts and BCAs have generally relied on four approaches in establishing equitable adjustments in specific cases.

Reasonable Cost Approach

The reasonable cost approach attempts to keep the contractor in the same (i.e., neither better nor worse) profit position on the unchanged work after the change than it was before the change. Since the Court of Claims decision in *Bruce Construction Corp. v. United States* (324 F.2d 516, Ct. Cl. 1963) in 1963, the reasonable cost approach has generally been considered the best approach for pricing an equitable adjustment. This approach should be used whenever accurate information is available concerning contractor costs affected by the modification.

The procedures contained in FAR 15.408, Table 15-2, Instructions for Submitting Cost/Price Proposals, especially Part III B, which provides instructions for calculating equitable adjustments for change orders, modifications, and claims, are consistent with the reasonable cost approach.

Sometimes the circumstances of the case clearly warrant an equitable adjustment, but the contractor may not have actual cost data or accurate estimates to support its claim. Two other approaches are sometimes used to resolve this problem: the total cost approach and the jury verdict approach. BCAs and courts have discouraged the use of these approaches unless the contractor is clearly entitled to an equitable adjustment and there is no better way to calculate the proposed equitable adjustment.

Total Cost Approach

The total cost approach infers that all costs incurred in excess of the original estimate were attributed to the contract change. The total cost method calculation is shown in Exhibit 11-3 below.

Exhibit 11-3
Equitable Adjustments Using Total Cost Approach

Cost of Work as Changed
Less: Cost of Work Included in Original Bid or Proposal
Plus: Profit
Equals Equitable Adjustment - Total Cost Approach

By implication, this approach assumes that any adverse impact of a change is caused solely by the government, leaving the contractor or third parties blameless. Such a simplistic view is certainly debatable. First, the contractor's original estimate may have been unrealistically low—either as an attempt to "buy in" to meet a competitive pricing situation or simply as an error. Or perhaps the incurred costs were attributed to the contractor's inefficient operations, poor purchasing practices, deviation from the work plan, or other faulty management practices rather than to the contract change. Perhaps the additional cost could be attributed to actions by third parties such as subcontractors, suppliers, or workers.

The courts have been cautious about using the total cost method. One decision (*WRB Corp. vs. United States*, 183 Ct. Cl. 409 (1968)) stated the following criteria for its use:

No Other Method for Establishing the Equitable Adjustment Is Available: The contractor does not meet this criterion if it could have kept good records but did not do so. However, failure to keep records may be an excuse if the contract conditions are so chaotic that records could not be kept. An example is a contract with a lot of interrelated change orders issued in a very short time.

The Estimated Cost Included in the Original Bid or Proposal Price Must Have Been Realistic and Reasonable: The fact that the bid or proposal was lowest does not prove that its costs were reasonable or realistic. The contractor has the burden of proof to demonstrate the realism and reasonableness of the costs in its original bid or proposal. The contractor can improve its chances if it can prove cost realism by expert testimony. The contractor is also helped if its price was close to other competitors and the government estimate. The contractor may be unable to prove that the costs in its bid or proposal were reasonable. It may, in the process of trying, provide acceptable data on what the cost should have been for the work as unchanged. If so, this is a starting point for ordinary price adjustment and abandonment of the "total cost" method.

The Costs for the Changed Work Must Be Reasonable: The courts and BCAs do not use a presumption of reasonableness for costs with the total cost method. The contractor must show cost reasonableness by a preponderance of the evidence.

The Cost Increases Must Be Attributed to Government Caused Change: No portion of the claim can include costs attributed to the contractor's uneconomical, inefficient, or ineffective practices.

It is extremely difficult for a contractor to support a claim successfully using the total cost theory. Some BCAs and courts have refused to allow the claim if the contractor fails to meet any of these four criteria. Others may allow the claim if the contractor meets most of the criteria.

A contracting officer might, in very extreme circumstances, use the total cost method to settle a claim at the local level. But the contracting officer should be extremely conservative in applying this method because it is highly controversial.

The total cost approach is often applied to an entire contract rather than just a portion of the contract. The same cautions and pitfalls apply in such instances.

The general objections to the total cost approach have given rise to what has become known as the "modified total cost" approach. Because it is rare that the difference in the price versus the actual cost can be attributed solely to one party, this approach allocates a share of the "blame" or cause of the change between the two parties and assigns the cost differential (price versus actual cost) accordingly.

Jury Verdict Approach

The government uses the jury verdict method when the contractor is clearly due an adjustment but there is no clear way to identify the associated costs for reasonable cost analysis. Both sides attempt to isolate the costs identifiable with the change in such a way that a third party (court or BCA) is able to pass judgment on their reasonableness and the general allowability of the adjustment.

Both the contractor and the government have an opportunity to present the available evidence to identify costs solely with the change. Each side can—and often does—include the opinions of qualified experts (e.g., estimators). Each side has the opportunity to directly challenge the facts and judgments presented by the other side. A court or BCA—acting similarly to a jury—then reaches a decision on an equitable adjustment.

In some situations, a contracting officer might use the jury verdict method to settle a claim at the local level.

The jury verdict approach is generally deemed better than the total cost approach because it focuses on the costs associated only with the change order; moreover, it can be applied both prospectively and retrospectively. In contrast, the jury verdict approach is generally deemed less desirable than the reasonable cost approach. Good business practice and the findings of the courts and BCAs require that a reasonable cost approach be used when adequate cost information is available.

Reasonable Value Approach

Until 1963, reasonable value was the basis frequently used to estimate the change in contract value that resulted from the contract modification. This approach was tested and to a large extent rendered obsolete by the 1963 Court of Claims decision in *Bruce Construction v. United States*.

In that case, Bruce Construction claimed a $42,425.98 price increase for replacing concrete blocks in a construction project with sand blocks. Based on market prices, that claim appeared reasonable because the market price for sand blocks was generally higher than the market price for concrete blocks. In fact, Bruce purchased sand blocks for the price of concrete blocks. The Court rejected the claim, finding that cost is the best measure of value.

As a result of the Court of Claims decision, the reasonable value approach has been replaced by the reasonable cost approach.

FORMAT FOR SUBMITTING PROPOSALS FOR EQUITABLE ADJUSTMENTS

Table 15-2, Part III B, in FAR 15.408 provides instructions for calculating equitable adjustments for change orders, modifications, and claims.

FAR 15.403-4 (a) iii requires the contractor to submit certified cost or pricing data if the expected value of a contract modification exceeds $550,000. This $550,000 is exceeded if the sum of the expected costs for the additions and deletions exceeds $550,000. (For example, deleting $400,000 and adding $200,000 requires submission of the data.) In submitting certified cost and pricing data, the contractor must follow the procedures delineated in FAR 15.408, Table 15-2, Instructions for Submitting Cost/Price Proposals. This formal procedure is a methodical way to document the calculation of the equitable adjustment. Furthermore,

Part III B provides instructions for calculating equitable adjustments specifically for change orders, modifications, and claims.

Although the instructions apply only to the submission of certified cost or pricing data, they are an excellent resource for calculating pricing proposals for all change orders. These instructions are consistent with the reasonable cost approach for calculating equitable adjustments. In accordance with the Part III B instructions, the net cost of a contract modification is calculated as follows: N = A - D + C

Where

A(dded) = Current *estimate* of the cost to complete added work

D(eleted) = Current *estimate* of the cost to complete deleted work not yet performed

C(ost) = Actual cost of all deleted work already performed

N(et) = Net change in cost related to a contract modification.

Equitable adjustment calculations, pursuant to the FAR Part III B instructions, are best demonstrated using the following case illustration.

CASE ILLUSTRATION: FMI SERVICES, INC.—EQUITABLE ADJUSTMENT

On January 4, 20X6, the Federal Bureaucratic Affairs Agency (FBAA) awarded a firm fixed price contract (number 222-04-2579) to FMI Services, Inc., for the production and delivery of 175 Super Devices at $115,000 each, for a total contract price of $20,125,000. The contract performance period requires that all deliveries be accomplished by November 30, 20X6.

Prior to agreement, FMI prepared a cost/price breakdown to determine the anticipated cost and profit for the entire effort. This cost/price breakdown (see Exhibit 11-4) would be the project budget, serving as a benchmark to monitor financial performance.

Exhibit 11-4
FBAA Contract 222-04-2529: Original Budget

Costs	$18,712,093.75
Profit	$ 1,412,906.25
Selling Price	$20,125,000.00

By September 30, 20X6, FMI had delivered a total of 115 Super Devices.

On October 3, Malachy Gaughan, FMI's Controller, released the actual results through September 30, 20X6, and the anticipated results from budget data for the remainder of the contract performance period. This latest report (see Exhibit 11-5) provided a revised budget for contract performance based on the actual experience through September 20X6.

Exhibit 11-5
FBAA Contract 222-04-2529: Revised Budget

	Actual Costs Through Sep. 30, X6	Oct. 1 Through Nov. 30, X6	Projected Results of Operations Through Nov. 30, X6	Original Budget (from Exhibit 11-4)	Anticipated Cost Overrun Through Contract Completion
Cost	$13,873,600	$7,238,400	$21,112,000	$18,712,094	$2,399,906
Profit			$ 987,000-	$ 1,412,906	$2,399,906-
Selling Price			$20,125,000	$20,125,000	$0

FMI now anticipates a loss, because the anticipated cost ($21,112,000) will exceed the selling price ($20,125,000) by $987,000.

Gaughan provided the following explanations for the $2,399,906 cost overrun:

Original estimate for hourly labor rate was $27.50. But after contract award FMI found it necessary to pay $30 per hour, an hourly rate that will prevail through the remainder of the contract performance period.

Original estimate for one of the major components, Alpha, was $2,500 each. But after contract award FMI found it necessary to pay $3,000 each, a unit price that will prevail to fulfill the remaining production of 60 Super Devices.

Original estimate for factory overhead and G&A overhead was 175% of direct labor cost and 13% of cost input, respectively. After nine months into the current fiscal year, FMI found that the actual indirect cost rates are higher. Factory overhead is currently 185% of direct labor costs and G&A is 16% of cost input. These higher rates will most likely prevail for the remainder of the fiscal year.

FMI production manager, Mark Sanchez, voiced disappointment on the results of the contract, but stoically accepted the anticipated loss on Contract 2579.

Three days later, on October 6, FBAA issued the following change order:

Remove component Alpha from all 175 units, replacing it with an enhanced (version of) Alpha. FBAA will be responsible for defraying the transportation cost in and out for the 115 units (previously delivered), which will be returned to FMI for retrofitting.

Sanchez reported that the change could be accomplished and that FMI could still meet the November 30 final delivery date. He then met with Gaughan to discuss plans for complying with the change order. Gaughan said that FMI would be entitled to an equitable adjustment for the increased cost caused by the change. He also said that the increased cost would include indirect costs for factory overhead and G&A overhead.

Sanchez instructed Gaughan to "get a proposal together for an equitable adjustment." Gaughan carefully read FAR 15.408, Table 15-2, Instructions for Submitting Cost/Price Proposals, particularly Part III B, which provides instructions for calculating equitable adjustments specifically for change orders, modifications, and claims. He felt he could use some of the material from the cost accounting report, but he also performed some fact-finding about the cost of "work added" and "work deleted"—key words that he noted in the instructions.

His research disclosed that:

FMI would not have to buy Alphas for the 60 units not yet delivered, but would need to purchase 175 enhanced Alphas (115 for the reworked units and another for the 60 units not yet delivered).

The now-obsolete Alphas have no residual value.

The current vendor quotation for 175 enhanced Alphas is $4,000 each, for a total of $700,000.

The obsolete Alphas would have to be removed from the 115 units delivered.

Gaughan continued his fact-finding by consulting with Sanchez to determine the labor hours involved in removing the obsolete Alphas and installing the enhanced Alphas. Sanchez said, "We'll need 5 hours per unit to remove the Alphas from the 115 units already delivered. That's a total of 575 hours at $30 per hour for a total of $17,250 in direct labor costs. Then we're going to have to install the enhanced Alphas on all 175 units—both the 115 units previously delivered and the 60 units yet to be delivered. That'll take about 150 hours per unit, or a total of 26,250 labor hours at $30 per hour, for another $787,500 of direct labor costs."

Gaughan decided that the indirect cost rates experienced during the first nine months of the fiscal year would still prevail for the remainder of the fiscal year. He decided to use the factory overhead (185% of direct labor costs) and G&A (16% of cost input) in his proposal.

Using FAR 15.408, Table 15-2, paying strict attention to the Part III B Instructions, Gaughan prepared the equitable adjustment proposal (shown as Exhibits 11-6(a) and 11-6(b)) and shared it with Sanchez.

Sanchez commented that the proposed equitable adjustment, as computed in accordance with the Part III B Instructions, covered only the cost associated with the change.

Sanchez asked if the equitable adjustment could include profit. Gaughan replied, "Yes, but only on the changed work. We're going to have to accept our loss on the unchanged work, but at least we'll be able to get some profit on the changed work."

Gaughan then went on to explain that by using FBAA's "structured profit approach" (see Chapter 10), a fair and reasonable profit would be $149,036, and that the total price of the proposed equitable adjustment would be $3,150,000. Gaughan then presented an analysis (see Exhibit 11-7) showing that if FBAA accepted the proposed equitable adjustment, the total price of the contract would be $23,275,000.

Exhibit 11-6(a)
FBAA Contract 222-04-2529: Proposed Equitable Adjustment

FMI Services, Inc.
Cost/Price Breakdown
Contract Number FBAA 222-04-2002
Change Order Number 0001
Proposal for Equitable Adjustment

Column 1 Cost Elements	Column 2 Estimated Cost of All Work Deleted Schedule A-1	Column 3 Cost of Deleted Work Already Performed Schedule A-2	Column 4 Net Cost to Be Deleted Schedule A-3	Column 5 Cost of Work Added Schedule A-4	Column 6 Net Cost of Change Schedule A-5
	Include the current estimates of what the cost would have been to complete the deleted work not yet performed (not the original proposal estimates), and the cost of deleted work already performed.	Include the incurred cost of deleted work already performed, using actuals if possible, or, if actuals are not available, estimates from your accounting records. Attach a detailed inventory of work, materials, parts, components, and hardware already purchased, manufactured, or performed and deleted by the change, indicating the cost and proposed disposition of each line item. Also, if you desire to retain these items or any portion of them, indicate the amount offered for them.	Enter the net cost to be deleted, which is the estimated cost of all deleted work less the cost of deleted work already performed. Column (2) minus Column (3) equals Column (4).	Enter your estimate for cost of work added by the change. When nonrecurrent costs are significant, or when specifically requested to do so by the Contracting Officer, provide a full identification and explanation of them. When any of the costs in this column have already been incurred, describe them on an attached supporting schedule.	Enter the net cost of change, which is the cost of work added, less the net cost to be deleted. Column (5) minus Column (4) equals Column (6). When this result is negative, place the amount in parentheses.
Direct Material					
Material—Alpha	$437,500	$287,500	$150,000		($150,000)
Material—Enhanced Alpha				$700,000	$700,000
Direct Material	$437,500	$287,500	$150,000	$700,000	$550,000
Direct Labor					
Install Alpha	$262,500	$172,500	$90,000		($90,000)
Remove Alpha				$17,250	$17,250
Install Enhance				$787,500	$787,500
Direct Labor (Applied to Direct Labor Cost)	$262,500	$172,500	$90,000	$804,750	$714,750
Factory Overhead	$485,625	$319,125	$166,500	$1,488,788	$1,322,288
Cost Input (Applied to Cost Input)	$1,185,625	$779,125	$406,500	$2,993,538	$2,587,038
General and Administrative (G&A) Overhead	$189,700	$124,660	$65,040	$478,966	$413,926
Total Cost	$1,375,325	$903,785	$471,540	$3,472,504	$3,000,964

Exhibit 11-6(b)

FBAA Contract 222-04-2529: Proposed Equitable Adjustment (Supporting Schedules)

	Qty	Material Cost per Unit	Hours per Unit	Total Hours	Labor Rate	Indirect Cost Rate	Column 2 Estimated Cost of all Work Deleted
Schedule A-1							
Component Alpha removed from All 175 units							
Column 2 - Estimated Cost of All Work Deleted							
Direct Material Material - Alpha	175	$2,500.00					$437,500.00
Direct Labor Install Alpha	175		50	8750	$30.00		$262,500.00
Factory Overhead Applied to Direct Labor Cost						185%	$485,625.00
Cost Input							$1,185,625.00
General and Administrative (G&A) Overhead Applied to Cost Input						16%	$189,700.00
Total Cost							$1,375,325.00
							Column 3 Cost of Deleted Work Already Performed
Schedule A-2							
Component Alpha Removed from the 115 units Already Delivered							
Column 3 - Cost of Deleted Work Already Performed							
Direct Material Material - Alpha	115	$2,500.00					$287,500.00
Direct Labor Install Alpha	115		50	5750	$30.00		$172,500.00
Factory Overhead Applied to Direct Labor Cost						185%	$319,125.00
Cost Input							$779,125.00
General and Administrative (G&A) Overhead Applied to Cost Input						16%	$124,660.00
Total Cost							$903,785.00
Schedule A-3							**Column 4 Net Cost to be Deleted**
Component Alpha Not Needed in 60 Units Not Yet Delivered							
Column 4 - Net Cost to Be Deleted							
Direct Material Material - Alpha	60	$2,500.00					$150,000.00
Direct Labor Install Alpha	60		50	3000	$30.00		$90,000.00
Factory Overhead Applied to Direct Labor Cost						185%	$166,500.00
Cost Input							$406,500.00
General and Administrative (G&A) Overhead Applied to Cost Input						16%	$65,040.00
Total Cost							$471,540.00
Schedule A-4							**Column 5 Cost of Work Added**
Component Enhanced Alpha to Be Installed on All 175 Units							
(retrofitted on 115 units and installed on 60 units)							
Column 5 - Cost of Work Added							
Direct Material Material - Alpha	175	$4,000.00					$700,000.00
Direct Labor Remove Alpha	115		5	575	$30.00		$17,250.00
Direct Labor Install Entrance	175		150	26250	$30.00		$787,500.00
Factory Overhead Applied to Direct Labor Cost						185%	$1,488,787.50
Cost Input							$2,993,537.50
General and Administrative (G&A) Overhead Applied to Cost Input						16%	$478,966.00
Total Cost							$3,472,503.50
Schedule A-5							**Column 6 Net Cost of Change Equitable Adjustment**
Equitable Adjustment							
Cost of Changed Work							
Column 6 - Net Cost of Change							
Direct Material Material - Alpha	(60)	$2,500.00					($150,000.00)
Direct Material Material - Enhanced Alpha	175	$4,000.00					$700,000.00
Direct Labor Install Alpha	(60)		50	(3000)	$30.00		($90,000.00)
Direct Labor Remove Alpha	115		5	575	$30.00		$17,250.00
Direct Labor Install Entrance	175		150	26250	$30.00		$787,500.00
Factory Overhead Applied to Direct Labor Cost						185%	$1,322,287.50
Cost Input							$2,587,037.50
General and Administrative (G&A) Overhead Applied to Cost Input						16%	$413,926.00
Total Cost							$3,000,963.50

Exhibit 11-7
FBAA Contract 222-04-2529: Impact of Equitable Adjustment on Contract Price

	Revised (Pre-Change) Budget (See Exhibit 11-5)	Equitable Adjustment	Post Change Estimate
Cost	$21,112,000	$3,000,964	$24,112,964
Profit or Loss (-)	$ 987,000-	$ 149,036	$ 837,964-
Selling Price	$20,125,000	$3,150,000	$23,275,000

Gaughan went on to explain, "We would have probably lost $987,000 had we performed the contract without the change. The change enables us to negotiate a price sufficient to cover the $3,000,964 anticipated cost increase for the change plus another $149,036 for profit on the change. We'll still lose $837,964 on the overall contract, but hopefully we'll at least make a profit on the change."

Under the terms of the proposed equitable adjustment, neither FMI nor the government is in a better or worse position as a result of the change. FMI may be able to earn a profit on the new work, but will still sustain a loss on the unchanged work.

EQUITABLE ADJUSTMENTS FOR GOVERNMENT-CAUSED DELAYS

Sometimes government action (or inaction) delays contract completion, extending the contract performance beyond the anticipated completion date. In many, if not most (or all), of these delays the contractor will incur additional costs during the delay period. Certain fixed overhead costs will go marching on even during the delay period. Furthermore, in the absence of replacement work or an equitable adjustment, the incremental overhead costs will be "unabsorbed," i.e., not covered by any revenue.

The problem of unabsorbed overhead is a major source of court and BCA cases. There is no question that contractors incur extra costs during these government delays. When they do occur, the contractor must establish two major points:

1. *The government caused delays, entitling the contractor to an equitable adjustment.* In these instances, the contractor can usually establish that the government caused delays. The contractor may find it more difficult to show that it should get an equitable adjustment for its unabsorbed overhead. In long delays, the government might claim that the contractor could have obtained other work but did not. It might also try to show that other customers paid the overhead not absorbed by the government.
2. *The amount of the claim for the unabsorbed overhead is justifiable.* The contractor has a significant problem justifying the amount of the claim for the unabsorbed overhead. It is often difficult to show how much, if any, of the overhead was actually unabsorbed. Contractors have tried various methods over the years to support these delay claims. The Eichleay formula has been moderately successful.

There are different methods of calculating the unabsorbed overhead cost. Perhaps the most widely employed method is the Eichleay formula, named for the Eichleay Corporation. Eichleay successfully used this formula many years ago in a claim before the Armed Services Board of Contract Appeals. Since then, BCAs and courts have generally ruled that the Eichleay formula is an acceptable method for computing unabsorbed overhead resulting from government-caused delay.

Basic Eichleay Formula

Under the basic Eichleay formula, the normal fixed overhead allocable to a contract is identified and expressed in terms of a daily rate. The daily rate is then multiplied by the days of delay to arrive at the total amount of unabsorbed overhead.

To demonstrate the basic Eichleay calculation, let's assume the following:

A = Total billings on the delayed contract: $930,000

B = Total billings on all contracts between award and completion of the delayed contract: $3,100,000

C = Relevant overhead (usually fixed overhead) between award and completion of the delayed contract: $391,500

D = Number of days between award and completion of the delayed contract, including the delay: 270 days

E = Number of days that performance was delayed: 30 days

The Eichleay formula attempts to assign unabsorbed overhead to the delayed contract in four sequential steps:

Step 1   Determine the ratio of billings applicable to the delayed contract to all firm billings.

A/B = $930,000/$3,100,000 = 30%

Step 2   Determine the unabsorbed overhead applicable to the delayed contract.

Results of Step 1 x C = 30% x $391,500 = $117,450

Step 3   Determine the daily unabsorbed overhead applicable to the delayed contract.

Results of Step 3/D = $117,450/270 days = $435

Step 4   Determine the unabsorbed overhead applicable to the delayed contract—the *equitable adjustment for the delay.*

Results of Step 4 x E = $435 x 30 days = $13,050

Modifications to the Basic Eichleay Formula

Although the basic Eichleay formula is widely used, it may—unless appropriately adjusted—yield inequitable results. The basic Eichleay calculation is based on the following assumptions:

- Overhead costs include only fixed costs.
- The contractor cannot replace the suspended work with other work.
- There is a total work stoppage.
- The cost of the delay is the same regardless of the percentage of contract completion. (The formula will produce the same result whether the contract is 1 percent or 99 percent complete.)
- The facilities are operating at or near capacity.

If the current situation does not conform with these assumptions, the contractor should consider some modified form of the formula or an alternative approach. The *Defense Contract Audit Agency (DCAA) Manual 12-805* suggests three adjustments to the basic Eichleay formula to produce more equitable results:

Eichleay Formula Adjusted for a Partial Replacement of Work. Consider reducing the number of delay days if you replace a portion of the work.

> Example: Assume the same basic facts described above except that the contractor replaces 30 percent of the work, leaving 70 percent unreplaced. You can compensate for the partial loss by considering only 21 delay days (70 percent of the 30 days). The resulting equitable adjustment would be $9,135, as follows:
>
> The Equitable Adjustment for the Delay (per Step 4 above)
> $435 x 30 days = $13,050
> Less: Adjustment for Replacement Work
> 30 days x 30% = 9 days
> $435 x 9 days = $ 3,915 -
>
> ***Equitable Adjustment to Reflect Partial Replacement of Work***
> $435 x 21 days = $ 9,135

Eichleay Formula Adjusted for a Partial Work Stoppage. Consider reducing the number of delay days if the contractor experiences a partial work stoppage.

> Example: Assume the same basic facts described above except that the contractor experiences a 60 percent work stoppage during the 30 days, enabling a 40 percent work continuance rate. You can adjust for the partial stoppage by considering only 18 delay days (60 percent of the 30 days). The resulting equitable adjustment would be $7,830, as follows:
>
> The Equitable Adjustment for the Delay (per Step 4 above)
> $435 x 30 days = $13,050
> Less: Adjustment for Partial Work Continuance
> 30 Days x 40% = 12 days
> $435 x 12 days = $ 5,220

Equitable Adjustment to Reflect Partial Work Stoppage
$435 x 18 days = $ 7,830

Eichleay Formula Adjusted for Less Than Capacity Operation. If the value of total contractor billings during the contract period has been depressed from full capacity, consider adjusting the value of the billings upward to approximate what the value would have been.

Example: Assume the same basic facts described above except that your firm's billings during the contract period have been depressed from full capacity. Further investigation shows the following for the six-month period March 1 thru August 31:

A = Total billings on the delayed contract $ 580,000

B = Total billings on all contracts $2,145,000

C = Fixed overhead   258,000

The resulting equitable adjustment would be $7,740, as follows:

Step 1   Ratio of Billings Applicable to the Delayed Contract to All Firm Billings

A/B = $580,000/$2,145,000 = 27%

Step 2   Unabsorbed Overhead Applicable to the Delayed Contract

Results of Step 1 x C = 27% x $258,000 = $69,660

Step 3   Daily Unabsorbed Overhead Applicable to the Delayed Contract

Results of Step 3/D = $69,660/270 Days = $258

Step 4   Unabsorbed Overhead Applicable to the Delayed Contract—the **Equitable Adjustment for the Delay**.

Results of Step 4 x E = $258 x 30 days = $7,740

Rarely (probably never) will the government gratuitously compensate a contractor for its unabsorbed overhead cost. The contractor will have to take the initiative to prepare a proposal for an *equitable adjustment* requesting additional compensation. In preparing the proposal for an equitable adjustment, the contractor must

* Carefully document and explain the rationale for its basic Eichleay calculation and any adjustments.
* Demonstrate how the government caused the delay.
* Explain why it was required to stand by during the delay. (The contractor's "stand by" explanation is enhanced if the work was suspended for an uncertain or unspecified duration and the contractor had to be prepared to resume work immediately.)

The contractor should also show the mitigation of damages by taking on replacement work. When appropriate, show how it was impossible or impractical to fully or partially take on additional work. To prevent recovery, the government must either show that:

- It was not impractical for the contractor to obtain other work to which it could reallocate its indirect costs; or
- The contractor's inability to obtain other work was caused by some circumstance other than the government-caused delay.

It might first appear that the calculation of an equitable adjustment is difficult and possibly onerous. A more careful and thoughtful reading, however, reveals that the courts, the BCAs, and the FAR writers have made commendable efforts to keep both the government and contractors whole.

APPENDIX A

Checklist for Adequacy of Submitted Cost and Pricing Data

GENERAL (FAR 15.408 (L), TABLE 15-2—SECTION I)

1. Does the contractor's proposal contain a signed cover page covering all the items in Section IA of Table 15-2?
2. Does the proposal contain a summary of total costs by cost element, cross-referenced to each proposed line item?
3. Does the proposal identify cost or pricing data (i.e., data that are verifiable and factual), and an explanation of the estimating process? When applicable, the following items should be specifically identified:
   a. Judgmental factors and the methods used in the estimate, including those used in projections from known data; and
   b. The nature and amount of any contingencies.
4. Does the contractor's proposal contain an index referencing all cost or pricing data, and information accompanying or identified in the proposal?
5. Does the proposal identify and describe any forward pricing rate agreements (FPRAs) used?
6. Does the proposal describe the location and point of contact for any cost or pricing data identified but not included in the proposal?
7. Does the proposal disclose any other activity that could materially impact the costs (i.e., existing excess material, company reorganizations, new technology, labor union discussions, significant increase in production and sales, etc.)?

MATERIALS, PURCHASED PARTS, SUBCONTRACTED ITEMS (FAR 15.408 (L), TABLE 15-2—SECTION II A)

8. Does the proposal identify the basis for the kinds, quantities, and cost of all material elements proposed?
9. Is there a consolidated priced summary of individual material quantities, or a consolidated priced bill of materials? Although not required, government reviewers (e.g., auditors) prefer the bill of materials to be in descending value order.
10. For each subcontract over $500,000, does the proposal show: source, deliverable, quantity, price, type of subcontract, degree of competition, basis for selecting the vendor, and basis for establishing the reasonableness of the price?
11. When required, has the subcontractor's cost or pricing data been submitted with the contractor's initial proposal? If available, the contractor should provide the results of review and evaluation of subcontract proposals.

12. Though not required, has the contractor provided reasons for omitted data or reviews, with dates when the data or reviews will be available?
13. Does the proposal provide justification when claiming an exception from submitting cost or pricing data?
14. If the proposal contains costs based on other factors, (e.g., scrap or yield factors), are those other factors and their basis for justification explained?

DIRECT LABOR (FAR 15.408 (L), TABLE 15-2—SECTION II B)

15. Does the proposal contain a time-phased (e.g., quarterly, annual) breakdown of labor rates and hours by category or skill level?
16. Is there a basis for the estimates of the rates and hours (i.e., historical experience, engineering estimates, learning curves, etc.)?
17. If labor is the allocation base for indirect costs, does the proposal summarize this data for each overhead pool and year?

INDIRECT COSTS (FAR 15.408 (L), TABLE 15-2—SECTION II C)

18. If there is no FPRA or indirect rate proposal, does the proposal show how indirect rates were estimated and applied? Support for the indirect rates could consist of cost breakdowns, trends, and budgetary data.

OTHER COSTS (FAR 15.408 (L), TABLE 15-2—SECTION II D)

19. Does the proposal identify all other costs by category and basis for pricing

FACILITIES CAPITAL COST OF MONEY (FCCM)

20. If the proposal claimed facilities capital cost of money, was form CASB-CMF submitted?
21. Was the calculation for the proposed amount shown?

PROFIT OR FEE

22. Contractors are encouraged to provide the rationale for proposed profit. (Record of Weighting Guidelines Application, with rationale, may be used.)

CHANGE ORDERS

23. Does the change order propose rates and hours by category or skill level?
24. Does the change order provide:
    a. The identification of the actual, or estimated, cost of deleted work already performed?
    b. An estimate of the cost to complete deleted work?
    c. An estimate of the cost to complete added work?

Index

A

acquisition methods, 32
adapting to established prices, 10
adequate price competition, 13–15
advance agreements, 47–48
allocability, 150, 154
allocable costs, 48–49
allocation bases, overhead cost, 143–145
allocation methods
   general and administrative expense, 159
   overhead cost, 139, 143
allowability
   facilities capital cost of money, 168
   general and administrative expense, 158–159
   overhead cost, 150, 154–155
allowable costs, 46–47
anticipated volume, general and administrative
   expense, 164
Anti-Deficiency Act, 3
Applicability and Disclosure Statement
   Requirements, 66
Armed Services Pricing Manual, 37
assessing proposed average wage rates, direct
   labor cost, 105
Asset Related Standards, 64
average rates, direct labor cost, 103–104

B

base analysis, general and administrative
   expense, 164
basis of allocation, 150, 155
BCA. *See* board of contract appeals
bill of materials, 120–121
Blanket Purchase Agreements (BPA), 3–4
BLS. *See* Bureau of Labor Statistics
board of contract appeals (BCA), 187
bonuses, 159

BPA. *See* Blanket Purchase Agreements
Bureau of Labor Statistics (BLS), 38
buy-ins, 11–12, 15–16

C

capital investments, 179–180
CAS. *See* Cost Accounting Standards
CASB. *See* Cost Accounting Standards Board
catalog price, 35
Certificate of Current Cost or Pricing Data, 88
Certificate of Independent Price
   Determination, 15
certified cost or pricing data, 72–73
Changes and Changed Conditions
   (Construction) clause, 188
Changes clause, 187
Changes–Cost-reimbursement clause, 187
Changes–Fixed-Price clause, 187
Changes–Time-and-materials or Labor Hour
   clause, 187
Code of Federal Regulations, 62
commercial items, price paid for, 35
commercial products, 23
commercial-type products, 23
competition, full and open, 1–2
competitive acquisition, 20–21
competitive offers, 4–5
competitive proposals
   competitive acquisition, 20–21
   definition, 17
   negotiation, 19–20
   sole source acquisition, 21–22
Comptroller General, 16
computer and consultation services, 133
conditions in offeror's work force, 104
Consistency and Modified Coverage Standards,
   63
contract clauses, 89–90